TEXAS POLITICS

GOVERNING the LONE STAR STATE

Second Edition

Cal Jillson
Southern Methodist University

McGraw Hill **Learning Solutions**

Boston Burr Ridge, IL Dubuque, IA New York San Francisco St. Louis
Bangkok Bogotá Caracas Lisbon London Madrid
Mexico City Milan New Delhi Seoul Singapore Sydney Taipei Toronto

TEXAS POLITICS
GOVERNING the LONE STAR STATE, Second Edition

1 2 3 4 5 6 7 8 9 0 QPD QPD 0 9 8

ISBN-13: 978-0-07-353837-2
ISBN-10: 0-07-353837-X

Learning Solutions Manager: Richard Barchak
Learning Solutions Representative: Trish Mish
Production Editor: Carrie Braun
Printer/Binder: Quebecor World

"Texas is a state of mind. Texas is an obsession. Above all, Texas is a nation in every sense of the word. . . . Like most passionate nations Texas has its own private history based on, but not limited by, facts."

John Steinbeck, Travels with Charley, *1962, pp. 201–202*

Table of Contents

Preface

This brief text on Texas politics, entitled ***Texas Politics: Governing the Lone Star State***, was a joy to write. That joy turned to quiet satisfaction as teachers and students of Texas politics found the first edition of this book accessible, informative, and, yes, fun. In this thoroughly revised second edition, we treat Texas politics as serious business, but we also recognize that it is a great show. Decisions that Texas political leaders make about taxes, education, health care, and child services directly affect the quality of people's lives and their prospects of future success and security. But for the serious political junkie, it does not get any better than the great redistricting fight, the four-way governor's race of 2006, or Tom Craddick's bare knuckle fight to retain the speakership of the Texas House. I have tried to capture the structure and dynamics, the prose and the poetry, the good, the bad, and the ugly of Texas politics.

This book has been used both as a stand alone text or as a supplement to an American government text in a combined American Government/ Texas Government course. In stand alone Texas politics courses it has most commonly be used in conjunction with a comparative state politics book. In the combined course the chapter order and content of ***Texas Politics*** map directly onto the chapter order and content of most major American Government texts. In either case, my goal is to help teachers and students understand and enjoy Texas politics.

Texas Politics approaches the politics of the Lone Star State from historical, developmental, and analytical perspectives. Each chapter opens with a discussion of the origins and development of the subject of the chapter, whether that subject is the Texas Constitution, the status of party competition in the state, or the role and powers of the Governor. Once we know how some aspect of Texas politics has developed over time, we can ask how and how effectively it works today. And then, inevitably, the discussion must shift to alternatives, to political change and reform. This text will allow teachers to share with their students the evolution of Texas politics, where we stand today, and where we seem to be headed.

I have chosen to write a brief text, rather than a book twice its size, because I believe that less is more in this instance. Faculty know too much that is fascinating and students have too many interesting questions for any book to try to anticipate and address them all. What I have done in the space that I have allowed myself is to describe how Texas politics works, how it came to work that way, and what general range of possibilities, both for continuity and for change, the future seems to hold. Where the conversation goes from there is up to students and their teachers, as it should be.

To students, I have tried to say more than that politics is important because it affects your lives in important ways and continuously. I have tried to provide a sense of how politics works and how people can become involved in it so that when an issue arises that you feel strongly about you will feel empowered. Politics is not just a spectator sport. It is a game that we are all entitled to play. Those who play Texas politics do not always win, but those who do not play almost always lose. To faculty teaching Texas politics, I have tried to help you communicate to your students what we know as political scientists and how much fun we had discovering it and sharing it.

Instructors and students will find an unmatched range of pedagogical aids and tools built into *Texas Politics*. Each chapter opens with a number of focus questions (usually five or six) and concludes with a Chapter Summary, a list of Key Terms, Suggested Readings, and Web Resources. The focus questions are listed at the beginning of the chapter and then again in the margins of the chapter where the information answering the question is to be found. Key Terms are bolded in the text, listed at the end of the chapter, and included in a Glossary at the end of the book. Each chapter presents several carefully designed tables or figures and a cartoon to highlight the major ideas, issues, and institutions discussed. Each chapter also contains a "Let's Compare" feature in which Texas is compared to other states on some important dimension or issue, such as urbanization, voter turnout, gubernatorial powers, and tax rates.

Texas Politics is organized in ten chapters. Chapters 1 and 2 trace the state's political history and place Texas within the broader context of American federalism. Chapter 1 describes the history and settlement of Texas and the cultural, economic, and political developments to the modern period. Chapter 2 describes the constitutional history of Texas, lays out the major provisions of the Texas Constitution, and describes how Texas fits into the American federal system.

Chapters 3 through 5 deal with political behavior. Chapter 3 deals with voters, campaigns, and elections. Key topics include, voter registration, turnout, campaign finance, and the conduct of Texas elections. Chapter 4 describes the resources and activities of interest groups in Texas and the generally ineffectual attempts to regulate them. Chapter 5 describes structure, history, and prospects of Texas political parties.

Chapters 6 through 9 detail the major political institutions of Texas: the legislature, the Governor and the executive branch, the judicial system, and local governments. Chapter 10 describes the budgetary process, major sources of tax revenues, and the major programs and expenditures of Texas state government. Special attention has been given to recent controversies over school finance, immigration, and redistricting. The personalities and issues of the 2006 and 2008 Texas elections are explored throughout.

Finally, I would like to give special thanks to the McGraw-Hill team that brought this book to print. Mark Georgiev, as Senior Sponsoring Editor, continues to have faith in the book. Carrie Braun gently but very efficiently coordinated the development of this project, Marisa Myers Bernste kept the reader front of mind as she copy-edited the manuscript, and Rich Barshak and Shirley Grall brought the book to press.

Equally important were the reviewers who kept this project focused on the major issues of Texas politics. Present at the creation were: Nancy Bednar, Del Mar College, Bob Bezdek, Texas A&M University, Corpus Christi, Paul Blakelock, Kingwood College, Gary Brown, Montgomery College, Cecillia Castillo, Texas State University, San Marcos, Brian Farmer, Amarillo College, Robert Holder, McLennan Community College, Timothy Hoye, Texas Women's University, Jerry Polinard, University of Texas, Pan American, and Robert E. Sterken, Jr., The University of Texas at Tyler. Each is a Texas politics expert in his or her own right and I was proud to have their advice and guidance. Special thanks go to Gary Brown who was always there when we needed a really well-trained eye really fast.

Southern Methodist University has, as always, been supportive of my work and the Political Science Department has created a great working environment. Harold Stanley, Dennis Simon, and Matt Wilson teach me something about Texas politics every day. Beyond all of these, my wife Jane has provided the peace, security, and support that make life a joy.

CHAPTER 1

Texas and the Texans: Then and Now[1]

Focus Questions

Q1. Where does the larger-than-life Texas mystique come from?

Q2. How has the geography of Texas affected the state's development?

Q3. How has the Texas economy evolved over the state's history?

Q4. How has the ethnic mix of the Texas population evolved over time?

Q5. What factors will determine the future prosperity and stability of Texas?

Texas is a big, complex, multifaceted, and utterly fascinating state. In both myth and reality, Texas is larger-than-life. It is the second largest state in the union (behind only Alaska) and the second most populous (behind only California). No other state can summon an equally romantic history; beginning with the Alamo, a decade as the independent Republic of Texas, the cattle drives, the oil fields, and J.R. Ewing's "Dallas." Only California, Florida, and New York can boast anything similar—a brand name—an image that has implanted itself in the popular mind.

> **Q1.** Where does the larger-than-life Texas mystique come from?

Throughout its history, Texas has attracted a volatile mix of adventurers, talented rascals on the rebound, and hardworking men and women searching for a fresh start. As early as the 1820s, the message *G.T.T.* (Gone to Texas) was scribbled on log cabins and boarded-up storefronts of Americans looking for a new beginning.[2] Stephen F. Austin, the founder of **Anglo** Texas, was born in Connecticut and schooled in Kentucky before settling in Texas. Sam Houston was born in Virginia and raised in Tennessee where he became governor before scandal drove him into Indian country and then on to Texas. Bowie came from Kentucky, Crockett from Tennessee, Fannin and Lamar from Georgia, and Travis from South Carolina. A few found Texas by traveling south: Anson Jones from Massachusetts, David Burnet from New Jersey, and Deaf Smith from New York.

Anglo A Spanish term referring to non-Hispanic whites.

Yet, history has not treated Texans gently. Texans had to fight for independence against a dangerous and arbitrary Mexican government. After ten rocky years of independence and fifteen as an American state on the distant frontier, Texas threw in its lot with the Confederacy. The **Civil War** left Texas defeated, occupied, and deeply traumatized. **Reconstruction** produced a sullen standoff between white Texans and their state government. Once white Texans regained control of their state in the 1870s, they wrote a constitution designed, above all else, to make government too weak and diffused to further threaten them. Modern Texans depend on that same government to confront and solve the vastly more complex problems of the 21st century. We will ask whether this 19th century constitution serves Texas well today.

In Chapter 1 we describe the people, culture, geography, and economy of Texas. How did Texas, a late arrival as the 28th state, become "the great state of Texas," or what Texas humorist Molly Ivins simply called "the great state" (assuming, obviously, that the Texas part was obvious)? Who settled Texas? When did they come? Where did they come from and where did they settle? How did they wrestle a living from the land? And what kind of society and polity did they intend to build?

Civil War   The U.S. Civil War, pitting the northern states against the southern states, occurred between 1861 and 1865.

Reconstruction   The period of post Civil War (1867 to 1872) military occupation of the South during which the North attempted to reconstruct southern social, political, and economic life.

ORIGINS AND SETTLEMENTS

The land that became Texas had been home to native peoples for at least 12,000 years.[3] Only in the 16th and 17th centuries did European exploration, conquest, and colonization impinge upon these first Texans. As late as 1800, 20,000 Native-Americans, including mighty tribes like the Comanche and Apache, lived in and ranged across Texas. About 3,500 Spanish Mexicans lived north of the **Rio Grande,** about half in San Antonio and most of the rest in La Bahia (Goliad) and Nacogdoches. Anglos and blacks were almost entirely absent.[4]

By 1900, 2.35 million whites and 620,000 blacks lived in Texas. About 71,000 Hispanics (4 percent of the total population) lived in South Texas, most between the Neuces and the Rio Grande, and the Indians largely were gone (0.5 percent). The Anglo settlement of Texas (or conquest of northern Mexico, depending upon your taste and perspective) was one of the most stunning population movements in history.

Rio Grande   Spanish for Grand River, the Rio Grande forms Texas's southern border with Mexico from El Paso to Brownsville.

Native Peoples

The first Texans were big game—*really* big game—hunters. They tracked mammoth and giant bison across the plains of what today is north central Texas. As the last ice age receded about 7,000 years ago, these prehistoric animals disappeared and the native peoples became hunters and gatherers focusing on smaller animals, including deer and gazelle, as well as fish, nuts, berries, and useful plants. Settled agriculture began among some native tribes, especially in east and northeast Texas, around 400 A.D. Hunting, fishing, and gathering from nature were still important, but crops of corn, beans, and squash provided flexibility and variety to native diets.

Intruders arrived early in the 16th century. The Spanish came first, but others, more numerous and more powerful, followed. Native people successfully resisted the Spanish attempts to draw them to the missions of early Texas, but they could not resist the rising Anglo immigration of the 19th century. The Caddo, Tonkawa, and Karankawa of Central and East Texas were subdued by the 1850s.[5] By the late 1870s, the Apache and the Comanche were forced from the Hill Country and High Plains north into Oklahoma and west into New Mexico.[6]

Spanish Explorers and Mexican Settlers

The Spanish explorer Alvar Nunez Cabeza de Vaca is one of history's most intriguing figures. Initially shipwrecked in Florida, his party built barges and put to sea only to wreck again on Galveston Island. Cabeza de Vaca spent nearly eight years (1528–36) living among and trading with native tribes throughout Texas and the Southwest as far as the gulf of California. His tales of prosperous lands and cities of gold piqued the interest of Spanish officials in Mexico City. Francisco Vasquez de Coronado was dispatched to make a more systematic survey. Coronado and a force of 2,000 Spaniards and Mexican-Indians spent nearly three years (1540–42) exploring Texas and the Southwest, penetrating as far as central Kansas. Coronado's failure to find the fabled Seven Cities of Cibola cooled Spanish interest in their northern provinces for more than a century.[7]

A brief incursion into Texas in the 1680s by the French trader and explorer, Rene-Robert-Cavelier, Sieur de La Salle, finally spurred the Spanish to expand their mission activities beyond the **Rio Grande Valley** as far North as San Antonio and as far East as Nacogdoches.[8] Still, as the 19th century dawned, Texas remained the lightly populated northernmost province of Spanish Mexico. Then, in 1810, Mexico rebelled against Spain and after a decade of warfare won independence in 1821. Even as Mexicans celebrated independence, an Anglo tide was rising in Texas.

Rio Grande Valley
Texas's four southernmost counties, often referred to simply as "the valley," are heavily Hispanic. The phrase is sometimes used more expansively to refer to all of South Texas.

American Settlers

Americans began drifting into Texas in small numbers beginning about 1815. The first major Anglo settlement, organized by Moses Austin and carried forward by his son, Stephen F. Austin, was established in 1823. Austin was authorized by Mexican authorities to offer up to one square league (4,428 acres) to settlers willing to occupy and work the land. Settlers were expected to be (or be willing to say they were) Catholics, to become Mexican citizens, and to foreswear slavery. As Anglo numbers grew, Mexican authorities worried about how to control these independent, even rebellious, immigrants. Attempts to limit immigration and to enforce laws requiring Catholicism and prohibiting slavery irritated the Anglos and tensions grew.[9]

General Sam Houston on horseback.
© Bettmann/CORBIS

The election of Antonio Lopez de Santa Anna as president of Mexico in 1834 was initially seen as promising. Texans believed that Santa Anna supported their autonomy within a loose federal state. But Santa Anna soon sought to consolidate power by centralizing control over all of Mexico, including Texas. Hostilities broke out between Texans and elements of the Mexican Army near San Antonio in October 1835. The first fight was the famous "Come And Take It" skirmish in which residents of Gonzales, about 70 miles East of San Antonio, defended a small cannon against Mexican cavalry sent to seize it. A wild Texan charge (it would not be the last) dispersed the Mexicans and retained the cannon, at least for a time.

By early 1836, Santa Anna had crossed the Rio Grande at the head of a large army. The real fight for Texas was about to begin. The Texans were bloodied early, first at the Alamo (March 6, 1836) and then in the slaughter at Goliad (March 27, 1836). These early defeats sent thousands of panic-stricken Anglo Texans fleeing eastward in what came to be known as the "Runaway Scrape." General Sam Houston's ragtag Texas army also retreated eastward, stopping where possible to train the unruly volunteers in marching, close order drill, and firing by companies.

Confident of victory, Santa Anna sent three columns in pursuit of the bedraggled Texans. One column was sent to capture the provisional government of Texas and two were to find and destroy the Texas army. Santa Anna accompanied the lead elements of the pursuit. Yet, within weeks, Houston's army outmaneuvered Santa Anna's force, caught them napping (literally), and routed them at San Jacinto (April 21, 1836). Santa Anna himself was captured on April 22 and forced to sign treaties recognizing Texas independence and withdrawing the remaining Mexican armies south of the Rio Grande. A tentative independence had been won, but danger and uncertainty lurked all about.

Republic of Texas
Texas was an independent nation from 1836 until it became a U.S. state on December 29, 1845.

The **Republic of Texas** experienced a decade-long rollercoaster ride of independent nationhood. Continued immigration and expansion vied with two Mexican invasions, frequent flirtations with bankruptcy, hyperinflation, and political instability to shape the new nation's future. Once Texas began to stabilize under the strong hand of President Sam Houston in the early 1840s, the U.S. grew wary of Texas as a competitor for influence over the West. To forestall this competition, U.S. President James K. Polk welcomed Texas into the Union on December 29, 1845. Polk's action sparked the Mexican-American War (1846–1848) and secured for the U.S. not only Texas but all of the American southwest and California.[10]

The Slaves

Spain and Mexico outlawed slavery by the 1820s, so Anglos were reluctant to bring slaves into Texas before the 1830s. Once Texas secured its independence many southern slaveholders moved to Texas. Texas entered the union as a slave state and the expansion of slavery in Texas continued through the 1850s. Most Texas slaves worked on cotton plantations east of a line running from Dallas through Austin to Corpus Christi.

In February 1861, Texas seceded from the United States to become the westernmost member of the Confederate States of America. Though Governor Sam Houston (in his seventh term as President or Governor of Texas) opposed secession, a majority of Texans embraced the Confederate cause. The Civil War and Reconstruction had a tremendous impact on Texas. Following Reconstruction, white Texans struggled to restore and then maintain the social, political, and economic primacy that they had enjoyed before the Civil War.

THE POLITICAL CULTURE OF TEXAS

These formative decades stamped Texas political life with a distinctive feel and character. By the time Texas won its independence from Mexico in 1836, Anglo Texans outnumbered Texans of Spanish or Mexican origin by ten to one. Anglo immigrants brought to Texas assumptions about and attitudes toward politics that they had learned in the United States. Most of the immigrants came out of the American South.

Scholars use the term **political culture** to denote widely shared attitudes toward politics.[11] Political scientist Daniel Elazar has traced the roots of the American political culture back into the colonial period. By the 1830s, this American political culture (in the U.S. and Texas) had matured into a broad commitment to democratic capitalism for white men. Democratic capitalism joins elements of equality and community with elements

Political culture Widely held ideas concerning the relationship of citizens to their government and to each other in matters effecting politics and public affairs.

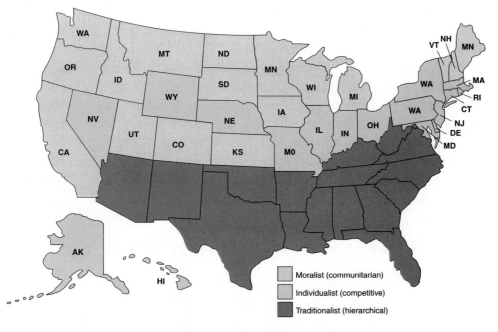

Moralist (communitarian)
Individualist (competitive)
Traditionalist (hierarchical)

Virginia Gray and Russell L. Hanson (eds.), *Politics in the American States: A Comparative Analysis,* 9th ed. Washington, D.C.: CQPress, 2008, p. 21. Adapted in part from Daniel Elazar, *American Federalism: A View from the States,* 3rd ed. New York: Harper and Row, 1984, p. 136.

of competition and hierarchy. Intriguingly, Elazar identifies three regional political subcultures that draw from the broader American political culture, each in a distinctive way.

New England and the northern states draw most heavily from the egalitarian and communitarian strains (think town meetings) to form what Elazar called a moralistic political culture. Today, we would probably call this a communitarian political culture, as moralistic tends to have strong religious overtones for us. Citizens in a moralistic political culture take politics seriously, participate at high levels, and approve higher taxes so that more public needs can be met. The Middle Atlantic and Middle Western states draw most heavily from the competitive strain (think Lincoln, rail-splitter to president) to produce an individualistic political culture. Citizens in an individualistic political culture assume that politics, like business, is a competitive arena in which advancement can be sought, services can be delivered, contracts can be awarded, and benefits can be received. The South draws most heavily from the hierarchical strain (think *Gone with the Wind*) to produce a traditionalistic political culture. In a traditionalistic political culture, participation is low, government is small and taxes low, elites govern, and the maintenance of social order is paramount.

The first Anglo Texans came mostly out of the American South and settled in East Texas and the Gulf Coast region. The dominant southerners favored states' rights and the leadership of established elites. Midwesterners came somewhat later, in smaller numbers, and settled in North Texas, the Panhandle, and West Texas. They favored small government, low taxes, and individual opportunity. History, migration and immigration, urbanization, and economic change have mixed and modified these regional political subcultures. Nonetheless, scholars and political observers agree that the Texas political culture has always been and remains Southern traditionalism with an admixture of Western and Midwestern individualism.

As we shall see throughout this book, despite historic change, the Texas political culture has been remarkably stable. Texas was once a rural agricultural state in which planter interests dominated the ruling Democratic party. Today, Texas is an urban industrial state in which business interests dominate the ruling Republican party. But throughout, political participation has been limited, citizens have been disengaged, the lobby has dominated Austin, and taxes have rested lightly on the state's social and economic elite.[12] The state motto, "Don't Mess With Texas," might well be "Let the Big Dogs Hunt."

THE PHYSICAL GEOGRAPHY AND EARLY ECONOMY OF TEXAS

Q2. How has the geography of Texas affected the state's development?

Texas is a vast and varied state. It spans more than 267,000 square miles. At its widest points, it is 773 miles from east to west and 801 miles from north to south. On this broad canvass, wave after wave of immigrants found their future.[13]

The geography of Texas presents three main regions. South Texas, often called the Lower Rio Grande Valley, or simply "the Valley," is semi-arid brush country south of an arc that runs from Corpus Christi to San Antonio to Del Rio. The rest of Texas is separated into two distinct regions, with several sub-regions in each, by the Balcones Escarpment. The **Balcones Escarpment** is a geological faultline that runs east from Del Rio to San Antonio and then north to the Red River, passing west of Austin, Killeen, and Fort Worth. It separates the humid, well-watered, lowlands of East Texas from the drier, upland, prairies and plains of West Texas.

Balcones Escarpment
A geological fault line that separates the lowlands of East Texas from the prairies and plains of West Texas.

The Regions of Texas. *Texas Natural Resources Information System*

South Texas

South Texas was home to many Native-American tribes and to the first European settlers in Texas. The limited natural resources of this harsh land supported their modest needs. By 1750, cattle ranches operated on both sides of the Rio Grande. Indian raids, cattle rustling, and the political instability surrounding the war for Mexican independence resulted in cattle ranging free throughout South Texas. Before the American Civil War, these famed longhorns fed Texans and modest herds were driven east to New Orleans and, somewhat later, north to Midwestern markets and railheads.

The ranching culture looms large in the Texas mind, if not so large as it once did in the Texas economy. The legendary **King Ranch,** south of Corpus Christi, still covers an expanse of 825,000 acres, larger than the state of Rhode Island.[14] Increasingly though, these historic ranches are being divided up, sold off, and set to other purposes. Nonetheless, parts of "the Valley" became a thriving truck farming economy of citrus fruits and vegetables once Anglo farmers introduced large scale irrigation in the 1920s. The majority of the sparse, mostly Hispanic, population has remained desperately poor. Only in the past couple of decades has the economy of San Antonio expanded beyond the military and tourism to manufacturing, health care, and the biosciences.

King Ranch   Founded in 1853 by Captain Richard King, the 825,000 acre King Ranch south of Corpus Christi epitomizes the huge dry land cattle ranches of Texas.

Q3. How has the Texas economy evolved over the state's history?

East Texas

East Texas was the population and wealth center of the state for much of the 19th century. White immigrants from the American South and their

"No one is making you do anything you don't want. I'm just saying we're all headed for Dodge City and we think you should come along."

LEO CULLUM/The New Yorker

slaves brought a rich cotton culture to East Texas in the 1820s and 1830s. Prior to the Civil War and for decades thereafter, agriculture, especially "King Cotton," rivaled and even surpassed ranching as a mainstay of the Texas economy. The cotton culture was a slave-based economy and society of plantations and small towns. Even after slavery ended and cotton gave way to poultry, timber, and oil and gas, the social structure of East Texas remained rural and segregated. Economic leadership passed to other regions of the state.

Gulf drilling rig. © *Digital Vision/PunchStock*

The Gulf Coast

The Gulf Coast, from the Louisiana border to Corpus Christi, is low grasslands and swamps with plentiful rainfall. During the 19th century, the Gulf Coast was an extension of East Texas. Cotton, rice, and grains were the principal crops. The 20th century brought tremendous change to the Gulf Coast. On January 10, 1901, A.F. Lucas brought in the **Spindletop** oil field near Beaumont. Oil wells had been operating in Texas for decades, but Spindletop was much bigger and more productive. Within a year, Spindletop was the most productive oil field in the world. Additional discoveries throughout Texas and then in the Gulf made Texas the oil capitol of the world for the first three-quarters of the 20th century. With Houston at its core, the Gulf Coast became an energy, petrochemical, manufacturing, and shipping center for Texas and the nation.

Spindletop A.F. Lucas's spindletop well near Beaumont came in on January 10, 1901, kicking off the 20th century Texas oil boom.

North Texas

As the railroads came south to Texas after the Civil War, they converged on Dallas and then Fort Worth. North Texas, home to some of the state's most fertile land, the Black and Grand Prairies, became the center of the state's cotton culture. Dallas was a commercial, banking, and insurance center by the late-19th century. Fort Worth, just thirty miles west of Dallas, became the commercial center for much of West Texas. Fort Worth's economic connection to the West Texas ranch economy was reinforced when the Armour and Swift meatpacking companies moved into Fort Worth in 1901.

World War II ushered in a period of tremendous growth in and around the Dallas-Fort Worth "Metroplex." Population more than doubled between 1940 and 1960 and manufacturing employment grew even faster. The postwar years brought rapid expansion of defense, construction, and aerospace industries and the Texas oil industry expanded into oil services, pipelines, shipping, and petrochemicals.

The Hill Country

Originally settled by German immigrants beginning about 1840, this beautiful but difficult area of central Texas remains distinctive today. Never easy for agriculture, the Hill Country has been home to ranchers that ran sheep, goats, and cattle as the terrain and foliage allowed. In recent decades, the region's beauty has drawn vacationers and retirees. Fredericksburg remains the ethnic German heart of the Hill Country.

West Texas

Permian Basin   A geological formation in West Texas, around Midland, where oil discoveries were made in the 1920s that remain productive today.

After the Apache and Comanche were subdued in the late-1870s, this rugged country was settled by farmers and ranchers, many of them from the American Midwest. By the mid-1880s, large ranches overspread West Texas, the railroads had arrived, and cattle moved to the urban markets of the Midwest and East by the tens of thousands. After World War II, ranching gave way to large-scale irrigated agriculture on the high plains of West Texas. Today, the panhandle and high plains are the heartland of Texas agriculture and of its modern cotton culture. From the wheat fields of the panhandle, through the heavily irrigated cotton to the South, the oil and gas fields of the **Permian Basin,** and the ranch lands of lightly populated Southwest Texas, the cowboy, vaquero, rancher, farmer, roughneck traditions of Texas still live.

BECOMING MODERN TEXAS

Texas is no longer an overwhelmingly Anglo, sparsely populated, rural state defined by cattle, cotton, and oil. This old Texas has receded before a new Texas that is vibrantly urban and vastly more diverse. The new Texas is urban, majority-minority, and vibrantly entrepreneurial. It has great potential, but that potential will not be realized automatically. Texas political authorities and citizens will have to see the future coming and respond thoughtfully to insure that "the great state" continues to merit that appellation in the 21st century.

Cultural Diversity

Q4. How has the ethnic mix of the Texas population evolved over time?

Dramatic social change has been a constant in Texas history. Figure 1.1 puts contemporary social change in historical perspective. We see that as late as 1800, Indians comprised 80 percent of those living in what would become Texas, with Hispanics comprising the remaining 20 percent. But vast change was coming.

Though data are sketchy for the first half of the 19th century, it is clear that the Indian presence in Texas plummeted, the Hispanic presence lagged, while Anglo and black numbers soared. By 1850, Anglos accounted for 65 percent of Texans and blacks for another 26 percent. Indian and Hispanic numbers had fallen to five percent and would drift even lower as the end of the century approached. Anglo numbers continued to rise through-

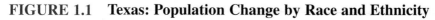

FIGURE 1.1   **Texas: Population Change by Race and Ethnicity**

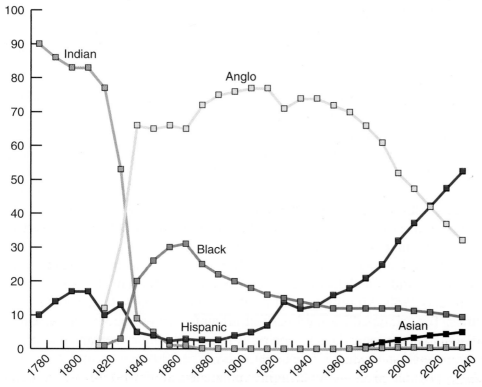

Source: Population estimates prior to 1850 are compiled from best available sources. U.S. Census Bureau, Texas: Race and Hispanic Origin: 1850 to 1990, Table 58. Randolph B. Campbell, Gone To Texas: A History of the Lone Star State (New York: Oxford University Press, 2003), pp. 470, 472. Projections for 2010 to 2040 come from the Population Estimates and Projection Program, Texas State Data Center, UT, San Antonio. See http://txsdc .utsa.edu/tpepp/2004.

out the 19th century. In 1900, Texas was about 75 percent Anglo, 20 percent black, and four percent Hispanic. Native-American numbers were vanishingly small. In 1940, when the U.S. Census began reporting Hispanics separately from whites, Anglos were still 74 percent, blacks 14.4 percent, and Hispanics 11.5 percent.

After 1950, slowly at first, but then more rapidly, the racial and ethnic make-up of Texas began to change. The Anglo share of the population began to fall, the black share continued its slow decline, and the Hispanic share began to rise more quickly. Population data from the U.S. Census Bureau and the Texas State Data Center show that Anglos were 66 percent of the population as late as 1980, 61 percent in 1990, 52 percent in 2000 (they fell below 50 percent in 2005), and are projected to be 42 percent by 2020 and 32 percent by 2040. Blacks have held steady at about 12 percent since 1980, but will slowly decline in coming decades. Projections suggest that blacks will make up 11 percent of the Texas population in 2020 and 9.5 percent by 2040.

The Hispanic share of the Texas population has doubled since 1970 and will continue to grow rapidly. In 1970, Hispanics composed 18 percent of the population; by 2005 it was 36 percent. Almost 30 percent of Texans speak Spanish at home. A majority of Texans will be of Hispanic heritage by the 2030s.

Asian Americans, a relatively new presence in Texas, constitute 3 percent of the population, but that will nearly double, to 5.1 percent by 2040. Native Americans remain a small proportion of the Texas population. The federal government recognizes three tribes, comprising about one-half of one percent of the state's total population. The Alabama-Coushatta live in

East Texas, the Tigua in West Texas, and the Kickapoo on the New Mexico border near Eagle Pass.

Urbanization

The first U.S. Census to include Texas was conducted in 1850 and reported that Texas was just 4 percent urban (towns of 2,500 or larger). Most Texans lived in small rural towns and on plantations, farms, and ranches. In 1900, Texas was still overwhelmingly rural. Only 17 percent of Texans lived in urban settings, compared to 73 percent of New Yorkers, 55 percent of Pennsylvanians, and 40 percent of Americans. Texas urbanized slowly through the early 20th century, until preparations for World War II spurred an exodus from rural Texas to the military bases and industrial plants in the urban triangle joining Houston, Dallas-Fort Worth, and San Antonio.

Table 1.1 shows that a number of Sun Belt states, including Texas, California, Florida, and Georgia, experienced rapid urban growth between 1940 and 1950. Migration from north to south also swelled the Sun Belt cities. Texas jumped from 45 percent urban in 1940 to 63 percent urban in 1950 and never looked back. The rural Texas of memory became the urban, commercial, and industrial Texas of today. The 2009 census update put the Texas population at nearly 25 million, 83 percent of whom lived in urban areas and 17 percent of whom lived in rural areas. Finally, Houston, San Antonio, and Dallas are three of the ten largest cities in the country and fully 60 percent of Texans live in a triangle that connects these three cities. All three of the cities have minority-majority populations.

TABLE 1.1
Let's Compare: The Move to the Cities in Texas and Other States

Texas urbanized slowly and late, but then with a vengeance. The majority of the U.S. population lived in cities by 1920, but the majority of Texans did not live in cities until some time in the 1940s. Unlike New York, Pennsylvania, Illinois, and California, which always revolved around their great cities, Texas and Florida are distinctly 20th century Sun Belt states. Only 17 percent urban in 1900, Texas is 83 percent urban today, exceeding the national average of 79 percent, and just a few points behind New York.

	1900	1910	1920	1930	1940	1950	1960	1970	1980	1990	2000
Nation	40	46	51	56	57	64	70	74	74	75	79
CA	52	62	68	73	71	81	86	91	91	92	94
TX	**17**	**24**	**32**	**41**	**45**	**63**	**75**	**80**	**80**	**80**	**83**
NY	73	79	83	84	83	86	85	86	85	84	88
FL	20	29	37	52	55	66	74	82	84	85	89
PA	55	60	65	68	67	71	72	72	69	69	77
IL	54	62	68	74	74	78	81	83	83	85	89
OH	48	56	64	68	67	70	73	75	73	74	77
MI	39	47	61	68	66	71	73	74	71	71	75
NC	10	14	19	26	27	34	40	46	48	50	60
GA	16	21	25	31	34	45	55	60	62	63	72

Source: U.S. Census Bureau, Urban and Rural Population: 1900–1990, *www.census.gov/population/censusdata/urpop0090.txt*. 2000 data came from U.S. Census Bureau, Statistical Abstract of the United States, 2008, p. 34, Table 29.

Economic Diversification

The Texas economy also continues to grow and evolve. The stock market collapse of early 2001 and the attacks of 9/11 later that year devastated the airline and hospitality industries and slowed the national and state economies. Corporate corruption, of which Houston's Enron provided the most glaring example, did further damage. The high tech industries around Dallas, Austin, and Houston took a beating in 2001 and 2002, but they have slowly rebounded and will be a major factor in the state's future growth. The bust in the housing market and economic slow down of late-2007 and 2008 hit Texas less hard than most other states.

Most recent job growth has been concentrated in the computer, education, and health fields. Jobs for computer software engineers, computer support specialists, network administrators, and specialists in desktop publishing are all growing by more than 50 percent between 2004 and 2014. In health care, medical assistants, respiratory therapists, and physical therapy aides will all grow by 40 to 50 percent. So will many teaching fields as well as certain areas of social and human service delivery.[15]

FUTURE CHALLENGES

Texas has a mythical self-image as a place where an individual willing to work hard can make a life and maybe a fortune. But while Texas is home to great wealth, it is also home to great poverty. Texas ranked only 37th

Q5. What factors will determine the future prosperity and stability of Texas?

TABLE 1.2
Texas Employment by Industry Sector, 2008

Industry Sector	2nd Quarter 2008
Goods Producing	
Agriculture*	61,785
Natural Resources	222,200
Construction	672,200
Manufacturing	926,500
Service Providing	
Trade, Transportation, and Utilities	2,145,800
Information	216,800
Financial Activities	653,800
Professional and Business Services	1,356,100
Education and Health Services	1,293,900
Leisure and Hospitality	1,021,200
Government	1,764,200
Other Services	356,900
TOTAL EMPLOYMENT	**10,691,385**

*Agricultural employment is available only in the Texas Quarterly Census.
Source: Texas Labor Market Review, August 2008, p. 2 and Texas Quarterly Census of Employment and Wages, 1st quarter 2008, p. 2. Both are at the Texas Workforce Commission website, www.tracer2.com

among the 50 states in median family income in 2007. Sixteen point three percent of Texans and 23.2 percent of Texas children live below the federally designated poverty line. Only seven states, mostly in the deep South and Southwest, have a greater proportion of poor citizens than Texas.[16] Texas also has a higher teen birth rate and a higher proportion of children without health insurance than any other state. The future prosperity of Texas depends upon insuring that more Texans are healthy, well-educated, and profitably employed.

Pro-Business Climate

Texas is generally rated near the top in the quality of its "business climate." It is home to more Fortune 500 companies than any other state in the union. Texans expect government to facilitate freedom and opportunity, mostly by staying out of people's way, and by keeping government small, taxes low, and regulations light. These are core preferences of the Texas political culture and are unlikely to change.

Texas often rates much lower, sometimes near the bottom, on "quality of life." Generally, a high quality of life involves good schools, attractive cities and towns, low pollution, and abundant outdoor recreation. Texas ranks near the middle on education spending, but much lower on the arts, health, welfare, and environmental spending.[17] The state's political leaders, often imagining that they must pick between a good business climate and an attractive quality of life, usually pick a good business climate. Future Texans will demand a better balance.

Educated Workforce

Texans understand that a strong economy requires an educated workforce. Yet, spending the money that it would take to insure excellent schools comes hard to Texans. Texas ranks 32nd among the states on the proportion of adults with Bachelor's degrees at 25.2 percent (below the national average of 27.5 percent). But shockingly, Texas ranks 50th among the states on the proportion of adults over 25 who have graduated from high school (or passed a GED). The national average is 84.8 percent, while Texas graduates 79.1 percent. Texas must do better.

Education reform and funding were the top issues during the 2005 regular legislative session and three special sessions in 2005 and 2006. In May 2006, the Texas Legislature finally passed and the Governor signed an education reform and funding bill that lowered local property taxes and replaced the money with an expanded business tax, a dollar a pack increase in the tax on cigarettes, and a number of smaller tax increases. Despite endless talk and years of political wrangling, Texas public schools ended up with little new money. More money for schools will be necessary to insure that the workforce of the future is well-trained.

Inclusion and Empowerment

As Texas continues to evolve ethnically and economically, it must insure that all of its citizens are included and empowered. By 2040, Anglos will constitute just one-third of the Texas population. Those that Anglo Texans have traditionally called minorities—blacks, Hispanics, Asians—will be two-thirds of the population, and Hispanics alone will be the new majority. Texas will not thrive unless most, ideally all, of its citizens thrive.[18]

The demographic future of Texas puts a heavy responsibility on all Texans. Anglo Texans, who will control most of the state's wealth long after their numbers wane, will be challenged to finance a state education system that prepares all Texans to contribute their full measure to our future prosperity. Texas's traditional minorities, and especially Hispanic Texans, will be challenged to increase their overall educational achievement and to enter more fully into the political community through naturalization (for those not already citizens), voter registration, voting, and officeholding.

CHAPTER SUMMARY

When history first took notice of Texas it was home to dozens of Native-American bands and tribes. They lived by hunting, fishing, and gathering as they were without horses, cattle, or domesticated animals beyond dogs. The Spanish arrived early in the 16th century and quickly established a broad but unobtrusive control of Texas. Almost three centuries later, as the 19th century opened, there were no more than 3,500 Spanish Mexicans north of the Rio Grande.

Anglos began streaming into Texas, 80 percent of them out of the American South, after the Louisiana Purchase brought the U.S. to its eastern border. By 1820, even before Austin led his settlers across the Sabine, Anglos outnumbered Spanish Mexicans. After Texas independence in 1836, Anglo immigrants and their slaves reached a floodtide that did not abate for decades. Cotton farming and cattle ranching were the basis of the Texas economy until oil took the leading role early in the 20th century.

The 20th century saw tremendous population growth. Texas became the second most populous state in the union and its economy evolved beyond natural resources to manufacturing, high tech, and services. The challenge of the 21st century in Texas is to expand inclusion and enhance equity as Anglo Texans go from being a large and dominant majority to being less than one-third of the population by 2040. For Texas to be healthy and prosperous in the 21st century, all Texans must be educated, empowered, and involved.

KEY TERMS

Anglo	Permian Basin	Rio Grande
Balcones Escarpment	Political culture	Rio Grande Valley
Civil War	Reconstruction	Spindletop
King Ranch	Republic of Texas	

SUGGESTED READINGS

Rodolfo Acuna, *Occupied America: A History of Chicanos*, 5th ed. (New York: Pearson Longman, 2004).

Randolph B. Campbell, *Gone To Texas: A History of the Lone Star State* (New York: Oxford University Press, 2003).

Gregg Cantrell, *Stephen F. Austin: Empresario of Texas* (New Haven, CT: Yale University Press, 1999).

William C. Davis, *Lone Star Rising: The Revolutionary Birth of the Texas Republic* (New York: Free Press, 2004).

T.R. Fehrenbach, *Lone Star: A History of Texas and the Texans* (New York: Macmillan, 1968).

James L. Haley, *Passionate Nation: The Epic History of Texas* (New York: Free Press, 2006).

Joel H. Silbey, *Storm Over Texas: The Annexation Controversy and the Road to the Civil War* (New York: Oxford University Press, 2005).

WEB RESOURCES

http://www.lsjunction.com/ The Lone Star Junction website contains great resources on Texas history and politics. It rewards exploration.

http://texashistory.unt.edu/ Like the Lone Star Junction, the University of North Texas's Portal to Texas History is well worth exploring.

http://www.census.gov/ The U.S. Census Bureau website contains an extraordinary range of information on population, income, race, and ethnicity, most of it by state.

http://www.texas.gov/ The general website for the state of Texas.

http://www.texasalmanac.com/ Published every year since 1957, a comprehensive source for all things Texas.

END NOTES

1. The mildly curious phrase, "Texas and the Texans," comes from the subtitle of T.R. Fehrenbach's classic history of Texas, *Lone Star: A History of Texas and the Texans* (New York: Macmillan, 1968).

2. Randolph C. Campbell's fine new history of Texas, entitled *Gone to Texas: A History of the Lone Star State* (New York: Oxford University Press, 2005), plays with the Gone to Texas theme throughout.

3. David J. Meltzer, *First Peoples in a New World: Colonizing Ice Age America* (Berkeley, CA: University of California Press, 2009).

4. Texas Almanac, 2008–2009, Elizabeth Cruz Alvarez, ed., (College Station, TX: Texas A&M University Press, 2008). For a brief history of Texas as well as the size and physical regions of the state, see pp. 17–78, 80–84.

5. Kelly F. Himmel, *The Conquest of the Karankawas and Tonkawas*, 1821–1859 (College Station, TX: Texas A&M University Press, 1999).

6. W. W. Newcomb, *The Indians of Texas: From Prehistoric Times to Modern Times* (Austin: University of Texas Press, 1961), pp. 346–362.

7. Manuel G. Gonzales, *Mexicanos: A History of Mexicans in the United States* (Bloomington: Indiana University Press, 1999), pp. 29–31.

8. Carey McWilliams, *North from Mexico: The Spanish Speaking People of the United States* (New York: Greenwood Press, 1990), p. 84.

9. Matt S. Meier and Feliciano Rivera, *A History of Mexican Americans* (New York: Hill and Wang, 1972), pp. 58–59.

10. PBS Video, "U.S. Mexican War, 1846–1848" (Alexandria, VA: PBS Video, 1998).

11. Daniel J. Elazar, American Federalism: A View From the States 2nd ed. (New York: Harper and Row, 1972), pp. 84–113.

12. Virginia Gray and Russell L. Hanson, *Politics in the American States: A Comparative Analysis,* 9th ed., (Washington, D.C.: CQ Press, 2008), p. 4.

13. C. Allan Jones, *Texas Roots: Agriculture and Rural Life Before the Civil War* (College Station, TX: Texas A&M University Press, 2005).

14. S.C. Gwynne, "The Next Frontier," *Texas Monthly,* August 2007, pp. 118–125, 178–181, 193–196.

15. Fiscal Notes, Office of Susan Combs, Texas Comptroller of Public Accounts. March, 2008, p. 11.

16. U.S. Census Bureau, *American Community Survey, State Ranking Tables,* 2007. See http://factfinder.census.gov/.

17. Kendra A. Hovey and Harold A. Hovey, *CQ's State Fact Finder, 2007: Ranking Across America* (Washington, D.C.: CQ Press, 2007), pp. 87, 91, 97, 242, 249.

18. Robert T. Garrett, "Groups: Texas' Income Gap Growing," *Dallas Morning News,* April 9, 2008, 8A.

CHAPTER 2

The Texas Constitution and American Federalism

Focus Questions

Q1. What restraints does federalism impose on Texas politics?

Q2. How do the U.S. and Texas Constitutions share political authority in Texas?

Q3. What similarities and differences have characterized Texas's seven constitutions?

Q4. What are the basic principles and key provisions of the current Texas Constitution?

Q5. Should constitutional reform be on the political agenda in Texas?

Federalism is an American invention. For most of human history, people thought that governments had to be highly centralized, as in monarchy or tyranny, or highly decentralized, as in loose confederations of sovereign states. The U.S. Founders thought that carefully written constitutions allowed two levels of government, national and state, to act over the same territory and people simultaneously. Yet, the Founders were practical men; they knew that shared powers invited conflict. The struggle between national and state actors for the power and resources to define and address the dominant issues of American political life is a permanent feature of American federalism.

Federalism A form of government in which some powers are assigned to the national government, some to the states, and some, such as the power to tax, are shared.

The United States Constitution and the fifty state constitutions, including the Texas Constitution, derive their authority from popular sovereignty: the freely granted approval of the people. **Constitutions** are basic or fundamental law, superior to and controlling of the everyday acts of government. Constitutions describe the structure of government, the powers of each office, the process by which officials are elected or appointed to office, and the rights and liberties of citizens. Constitutions both award and limit political authority.

Constitution Basic or fundamental law that lays out the structure of government, the powers of each office, the process by which officials are elected or appointed, and the rights and liberties of citizens.

The U.S. Constitution and the fifty state constitutions all mandate similar institutions. All employ separation of powers, checks and balances, bicameralism, and the explicit protection of individual liberties through a bill of rights. All have a chief executive, a bicameral or two-house legislature (except Nebraska, which gets by with a unicameral legislature), and a judicial system of trial and appellate courts. All explicitly protect the rights and liberties of citizens.

Despite these structural similarities, states vary widely in the powers given to their governments, the concentration or diffusion of those powers, and the precise limits and checks employed. As we shall see below, the Texas Constitution limits political power more than most state constitutions, distributes power broadly through a diffuse political system, and encourages political officials to check each other at every turn. By design, the Texas Constitution makes indecision easy and decision difficult.

In this chapter, we describe the balance of constitutional authority between the national and the state governments in the American federal system. We trace Texas constitutionalism from its origins in Spanish Mexico through the tumult of independence, statehood, and the American Civil War. We then explore the current (we cannot really say modern) Texas Constitution of 1876. We close with a discussion of the prospects for constitutional reform in Texas.

TEXAS: A STATE IN THE AMERICAN FEDERAL SYSTEM

Q1. What restraints does federalism impose on Texas politics?

The U.S. Constitution defines the balance of power in American federalism.[1] Article VI contains the famous "**supremacy clause,**" which declares "this Constitution, and the laws of the United States which shall be made in pursuance thereof; . . . shall be the supreme law of the land; and the judges in every state shall be bound thereby, anything in the Constitution or laws of any State to the contrary notwithstanding." This seems pretty definitive: national power trumps state power.

Supremacy clause
Article VI of the U.S. Constitution declares the U.S. Constitution, federal laws, and treaties to be the supreme law of the land.

Enumerated powers
The specifically listed, or enumerated, powers of the Congress and president found in Article I, section 8, and Article II, section 2, of the U.S. Constitution.

In practice, federalism is murkier than the supremacy clause suggests. The national government is a government of **enumerated powers,** powers specifically allocated to it in the Constitution. Within these areas of enumerated power—foreign policy, national defense, interstate and foreign commerce, and a few others—national authority is supreme. But where authority is not granted to the national government by the U.S. Constitution, state governments enjoy complete or plenary powers, unless specific powers are denied them by their state constitution. Traditionally, states have made most policy regarding education, public safety, health care, transportation, family law, business regulation, and much more.[2]

National Powers

Q2. How do the U.S. and Texas Constitutions share political authority in Texas?

The U.S. Constitution grants a number of specific or enumerated powers to the national government. Article I, section 8, and Article II, section 2, give the national government the exclusive power to conduct foreign policy; raise, support, and command an army and navy; establish a national currency; set uniform rules for naturalization and bankruptcy; and regulate interstate and foreign commerce. To be doubly clear that these are national powers and the states are not to intrude, Article I, section 10, specifically prohibits state involvement in foreign policy, national security and war-making, issuing money, or regulating interstate and foreign commerce.

Moreover, Article I, section 8, concludes with the "**necessary and proper**" **clause,** or elastic clause as it is sometimes known. The elastic clause gives the national government broad discretion to act in regard to its enumerated powers. It declares that Congress has the power "to make all laws which shall be necessary and proper for carrying into execution the foregoing [enumerated] powers, and all other powers vested by this Constitution in the government of the United States, or in any department or officer thereof." The U.S. Supreme Court interpreted the "necessary and proper" clause expansively in *McCulloch v. Maryland* (1819). Chief Justice John Marshall wrote: "Let the end be legitimate, let it be within the scope of the Constitution, and all means which are appropriate, which are plainly adopted to that end, which are not prohibited but consistent with the letter and spirit of the Constitution are constitutional."

Amendments to the U.S. Constitution also expanded national power over the states. The 13th (1865), 14th (1868), and 15th (1870) Amendments gave Congress the power to end slavery, define American citizenship, and ensure the right of black men to vote. The 19th Amendment (1920) gave Congress the power to enforce female suffrage, the 24th (1964) to suppress the poll tax, and the 26th (1971) to enforce the right of 18- to 20-year-olds to vote. Finally, the "due process" and "equal protection" clauses of the 14th Amendment have been used to make the rights and liberties outlined in the U.S. Bill of Rights apply against the state as well as the national governments.

Necessary and proper clause   The last paragraph of Article I, section 8, of the U.S. Constitution, states that Congress may make all laws deemed necessary and proper for carrying into execution the powers specifically enumerated in Article I, section 8.

Powers Reserved to the States

Many among the Founding generation worried that the new national government might oppress the states and their citizens. The very first Congress proposed and the states adopted ten amendments to the new Constitution—the Bill of Rights. The 10th Amendment declared that "the powers not delegated to the United States by the Constitution, nor prohibited by it to the states, are reserved to the states respectively, or to the people."

The political scientist Joseph Zimmerman has explained the scope and variety of the **reserved powers** of the states by dividing them into three categories: "the police power, provision of services to citizens, and creation and control of local governments."[3] States are operating within their general "police power" when they act to promote public health, welfare, safety, morals, and convenience. States also provide a wide range of public services, including police and fire protection, road construction, and education. And states have the constitutional authority to create and regulate local governments. The reserved powers of the states give them the authority, if they choose to use it, to govern much of daily life.

Moreover, the 11th Amendment (1798) to the U.S. Constitution explicitly recognizes the **sovereign immunity** of the states. The 11th Amendment

Reserved powers   The 10th amendment to the U.S. Constitution declares that powers not granted to the national government by the Constitution are reserved to the states or their citizens.

Sovereign immunity   The 11th amendment to the U.S. Constitution declares that states cannot be sued in their own courts except as federal or state law explicitly allows.

says "the judicial power of the United States shall not be construed to extend to any suit in law or equity, commenced or prosecuted against one of the United States by citizens of another state, or by citizens or subjects of any foreign state." This means that states, as sovereign entities, cannot be forced to appear in the courts of another sovereign, whether another American state or a foreign nation. Similarly, states cannot be sued in their own courts unless state law expressly provides for such suits. Despite these explicit constitutional protections, states have had to fight to maintain their powers and prerogatives in the federal system.

Shared Powers

While some powers belong exclusively to the national government, like the power to make war, and others belong exclusively to the states, such as the power to create local governments, other powers are shared. Both the national and state governments have the power to tax, borrow, and spend; to build and maintain roads and highways; to regulate commerce within their respective jurisdictions; and to administer social services. The Founders expected some conflict between the national government and the states, but they sought to limit conflict between the states.

Relations among the States

Article IV, sections 1 and 2, of the U.S. Constitution require the states to respect each other's civil acts, deal fairly with each other's citizens, and return suspected criminals who flee from one state into another.

Full Faith and Credit. Article IV, section 1, of the U.S. Constitution requires that "Full Faith and Credit shall be given in each State to the public Acts, Records, and Judicial Proceedings of every other State." Through this simple provision, the Founders sought to create a national legal system by requiring the states to recognize and respect each other's legal acts and findings. Nonetheless, over the course of American history, social issues such as religious toleration, slavery, and gay marriage have strained the reciprocity and cooperation between the states.

Privileges and Immunities. Article IV, section 2, of the U.S. Constitution declares that "the Citizens of each State shall be entitled to all Privileges and Immunities of Citizens in the several States." The U.S. Supreme Court has declared that the "privileges and immunities" clause guarantees that citizens visiting, working, and conducting business in other states enjoy "the same freedom possessed by the citizens of those States in the acquisition and enjoyment of property and in the pursuit of happiness; and . . . the equal protection of the laws."

Extradition. Article IV, section 2, provides for a legal process called extradition. "A person charged in any state with treason, felony, or other crime, who shall flee from justice, and be found in another state, shall on demand of the executive authority of the state from which he fled, be delivered up, to be removed to the state having jurisdiction of the crime." Extradition requests are a staple of television police dramas.

Historically, the U.S. Constitution gave the national government responsibility for military and foreign policy and left Texas and her sister states in charge of their own "internal police." But as the nation has grown in size, population, wealth, and complexity, the boundary line between the national government's "supremacy" within its areas of constitutional responsibility and the states' "reserved powers" has shifted and blurred.

During the 19th century, domestic policy was state and local policy. But the economic and social problems accompanying the Great Depression of the 1930s convinced most Americans that the national government had to play a larger role in social and economic policymaking. National influence over state governments and policy grew through the 1970s. Beginning with the Reagan administration in the 1980s, conservatives in the executive branch, Congress, and the courts sought to restore some domestic policy responsibilities to the states. This process has been called **devolution.**

Devolution The return of political authority from the national government to the states.

Nonetheless, the federal government continues to guide and direct the states in myriad ways. Fully one-third of the funds that Texas state government spends each year come from the federal government and these funds always have strings attached. In addition, the federal government frequently requires action by the states, in regard to education reform, pollution control, and prisoner treatment, among many other issues, without providing the funds to comply. These requirements are called **unfunded mandates** and are a particular irritant to the states.

Unfunded mandates States frequently complain that the federal government mandates actions, like improving education, without providing sufficient funds to fulfill the mandate.

THE CONSTITUTIONAL HISTORY OF TEXAS

Table 2.1 shows that Texans have lived under seven constitutions, five since statehood.[4] Hispanic and Anglo Texans lived under the Spanish imperial government of New Spain before Mexico achieved its independence in 1821. In 1824, Mexico adopted a federal constitution; in 1827, authorities in Mexico City approved a provincial constitution that rolled Texas into the northern Mexican province of Coahuila. Texas's independence brought adoption of the hastily prepared 1836 Constitution of the Republic of Texas. Texas's annexation to the United States in 1845 required another new constitution.

Q3. What similarities and differences have characterized Texas's seven constitutions?

Secession, military defeat, reconstruction, and readmission brought a series of short-lived Texas constitutions between 1861 and 1869. As soon as Reconstruction ended, Texans overturned the hated Constitution of 1869 and replaced it with a new constitution that made Texas state government weaker, more diffuse, and in the minds of its authors, less dangerous. The Texas Constitution of 1876 remains in effect today.

1827 *Coahuila y Tejas* Constitution

Spain ruled Mexico for nearly 300 years, until a decade long revolution (1810–1821) established Mexican independence. Neither Spain nor Mexico

TABLE 2.1
The Seven Constitutions of Texas

Constitution	Years in Effect
Coahuila y Tejas	1827–1835
Republic of Texas	1836–1845
U.S. Statehood	1845–1861
C.S.A. Statehood	1861–1865
Presidential Reconstruction	1866–1869
Congressional Reconstruction	1869–1876
Modern Texas	1876–present

established stable government on its lightly populated northern frontier.[5] Mexico attempted to do so by wrapping Texas into the northern Mexican state of Coahuila in 1824. Texans enjoyed a modest representation in the *Coahuila y Tejas* legislature, one of ten members initially and two of twelve once the provincial Constitution was completed in 1827. Texans felt outnumbered and ignored. They twice petitioned to be a separate Mexican state, but were turned down both times.

1836 Republic of Texas Constitution

Texans declared their independence from Mexico on March 2, 1836. In the chaotic days that followed the fall of the Alamo, as Houston struggled to build an army, Texas political officials worked to produce a new constitution. The Republic of Texas Constitution, adopted on March 17, 1836, reflected basic U.S. principles, including separation of powers, checks and balances, and bicameralism.

The president was limited to a single three-year term, but while in office he enjoyed many of the powers of the U.S. president. He was commander-in-chief of Texas military forces, though he was prohibited from commanding in person without the formal permission of the Congress. He was empowered to negotiate treaties and make senior appointments with the advice and consent of the Congress, and he had power to grant reprieves and pardons. The Congress of the Republic of Texas was made up of a House and Senate. Members of the House served one-year terms and senators served three-year terms, with one-third of the Senate elected annually. Supreme Court justices and state judges were elected by a joint-ballot of the Congress for a four-year term, and were eligible for re-election.

For individual Texans, slavery and freedom stood side-by-side in the Republic of Texas Constitution. Slavery was legalized and free blacks were forbidden to live in Texas without the express permission of Congress. All white men were assured a broad array of rights and liberties, including a homestead if he did not already possess one. All white men enjoyed the right to vote and to stand for office if they so chose.

The Constitution concluded with a Declaration of Rights (again addressed mostly to white men) that followed closely the U.S. Bill of Rights. It guaranteed freedom of speech, press, and religion. It guaranteed the right against self-incrimination, the right to a speedy trial, and the right against cruel and unusual punishment. It also guaranteed citizens against imprisonment for debt and declared that "monopolies are contrary to the genius of free government."

1845 U.S. Statehood Constitution

Texas joined the United States of America as the 28th state in 1845. The statehood Constitution was modeled on the U.S. Constitution and the constitutions of southern states already in the Union. Universal, white, male suffrage and slavery were again embraced. On the one hand, all white men, including Mexicans, which counted as progressive in 1845, were permitted to vote and to hold state and local office. On the other hand, slavery and the rights of slaveholders were reinforced. The legislature was forbidden to emancipate slaves without compensation or prohibit immigrants to Texas from bringing their slaves with them.

The governor's term was cut to two years, but re-election was permitted, so long as a governor served no more than four years in any six-year period. The legislature was to meet biennially (every other year) rather than annually. Members of the Texas House served two-year terms and members of the Senate served four-year terms. The Texas judiciary was comprised of district courts of original jurisdiction and a three-member Supreme Court to hear appeals.

The governor appointed, by and with the advice and consent of the Senate, the secretary of state, the attorney general, and members of the judiciary. The legislature, by joint ballot, elected a state treasurer and a comptroller of public accounts. The Bill of Rights, moved to the front of the document as Article I, included all of the protections afforded by the Constitution of 1836 and more. In addition to protection of individual rights and liberties, the Constitution of 1845 sought to protect citizens against predatory corporations and business practices. Monopolies were again prohibited, as were state chartered banks, and corporations were required to secure a legislative charter.

1861 C.S.A. Statehood Constitution

When Texas seceded from the Union and joined the Confederate States of America (C.S.A.), it needed a new constitution. The 1845 Constitution was simply amended to remove references to the U.S.A. and insert references to the C.S.A. Slavery was, of course, retained and slave-owners were forbidden to free their slaves without state government approval.

1866 Presidential Reconstruction Constitution

Within days of General Lee's surrender at Appomattox, President Lincoln was assassinated and Andrew Johnson became president. Lincoln was, of course, a Republican, but he had reached across party lines to select Johnson, a Tennessee Unionist senator, former Democrat, and slaveholder, as his running mate in the wartime election of 1864. Lincoln intended Johnson's selection as a signal to the nation that unity could and would be restored. But with Lincoln dead, President Johnson was left alone to shape post-war policy. Johnson required only that southern states renounce slavery and secession before rejoining the Union. Texas again sought to lightly revise its 1845 Constitution.

The Constitution of 1866 abolished slavery, renounced the ordinance of secession and the right of secession for the future, and repudiated wartime debts. However, blacks were denied the right to vote, hold office, serve on juries, or attend the public schools.[6] Republicans in Congress were outraged and grew increasingly assertive. In 1867, they seized control of the reconstruction process from President Johnson and demanded that new constitutions be written to assure equal rights to the former slaves. Most southern states, including Texas, resisted and the U.S. Congress eventually responded with force.

1869 Congressional Reconstruction Constitution

In March of 1867, Congress disbanded the southern state governments and divided the South into five districts for military occupation, with one composed of Texas and Louisiana. Each state was required to ratify the 14th Amendment and to draft a constitution that insured the political equality of black men. With white men who had actively supported the Confederacy barred from voting, black and white Republicans controlled the Constitutional Convention of 1868. Divisions soon emerged among Republicans over whether to move incrementally or immediately to black equality. Democrats opposed black equality. Moderate Republicans wanted to go slow while radical Republicans, led by convention chair Edmund J. Davis, favored full equality. Radicals won. Black men were assured equal rights with white men, including the right to vote, stand for office, serve on juries, and send their children to public schools.

The new Constitution centralized power in the hands of the governor and gave him a four-year term. The governor appointed most executive, judicial, and local officials; commanded the state militia; and controlled the state police. Salaries were generous, the state legislature met annually, and a new public school system required high taxes.[7] Most Republicans approved the new Constitution while those Democrats still eligible to vote were ready to adopt anything that would end military occupation and secure readmission to the Union. The Constitution was approved by the lopsided vote of 72,446 to 4,928.

In a much closer contest, radical Republican E.J. Davis narrowly defeated moderate Republican A.J. Hamilton (39,901 to 39,092) for the governorship. Davis used the full powers of the governor's office to restore order to postwar Texas, constitute loyal local governments, and provide free public education to all children. Davis' use of the state militia and police to protect the freedmen against violence offended many whites, and the high taxes required by the new public school system confirmed the worst fears of his opponents. As soon as Texas statehood was restored and former confederates returned to the electorate in 1872, Democrats returned to power in the legislature. In 1873, Democrat Richard Coke ousted Davis from the governorship.

1876 Texas Constitution

Initially, Governor Coke and the Democratic leaders in the Legislature sought only modest reforms to the Constitution of 1869. They acknowledged that the powers of government were great, but promised to use them in the interest of the state's resurgent white majority. Despite extensive debate, the politicians were unable to forge a proposal that could pass popular muster. White Texans had had their fill of a government strong enough to order them about. The legislature finally admitted defeat and called for a constitutional convention.

The Constitutional Convention of 1875 was determined to return to Texas's traditional preferences for limited government, low taxes, and local control. Delegates believed that the purpose of a constitution was to restrict political power. They proceeded very systematically to do precisely that. The governor's term was reduced from four years to two, his salary was cut from $5,000 to $4,000, and his power to appoint most statewide and local officials was removed.

The legislature was to meet biennially, the length of the sessions was strictly limited, and the legislator's pay was cut to just five dollars a day for the first sixty days of the session and two dollars a day thereafter—a decision meant to encourage them to get their work done and go home. The Texas Supreme Court was divided into two high courts. The new Supreme Court was limited to hearing appeals in civil cases and a Court of Appeals (renamed the Court of Criminal Appeals in 1891) was created to hear appeals of criminal cases. Finally, the administration of local schools, along with some state funds, was returned to local officials. Texas voters overwhelmingly approved the new Constitution, 136,606 to 56,652, in February 1876.

The Constitution of 1876, though frequently amended, still governs Texas. Texas elites have always favored small government, low taxes, and an open field for entrepreneurship and competition. And with the singular exception of the Republican Reconstruction Constitution of 1869, when the traditional Texas elites were temporarily sidelined, they have prevailed. Now we ask how well the Texas Constitution works today.

TABLE 2.2
Let's Compare: Texas to Nine Other State Constitutions

The longer and more detailed a state constitution, the more frequently it needs to be amended. Here we compare the age, length, and complexity of the Texas Constitution to those of nine other states. The Texas Constitution is among the longest (2nd among all 50 states) and the most frequently amended (3rd among all 50).

State	Effective Date	Word Length	Amendments	Amendment Per Year
Alabama	1901	350,000	799	7.49
California	1879	54,645	514	4.02
Florida	1969	51,456	110	2.89
Illinois	1971	16,510	11	.31
Massachusetts	1780	36,700	120	.53
New York	1895	51,700	217	1.93
Oklahoma	1907	74,075	175	1.75
Pennsylvania	1968	27,711	30	.77
Texas	**1876**	**90,000**	**456**	**3.47**
Wyoming	1889	31,800	97	.82

Source: Book of the States 2008 (Lexington, Ky: Council of State Governments, 2008), Vol. 40, Table 1.1, p. 10.

THE TEXAS CONSTITUTION TODAY

All fifty state constitutions, including the Texas Constitution, have the misfortune of being compared to the U.S. Constitution. The U.S. Constitution, in just 4,300 words in the original document, 8,500 including its 27 amendments, defines the structure and powers of the national government and the federal system. State constitutions are almost invariably longer, more detailed, and more frequently amended. As a result, they enjoy less respect than the U.S. Constitution.

In 2008, the average state constitution was over 36,000 words and had been amended 135 times. Alabama holds the dubious distinction of having the longest and most frequently amended constitution, at 350,000 words and 799 amendments. California's constitution, at nearly 55,000 words, has been amended more than 500 times. The Texas Constitution is about 90,000 words and has been amended 456 times (as of January 2008).[8]

Bill of Rights

Q4. What are the basic principles and key provisions of the current Texas Constitution?

Article I of every Texas constitution since statehood has been dedicated to guaranteeing an extensive list of personal freedoms. As we have seen, there has always been lots of overlap between the U.S. Bill of Rights and the Texas Bill of Rights. Both guarantee freedom of speech, press, religion, assembly, and petition. Both guarantee rights to a speedy trial before a jury of one's peers and protections against unreasonable searches, seizures, and double jeopardy.

But the Texas Bill of Rights offers some protections that the U.S. Bill of Rights does not. For example, in Texas, "no person shall be outlawed," "no person shall be committed . . . except on competent medical or psy-

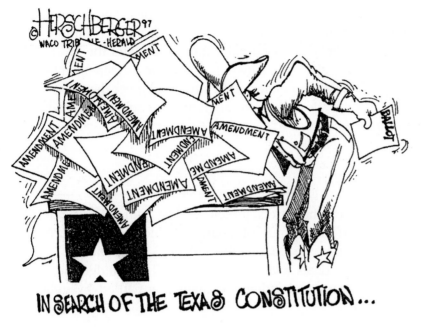

IN SEARCH OF THE TEXAS CONSTITUTION...

Waco/Tribune-Herald/Herschberger Cartoon Service

chiatric testimony," and "no person shall be imprisoned for debt." Thus reassured, Texans have, in recent decades, turned to the protection of gender and victim's rights. Texas added an equal rights amendment to the Constitution in 1972. Victim's rights provisions were added in 1989 and 1997. Victims of crime have the right to be present at all stages of the legal process, to confer with prosecutors, and to receive restitution and compensation where appropriate.

Legislative Branch

Article III of the Texas Constitution authorizes a Senate and a House of Representatives. It limits the Texas Legislature to biennial sessions of no more than 140 days. It requires a balanced budget and limits member salaries to $7,200 annually plus a modest per diem for days that members are actually in regular session, special session, or engaged in committee work. The explicit idea behind limiting the time the legislature is in session, the amount of money they can spend, and the salaries that legislators can draw for their work is to keep government small, cheap, and unobtrusive.

Executive Branch

Article IV of the Texas Constitution describes an executive branch in which power is both limited and fragmented. Although the governor is described as the state's "chief executive officer," he or she shares executive authority with five other statewide elected officials, two key policy making boards, and dozens of independent boards and commissions. The lieutenant governor, comptroller of public accounts, attorney general, agriculture commissioner, commissioner of the General Land Office, and the Texas Railroad Commission are all elected statewide, while the fifteen members of the State Board of Education are elected in single-member districts. Moreover, the legislature has made most administrative agencies independent of the governor's direct control.

Judicial Branch

Article VI describes the Texas judiciary. The judicial system in Texas includes seven different kinds of courts, including two courts of final appeal; the Texas Supreme Court deals with civil cases and the Texas Court of Criminal Appeals deals with criminal cases. Texas judges are elected to four or six-year terms and judicial vacancies are filled by gubernatorial appointment.

Local Government

Dillon's Rule   A legal concept holding that local governments are the creatures or creations of state governments.

Articles IX (Counties) and XI (Municipal Corporations) describe the role and powers of local governments in Texas. Local governments come in three basic types: county governments, municipal or city governments, and special districts. Under a legal principle known as "**Dillon's Rule**," local governments are subject to state authority as outlined in the Constitution.

Amendments

Constitutional amendments must be approved both by the legislature, in regular or special session, and the voters. A proposed amendment must receive an absolute two-thirds vote in both houses of the Texas legislature (100 votes in the House, 21 in the Senate). Then it must be approved by a majority of voters in the next statewide election. Texans have adopted 456 amendments and rejected 174, for an overall pass rate of 72.3 percent. Some states, California most famously, allow citizen initiatives to place potential amendments on the ballot. Texas does not.

THE PROSPECTS FOR CONSTITUTIONAL REFORM IN TEXAS

Q5. Should constitutional reform be on the political agenda in Texas?

Is Texas well served by a 19th century constitution written by and for a rural, agricultural, racist society still reeling from military defeat, social dislocation, and economic turmoil? Some argue that after more than 130 years and 456 amendments, the venerable Texas Constitution of 1876 is a shambles. Advocates of constitutional reform promise a shorter, clearer, more effective constitution. The reforms most frequently mentioned are consolidating executive authority, moving to annual legislative sessions, rationalizing the judiciary, and modernizing county government. But Texans have always been wary of strong (fearing that strong really means expensive) government. Major reform efforts failed in 1974 and 1990 and constitutional reform is not on the Texas political agenda today.

Constitutional Convention of 1974 and Its Aftermath

In the early 1970s, Texans seemed primed for constitutional reform. The Watergate affair in Washington and **Sharpstown scandal** in Austin produced a wave of reform sentiment. In 1972, Texas voters approved a constitutional amendment creating a constitutional revision commission to produce recommendations for submission to a constitutional convention. The convention was to be composed of the members of the Texas House and Senate meeting as one body.

The convention labored from January to July 1974 to produce a new constitution. The result was a sleek new document of just 17,500 words. It called for major institutional reforms, including an annual meeting of the legislature and appointment of state judges. But other issues, especially a **right-to-work** provision opposed by organized labor, a gambling provision opposed by conservatives, and a school funding provision opposed by rural interests, doomed the convention's work. The revised constitution fell three votes short of final passage in the convention and, hence, never reached the voters.

The 1975 regular session of the Texas Legislature repackaged major elements of the constitutional convention's work into eight separate amendments and submitted them to the voters for approval. Among these proposals were streamlining executive and judicial institutions, annual legislative sessions, modernizing county government, and tax reform. Conservative Democratic Governor Dolph Briscoe opposed the reforms, claiming that they could lead to an income tax, and all eight proposals went down to a two-to-one defeat.

Sharpstown scandal 1972 scandal in which Houston financier Frank Sharp and a number of prominent Texas politicians were accused of trading political for financial favors.

Right-to-work Legal principle prohibiting mandatory union membership.

The Future of Constitutional Reform in Texas

Reformers tried again in the early 1990s, but they did not get far. Senator John Montfort started the conversation in the early 1990s and Representative Rob Junell and Senator Bill Ratliff continued it later in the decade. They developed a plan to reduce the number of statewide elected officials to four (the governor, lieutenant governor, comptroller, and attorney general) and empower the governor to appoint the key executive branch department heads. Legislative terms were extended to four years for the House and six for the Senate. Proposals were also made to streamline the courts and to move from elected to appointed judges who would

Lt. Governor William Hobby addressing the Texas constitutional convention, 1974.

then stand for confirmatory election to subsequent terms. These proposals, while widely discussed, never even made it out of committee. One hears nothing of constitutional reform in Texas today.

Still, constitutional reform is a foundational democratic process and so it is meant to be difficult. In democratic theory, a constitutional convention is understood to be the whole people meeting to consider and reconsider the foundations of their government—not a process to be undertaken lightly. Because the convention represents the whole people, many believe that no prior limitations can be placed on it—everything is on the table—including the structure and process of government, the sources of government funding (including the income tax), the scope and jurisdiction of the courts and of local governments, and even the Bill of Rights and the liberties of individual citizens.

Now the fact that Texas is bound by the U.S. Constitution does place some limits on state constitutional reform. The U.S. Constitution guarantees Texas a republican form of government and the provisions of the U.S. Bill of Rights would still apply in Texas. And citizens of Texas would, of course, get to vote on whether to adopt a new constitution once it was proposed. Clearly, constitutional reform is serious and fundamental business and, as such, deserves the thoughtful attention of citizens and public officials.

CHAPTER SUMMARY

Federalism is a system of government that divides power between a national government and a series of subnational governments—in the U.S., these are the fifty states. The U.S. Constitution declares the national government "supreme" within the areas of its enumerated powers and reserves to the states all remaining political authority not denied to them by their own state constitutions. Not surprisingly, the national and state governments have struggled throughout American history to define the boundaries of American federalism.

All constitutions define and limit the powers of government. The U.S. Constitution and all fifty state constitutions do this by granting some powers, denying others, and deploying institutional features such as separation of powers, checks and balances, and bicameralism to limit and restrain government. Some states have sought to accomplish their public purposes through a broadly empowered, well-funded, and active set of state and local political institutions. Some have gone another way.

Texans have always favored limited government, low taxes, and local control. These commitments were evident in the Republic of Texas Constitution of 1836 and the U.S. Statehood Constitution of 1845. Texas's Civil War experience of military defeat, occupation by Union forces, and centralized government under the hated Constitution of 1869 deepened the people's commitment to limited government. Hence, limiting, even minimizing, government power was the dominant goal of the Constitution of 1876.

The Constitution of 1876, amended no less than 456 times, highlights a plural executive, a diffuse bureaucracy, a part-time legislature, and an elected judiciary that culminates in dual high courts. To this day, Texans are wary of powerful government, high taxes, and intrusions upon their individual rights and liberties. Yet, some Texans wonder whether their state government can provide excellent schools, a healthy economic environment, and an attractive quality of life without significant constitutional reform. We will explore these issues in the remainder of the book.

KEY TERMS

Constitution

Devolution

Dillon's Rule

Enumerated powers

Federalism

Necessary and proper clause

Reserved powers

Right-to-work

Sharpstown scandal

Sovereign immunity

Supremacy clause

Unfunded mandates

SUGGESTED READINGS

Dale Baum, *The Shattering of Texas Unionism: Politics in the Lone Star State During the Civil War Era* (Baton Rouge, LA: Louisiana State University, 1998).

Margaret Sweet Henson, *Lorenzo de Zavala: The Pragmatic Idealist* (Fort Worth, TX: Texas Christian University Press, 1996).

Janice C. May, *The Texas State Constitution: A Reference Guide* (Westport, CT: Greenwood Press, 1996).

Carl H. Moneyhon, *Texas After the Civil War: The Struggle of Reconstruction* (College Station, TX: Texas A&M University Press, 2004).

Joseph E. Zimmerman, *Interstate Relations: The Neglected Dimension of Federalism* (New York: Praeger, 1996).

WEB RESOURCES

http://www.tsha.utexas.edu/handbook/online.html The Handbook of Texas Online is a joint project of the General Libraries of UT, Austin and the Texas State Historical Association. This site provides the text of and articles about Texas constitutions.

http://www.capitol.state.tx.us/txconst/toc.html From the Research Division of the Texas Legislative Council, here is an updated version of the Texas Constitution including all amendments.

http://ww2.lafayette.edu/~publius/ Publius is the leading scholarly journal dealing with American federalism.

http://www.csg.org Website for the Council on State Governments contains a wealth of comparative data and topical discussion.

END NOTES

1. Daniel J. Elazar, *American Federalism: A View From the States* 3rd ed. (New York: Harper & Row, 1984). See also Thomas R. Dye, *American Federalism: Competition Among Governments* (Lexington, Mass: Lexington Books, 1990).
2. Virginia Gray and Russell L. Hanson, eds., *Politics in the American States: A Comparative Analysis,* 9th ed. (Washington, D.C.: CQ Press, 2008), pp. 31–36.
3. Joseph E. Zimmerman, *Contemporary American Federalism: The Growth of National Power* (New York: Praeger, 1992), p. 35.
4. All of the Texas constitutions can be found at: http://tarleton.law.utexas.edu/constitutions/text/
5. Margaret Sweet Henson, *Lorenzo de Zavala: the Pragmatic Idealist* (Fort Worth, TX: Texas Christian University Press, 1996), pp. 7–20.
6. Randolph B. Campbell, *Grass-Roots Reconstruction in Texas: 1865–1880* (Baton Rouge, LA: Louisiana State University Press, 1997), p. 10.
7. Carl H. Moneyhon, *Texas After the Civil War: The Struggle of Reconstruction* (College Station, TX: Texas A&M University Press, 2004).
8. *The Book of the States 2008,* vol. 40 (Lexington, KY: Council of State Governments, 2008), Table 1.1, p. 10.

CHAPTER 3

Political Participation in Texas: Voters, Campaigns, and Elections

Focus Questions

Q1. Why should Texans participate in the politics of their state?

Q2. What means have been used to limit suffrage in Texas history?

Q3. What laws and rules govern the right to vote today?

Q4. Which Texans exercise their right to vote and which do not?

Q5. How are political campaigns conducted in Texas?

Q6. What kinds of elections do we have in Texas?

Healthy democratic politics assumes the full and informed participation of citizens in the discussion of public issues and the selection of government officials. Active citizens are the irreplaceable participants in democratic politics. **Political participation** refers to all of the opportunities we have as individuals or as members of groups, associations, or political parties to join in shaping our common life. Intelligent candidates conducting informative campaigns before watchful citizens, who in turn cast thoughtful votes on election day, are the democratic ideal.

Opportunities for political participation in Texas are extensive. Talking about politics with friends and neighbors, studying the issues, joining civic groups, attending school board meetings, protesting at the local court house or the state capitol, stuffing envelopes for a candidate, giving money to a political party, voting, and stepping forward as a candidate for office are all forms of political participation. There are many ways, available to you and every other citizen, to make your voice heard and your opinions and interests felt on matters of public interest.

Yet, in politics, as in the rest of life, the ideal and the real often diverge. In real politics, candidates often are intelligent, but they do not always, or even usually, conduct informative campaigns. Rather, campaigns are often mud baths, filled with charge and counter-charge, as issues fade into the background. Citizens do not always watch closely, turn out to vote on election day, or make well-informed decisions. Some citizens are disengaged

Q1. Why should Texans participate in the politics of their state?

Political participation
All of those activities, from attending campaign events, to voting, and even running for office, by which individuals and groups undertake to affect politics.

More than 250 protesters rallied in front of Calvary Christian Academy in Fort Worth as Mr. Perry signed two bills dealing with abortion. Some were angry the bills were signed at a Christian school. *CHERYL DIAZ MEYER/Staff Photographer/The Dallas Morning News*

and ill-informed, others are turned off by the negative tone of campaigns, and many stay home on election day. Hence, the support, good-will, and legitimacy that should greet newly elected public officials are often replaced by alienation, skepticism, and suspicion.

Unfortunately, skepticism and suspicion about state politics has often been well-founded. Article I, section 2 of the U.S. Constitution gave the states the principal responsibility for registering voters, structuring campaigns, and holding elections. Many states, including Texas with its traditionalistic political culture, used this authority to exclude most poor and minority citizens from politics. Over the course of the 20th century, the federal government forced these states, usually much against their will, to treat their citizens equally.

THE EVOLUTION OF SUFFRAGE IN TEXAS

Suffrage   Another term for the legal right to vote.

Q2. What means have been used to limit suffrage in Texas history?

Today, virtually every adult citizen of Texas is allowed and even encouraged to register and to vote. It was not always so. The Texas Constitutions of 1836 and 1845 granted **suffrage**—the legal right to vote—to white men and Hispanic men and denied it to blacks, Indians and women. Hispanics, while legally citizens and entitled to vote, were subject to frequent discrimination. The South's defeat in the Civil War brought an end to slavery and a demand, embodied in the 13th, 14th, and 15th Amendments to the U.S. Constitution, that black men be recognized as citizens with the right to vote and stand for political office. Once Reconstruction ended, private groups and public officials worked systematically and over a period of decades to limit black and Hispanic participation in Texas public life.

Post-Civil War Exclusion

White Texans used every tool at their disposal, including physical intimidation and violence, economic pressure and threats, and formal constitutional and legal action, to regain political and social control of the state after the Civil War. Once the Democratic Party returned to power in the early 1870s, a restrictive voter registration system was enacted to exclude minorities and the poor.

Restrictions on Voter Registration

The voter registration system in place in 1900 was intended to be open to well-heeled whites and closed to all others. The voter registration rolls were open for just four months each year, October 1 through January 31. Campaigns occurred in the late summer and fall, with elections in November, so the voter lists were locked down nine months before the election was held. Generally, only the social and political elite, who followed politics year-round and knew the importance of electoral outcomes, were registered. By 1900, only about four percent of adult black men in Texas were registered to vote. And then the rules were tightened.

Poll Tax

Early 20th century Texas was a largely rural society in which exchanges of labor and barter of goods meant many poor families saw little real money over the course of a year. In 1902, Texas adopted a **poll tax** of $1.50 to register to vote. A small farm might clear $300 in a good year, so paying $1.50 to register to vote involved no small calculation. Most poor Texans decided to save their money and forego their vote. Most, but not all.[1]

Poll tax In 1902 Texas adopted a poll tax of $1.50 to discourage the poor and minorities from voting.

White Primary

In 1903, Governor Jim Hogg and the Texas legislature, led by Representative Alexander Terrell, sought further to limit minority influence in Texas politics. The Terrell election law altered the process by which parties nominated candidates by moving from party conventions to party primary elections. Texas was one-party Democratic, so winning the Democratic Party primary was tantamount to election. In 1906, the Texas Democratic Party held its first **white primary.** Only whites were permitted to vote in the Democratic Party primary, insuring that blacks had no role in choosing the state's officeholders.

Black leaders sued the state of Texas, arguing that the 15th Amendment to the U.S. Constitution prohibited racial discrimination in voting. In 1924, the U.S. Supreme Count agreed, in *Nixon v. Herndon,* that the state of Texas could not exclude blacks from voting in state sanctioned primary

White primary In 1906 Texas Democrats adopted a white primary, meaning that only whites were permitted to vote in the democratic primary.

Nixon v. Herndon (1924) U.S. Supreme Court held that Texas could not exclude blacks from voting in state sanctioned primary elections.

Grovey v. Townsend
(1935) U.S. Supreme
Court found that the
Democratic Party in
Texas was a private
organization and could
exclude blacks from its
primary elections.

Smith v. Allwright
(1944) U.S. Supreme
Court overturned *Grovey*,
declaring that political
parties are 'agencies of
the state' and must abide
by the 15th Amendment's
prohibition on racial
discrimination in voting.

U.S. v. Texas   (1966)
U.S. Supreme Court
struck down the poll tax
in state elections.

Preclearance   The
Voting Rights Act requires
states and communities
with a history of racial
discrimination in voting to
seek prior approval from
the Justice Department for
changes to their election
codes to insure against
dilution of minority
electoral impact.

elections. Democratic Party officials responded by declaring that the Democratic Party in Texas was a private organization, not an official organization of Texas government, and could define its membership as it saw fit. In the 1935 case of ***Grovey v. Townsend,*** the Supreme Court accepted the Texas Democratic Party's argument.[2]

Federal Intervention

Federal intervention on behalf of poor and minority voters began in the mid-1940s but took decades to complete. In 1944, the U.S. Supreme Court overturned its finding in *Grovey* to declare in ***Smith v. Allwright*** that political parties are "agencies of the state" and must abide by the 15th Amendment's prohibition on racial discrimination in voting. Despite this important ruling, several stout lines of defense against minority voter registration and political participation remained in place.[3]

Restrictive voter registration procedures and the poll tax limited minority participation into the 1960s, but then change came on in a rush. Texas resisted at every turn. In 1964, the 24th Amendment to the U.S. Constitution made the poll tax unconstitutional for national elections. Texas responded by developing a dual ballot, one for national elections where no poll tax was required, and another for state elections where the poll tax was still required. In 1966, the U.S. Supreme Court, in ***U.S. v. Texas,*** declared the poll tax unconstitutional in state elections too. By the early 1970s, the federal courts had struck down state laws requiring annual voter registration, an early end to voter registration, and lengthy residence requirements.

The Voting Rights Act and Its Amendments

The Voting Rights Act (VRA) of 1965, along with the Civil Rights Acts of 1964 and 1965, broke the back of racial segregation. The VRA outlawed literacy tests, required federal officials to facilitate minority voter registration, and required nine southern states with histories of racial discrimination in voting to submit any proposed changes to electoral laws to a **preclearance** process run by the U.S. Department of Justice. Preclearance was intended to block any changes that would, intentionally or not, dilute minority voter influence. Most provisions of the VRA are permanent, though funding levels and some specific enforcement provisions require periodic renewal. The VRA was reviewed and renewed in 1970, 1975, and 1982. In 1975, provisions were added requiring Texas and other states with large numbers of voters for whom English is not their native language to provide bilingual ballots and other assistance.

In 2006, President Bush and the leadership of both parties in Congress promised to extend the VRA for another 25 years. Southern Republicans in the House, led by representatives from Georgia and Texas, staged a revolt that threatened the renewal. Some opponents of renewal argued that great progress had been made in minority voter registration, participation, and office holding over the past 40 years and that it was unfair to subject southern states to special scrutiny any longer. Others opposed the language assistance provisions, arguing that knowledge of English is a requirement of citizenship and so should not be necessary for those truly eligible to vote. Eventually, the revolt was quelled and the VRA was renewed by a vote of 390 to 33 in the House and 98–0 in the Senate. President Bush signed the bill on July 27, 2006.

Congressional leaders look on as President George W. Bush signs the 2006 extension of Voting Rights Act. *Courtesy of www.whitehouse.gov*

MODERN VOTER REGISTRATION AND TURNOUT

Texas moved quickly, if a bit grudgingly, to comply with the original VRA. In 1967, the legislature designated the Secretary of State as the state's chief elections official, responsible for interpreting legislation, monitoring compliance, and distributing funds to local election officials. Local election officials, usually the county tax assessor-collector or a designated county election administrator, actually set up and conduct elections. In 1971, the state legislature adopted a thoroughly modern system of permanent voter registration. For a mix of old and new reasons, Congress remains concerned about the efficiency and integrity of the nation's voter registration, vote casting, and vote counting systems.

> **Q3.** What laws and rules govern the right to vote today?

Voter Qualifications

To be a qualified voter in Texas, one need only be a U.S. citizen over 18 years of age (though you can register at 17 years and 10 months if you will be 18 by election day) and a resident of the state and county for at least 30 days. Qualified voters must have been registered at least 30 days before the election. Texans do not register as Democrats, Republicans, or independents, as voters in more than half the states do. Texans simply register to vote and then on election day they decide which party to support.[4] In 2008 Texas had 13.3 million registered voters, which is about 75 percent of the state's voting age population.

Voter Registration

The Texas Secretary of State's website (see the Web Resources section at the end of this chapter) provides easy-to-follow information on how to register to vote. Texas voters can register at any time during the year, either in person or through the mail. In fact, a new voter can be registered by his or her spouse, parent, or child if that person is a registered voter. Registration, once established, is permanent so long as the voter's address remains the same. Voters who move within the same county can revise their voter registration information online. If you move from one county to another, you must re-register, but, again, the process is quite simple.

Motor Voter   A 1995 law, also known as the National Voter Registration Act, that permits persons to register to vote at motor vehicle and other state government offices.

In 1995, the U.S. Congress passed the National Voter Registration Act (better known as the **Motor Voter** law). Motor Voter allows qualified voters to register while they are getting or renewing a driver's license or applying for some other public service. The hope was that making voter registration more convenient would increase registration and, more importantly, voting. It did, modestly. In 2002, Congress passed—and President Bush signed—the Help America Vote Act (HAVA). HAVA established a new federal agency, called the Election Assistance Commission (EAC), to assist states in improving their voter registration, vote casting, and vote counting systems.

HAVA required each state, including Texas, to construct a statewide voter registration list. Each voting location is required to have at least one computer with access to the statewide list to check eligibility if a voter's name does not appear on the precinct's voter list. Voters whose eligibility is unclear must be allowed to cast a provisional ballot, which is counted when the voter's eligibility is confirmed, and the state is required to develop a system through which voters can check to see whether their provisional ballot has been counted. Finally, states must comply with education requirements to assure that new voters know how to use electronic, optical scan, and punch card voting systems. Congress spent more than $3.9 billion on new voting equipment between 2003 and 2008, with $190 million going to Texas, but questions remain about the accuracy and vulnerability to tampering of the new voting equipment.[5]

Voter Turnout

Voter turnout   That portion of the eligible electorate that actually turns up to cast a vote on election day.

Voter turnout is the proportion of the voting-age population (VAP) that actually cast a vote in a given election. American elections, even hard-fought presidential elections, have rarely reached 60 percent in recent decades. Off-year elections for the U.S. Congress and many top state races average around 35 percent. And countless local and special district elections attract less than 10 percent of potential voters.

Even by these modest U.S. standards, Texans are poor voters. Texans average six to eight percent under national averages. Texans have for decades averaged about 45 to 50 percent turnout in presidential elections and 25 to 30 percent in gubernatorial and congressional elections. Major metropolitan elections, such as those for mayor in Dallas, Houston, and San Antonio, usually draw between 10 and 20 percent of eligible voters. Special elections, such as those for constitutional amendments, municipal charter reform, and school bond elections, usually draw from 5 to 15 percent of eligible voters.[6]

Texas public officials have sought to improve turnout by making voting easier and more convenient. Absentee ballots, obtained and returned by

TABLE 3.1
U.S. and Texas Turnout (Among Eligible VAP) in National Elections

Presidential Elections				
Election Year	**U.S. Turnout**	**Texas Turnout**	**Texas Shortfall**	**Texas Ranking**
1960	63.1	41.2	–21.9	44
1964	61.8	44.6	–17.2	44
1968	60.7	48.7	–12.6	48
1972	55.4	45.3	–10.1	43
1976	53.5	46.3	–7.2	44
1980	52.6	44.9	–7.7	44
1984	53.1	47.2	–5.9	44
1988	50.2	44.2	–6.0	45
1992	55.2	49.1	–6.1	46
1996	48.9	41.1	–7.8	47
2000	51.2	43.1	–8.1	48
2004	58.3	50.3	–8	48
2008	61.7	52.4	–9.3	48*
Congressional Elections				
1962	46.3	26.1	–20.2	43
1966	45.4	20.8	–24.6	50
1970	43.8	27.5	–16.3	46
1974	36.2	18.5	–17.7	49
1978	34.9	23.3	–11.6	47
1982	38.1	26.4	–11.7	48
1986	33.4	25.5	–7.9	45
1990	33.1	26.8	–6.3	43
1994	36.0	31.3	–4.7	44
1998	32.8	24.3	–8.5	46
2002	34.2	27.3	–7.4	49
2006	43.6	33.5	–10.1	51

Source: U.S. Bureau of the Census, *Statistical Abstract of the United States* (Washington, D.C.: Government Printing Office), 1975, #729, p. 451; 1984, #439, p. 265; 1990, #444, p. 265; 1994, #451, p. 289; 1995, #462, p. 291; 2002, #396, p. 255; 2004–05, #410, p. 258; 2007, #406, p. 257; 2008, #405, p. 257. *Author estimate from early data.

mail, have long been available to citizens who knew in advance that they would be away from home on election day or otherwise unable to make it to the polls. In the late 1980s, the Texas legislature approved early voting. County election officials set early voting dates, beginning as much as three weeks before and concluding four days before the official election day. In recent Texas elections, about 40 percent of votes have been cast early, though in the 2008 General Election that number jumped to two-thirds.

THE DECISION TO VOTE (OR NOT)

Voting is a function of knowledge, experience, and confidence. Citizens who are older, well-educated, economically secure, and embedded in their community tend to vote in large numbers. Citizens who are younger, less well-educated, economically insecure, and new to their community tend to vote in much smaller numbers. Not surprisingly, politicians respond to those who vote, ignoring substantially, if not completely, those who do not vote.

> **Q4.** Which Texans exercise their right to vote and which do not?

TABLE 3.2
Let's Compare: Turnout Among Eligible Voters, 2006
by Age, Gender, Race and Ethnicity

Texas voters, both mature citizens and younger citizens, turn out at low rates. Young Texans vote at lower rates than young citizens in any other large state. Notice that nationally and in most states, young women turn out at somewhat greater rates than young men. Young blacks turn out at higher rates than either young whites or Hispanics.

	Voters Over 30	Voters 18–29	Women 18–29	Men 18–29	Anglo 18–29	Black 18–29	Hispanic 18–29
National	54	26	27	24	28	24	19
California	54	25	26	23	29	23	22
Texas	**45**	**17**	**18**	**16**	**17**	**26**	**15**
New York	49	19	19	19	20	18	17
Florida	50	18	20	17	19	23	11
Pennsylvania	53	25	25	25	26	18	*
Illinois	54	23	27	19	25	20	21
Ohio	59	31	34	29	33	23	*
Michigan	62	38	40	37	38	42	*
North Carolina	45	21	21	21	24	18	*
Georgia	48	29	36	22	31	27	*

Source: CIRCLE, *The Center for Information and Research on Civic Learning and Engagement*, University of Maryland, June 2007. *http://www.civicyouth.org.*
*Indicates that not enough data was available.

Who Votes

In Texas, voter turnout varies by age, income, education, race, and ethnicity. Wealthy Anglos vote at much higher rates than poor blacks and Hispanics. Even when one controls for income, Anglos vote at slightly higher rates than blacks and significantly higher rates than Hispanics. Though Anglos make up only 48 percent of the adult population while Hispanics make up about 36 percent and blacks 11.5 percent, Anglos still control statewide elections.

How can this be? First, one must be a citizen to vote. While 98 percent of Anglo and black Texans are citizens, only 70 percent of Hispanic Texans are citizens. Second, even among Hispanic citizens, voter turnout is only about half what it is for Anglo and black Texans. Figure 3.1 shows that while the numbers are changing slowly, Anglos still cast two-thirds of the votes in statewide elections. Blacks cast about 12 percent of votes, right in line with the black proportion of the Texas population. The Hispanic vote is increasing, but it is still just 20 percent of votes cast in recent elections.[7]

Analysts speculate in each election about whether the increasing Hispanic presence in the population will show up in electoral results. It will, eventually, but only as several processes play themselves out. First, some significant portion of the 30 percent of Texas Hispanics who currently are not citizens must become naturalized American citizens. Second, Hispanic citizens not currently registered to vote must register. And third, Hispanic turnout must increase. When Texas Hispanics do vote, they vote about two-to-one Democrat.[8]

FIGURE 3.1   Percent of Votes Cast in Texas Elections by Race and Ethnicity 1976–2006

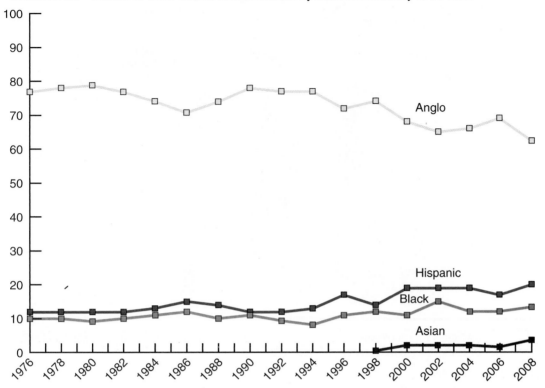

Note: Data is unavailable for 1978 and 1984. Average of votes cast by race and ethnicity in the previous and subsequent election has been inserted.
Source: Derived by the author from U.S. Census data. Go to Census, click on "V" in the alphabetical list. Data for 1976 comes from "Registration and Voting in 1976—Jurisdictions Covered by the Voting Rights Act Amendments of 1975," Table 1. Data for later years comes from "Reported Voting and Registration, by Race and Spanish Origin (Hispanic Origin after 1986), for States," 1980, Table 5; 1982, Table 16; 1986, Table 4; 1988, Table 4; 1990, Table 4; 1992, Table 4; 1994, Table 4a; 1996, Table 4a; 1998, Table 4a; 2000, Table 4a; 2002, Table 4a; 2004, Table 4a; 2006, Table 4b.

Low levels of voter registration and turnout are not without their costs. Politicians represent their constituents. Ideally, politicians would represent every person in his or her constituency with equal care and attention. But most politicians are more likely to listen to those they think support them, vote for them, or contribute to their campaign. How receptive would you expect a politician to be to each of three groups of constituents if one group consistently supports him, the second group splits its vote, and the third group mostly does not vote at all?

Illegal immigration is a different, though related, political issue. Yesterday's illegal immigrant might become tomorrow's legal(ized) citizen and voter. Democrats seek to represent the interest of Hispanic Americans in family unification (bringing additional family members to the U.S.) and civil liberties (not being targeted for special scrutiny) without appearing to be dismissive of border security. Republicans tend to focus on border control, as both law enforcement and national security issues, while trying not to alienate Hispanic voters or employers who depend on the labor of illegal immigrants.[9]

Hence, the immigration debate nationally—and in Texas—has focused on three key issues: border security, a guest worker program, and a path toward citizenship for illegal immigrants already in the country. U.S. House Republicans passed a bill in 2006 calling for tight border controls, with no guest worker program and no path to citizenship. The Senate, following President Bush's lead, passed a "comprehensive" immigration bill also requiring increased border security, but establishing a guest worker program, and a path to citizenship for most of the 11 to 12 million illegal immigrants now in the U.S. Though Congress partially funded a 700 mile border fence just before the 2006 congressional elections, it failed to pass comprehensive immigration reform in 2007. Immigration was a hot issue at the local and state levels of the 2008 campaign, but no resolution of this divisive issue is in sight.

Why Texans Don't Vote

We often think of Texas as a wealthy state, and, in some sense, it is. But Texas is also a state in which great poverty lives just out of sight of great wealth. Wealthy people participate in politics in all kinds of ways, including lobbying, voting, and contributing to campaigns, while poor people usually do not. Just a few formal and informal barriers are sufficient to dampen voting, especially among the poor, in Texas.

Formal Restrictions. Few formal or legal restrictions on voting exist in Texas. But, there are a few. Political scientist Michael McDonald has done a state-by-state study of the number of potential voters rendered ineligible by felony conviction. Texas allows former felons to reregister after they have completed all of their prison, parole, and probation time. McDonald reports that 490,016 felons and former felons were ineligible to vote in Texas during the 2008 state elections.[10]

While Texas formally excludes only felons and a few others from the electorate, it fails to take actions that other states have taken to increase voter turnout. Some states cluster elections to enhance voter interest, allow voters to register up to and including election day, and schedule elections over several days to facilitate voter turnout. Texas has yet to adopt any of these reforms.

Informal Restrictions. Historical and cultural barriers act to limit political participation in Texas. A century of violence, intimidation, and legal exclusion of minority voters, reluctantly lifted under federal pressure, has left a legacy of nonparticipation. Lessons once learned are not easily forgotten. Language also acts as a barrier for some Hispanic voters. While the Voting Rights Act of 1975 requires that the needs of language minorities be addressed, voters not comfortable with English and not familiar with the electoral process still might be intimidated and discouraged.

Finally, voter turnout is highest in visible, important, competitive elections. Many Texas elections are quiet, even lazy, affairs. Elections in which Texans are asked to decide on a dozen statewide elected officials and perhaps two dozen obscure local county commissioners, city council persons, and judges also depress turnout. So do non-competitive elections in which one party dominates.

POLITICAL CAMPAIGNS

Campaigning in Texas takes time, stamina, and money. In local races it is still common for candidates to knock on doors and go to neighborhood meetings. But in state-wide races, candidates depend upon teams of professional campaign managers, hundreds (if not thousands) of activists and volunteers, and a multimedia strategy of yard signs, fliers, radio, and television to get their name and message before the voters. As professional managers have taken over campaigns, costs have rapidly escalated.[11]

> **Q5.** How are political campaigns conducted in Texas?

Campaign Staff: Professionals and Amateurs

For decades, presidential campaigns have largely bypassed Texas. Candidates of both parties come to raise money, but they rarely campaign here because party nominations have usually been locked up before the early March Texas primary rolls around. When primary campaigns do come to Texas, as in 2008, they break on the state like an afternoon thunderstorm and just as quickly they are gone. Texas campaigns are more like a long draught that comes and stays.

Major statewide races, such as those for governor, lieutenant governor, and U.S. senator, are organized and managed by a professional team of campaign strategists, pollsters, media specialists, and fundraisers. Oftentimes,

Senator Hillary Rodham Clinton of New York conferred with some future Texas voters prior to the March 4, 2008 Texas primary.

these campaign professionals are drawn not just from Texas, but from around the nation. Top campaign managers and their firms are the hired guns of modern politics.

Well-known candidates have established histories and records, but the campaign team can gauge public opinion on the major issues of the day, select the issues and issue positions that put the candidate in the best light, and design a media campaign that will present the candidate most effectively. The campaign team also engages in opposition research: studying the opponent's personal background, issue positions, and past political statements and votes, looking for weaknesses that might be exploited during the campaign.

Most voters do not see candidates for statewide office in person, but they can hardly avoid their campaign commercials and materials. Television, radio, and print advertisements have become increasingly targeted. Campaign operatives pour over survey data to determine which television programs and which radio stations their supporters watch or listen to regularly. They also try to determine which issues—jobs, taxes, judicial appointments, the environment—concern them most. Campaigns work very hard to find clusters of like-minded voters and target them with messages that will resonate with them and hopefully move them to the polls.[12] Campaigns usually find it much easier to identify and turn out their base voters than to mobilize nonvoters or convert opponents.

Every campaign, especially local campaigns but even well-funded statewide races, depends on amateurs, part-timers, and volunteers. Most people do not have the time, money, or inclination to dedicate themselves to politics. They can, however, make a modest contribution of time to take part in a phone bank, stuff campaign fliers into envelopes, or put up yard signs.

Young people, on the other hand, have more energy and fewer obligations than older people and are always welcome in political campaigns.

When volunteers do not appear in sufficient numbers, the inner-LBJ in most Texas politicians can be summoned. In Texas cities, get-out-the-vote money, also called street money or walking around money, can boost volunteerism. In South Texas, campaigns can hire politiqueras, temporary paid campaign workers to go door to door to pass out fliers, urge a vote, and even arrange a ride to the polling place, for $100 to $200 on election day.

Campaign Finance

Money has long been described as the mother's milk of politics. In Texas, baby is always hungry. A few candidates have personal wealth and are willing to put it to work in support of their political ambitions. Most have to raise campaign money from others and virtually all of them hate it. Political fundraising is awkward, time consuming, and fraught with moral ambiguity. Politicians commonly say that donors neither expect nor receive anything for their contributions, but most citizens cannot help but wonder.

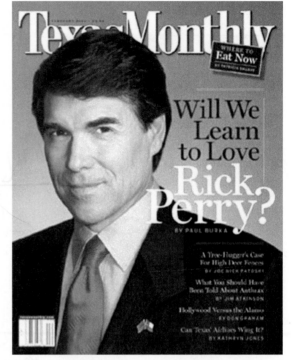

As this *Texas Monthly* cover suggests, though Rick Perry was the frontrunner throughout the 2006 campaign, he had questions to answer. TEXAS MONTHLY *cover courtesy of* TEXAS MONTHLY. *Copyright © 2002* TEXAS MONTHLY.

The 2002 Texas campaigns for governor and lieutenant governor put a spotlight on the role of personal wealth in campaigns. Most spectacularly, Democrat Tony Sanchez, a first-time candidate, poured nearly $70 million of his own money into a losing campaign to unseat incumbent Republican Governor Rick Perry. Perry spent nearly $30 million to hold his seat. In the lieutenant governor's race, Republican David Dewhurst drew heavily on his personal fortune in winning a $12 million race against Democrat John Sharp. Other statewide races cost anywhere from $1 to 6 or 7 million. Personal fortunes do not insure victory, but they certainly streamline and simplify the campaign process.

The 2006 governor's race was less about personal wealth and more about traditional fundraising prowess.[13] Governor Perry faced an unusual electoral challenge in 2006. The Democratic Party nominated former Houston city council member and one-term congressman Chris Bell. In addition to Bell, Perry faced two prominent independent candidates. One was popular entertainer and political novice, Kinky Friedman. Friedman was not a serious threat, but he did muddy the waters by playing to Texans' traditional disdain for politics and by appealing to the disaffected. The other was popular Republican Comptroller Carole Strayhorn. She decided to run as an independent when it became clear that she could not beat Perry in the Republican primary.

As the incumbent Republican governor of a red state, Perry was considered the favorite throughout the race. He raised more than half of the

Kinky Friedman drew big crowds on the campaign trail. *MARK MATSON/*Austin American-Statesman

$46 million raised by the four major candidates.[14] Perry entered the post-Labor Day stretch run of the campaign with a war chest of $10 million on hand. Perry organized his re-election fund raising around a group he called the Century Council. The Century Council was composed of 85 donors, each of whom gave at least $100,000 between 2002 and 2006. The Council provided about $10 million, or about 35 percent, of the $29 million total that Perry spent during the campaign. Perry had twice as many donors contributing $25,000 and up as Bush had either in 1994 and 1998 and five times as many as Ann Richards had in 1990 and Bill Clements had in 1986.[15]

While Perry's three challengers ultimately held him to less than 40 percent of the total vote, none ever posed a serious threat to him. Carole Strayhorn raised $12.6 million for the campaign, but as an independent candidate she had to win votes one at a time by convincing Democrats and Republicans to abandon their normal voting habits. Chris Bell, the Democratic party nominee, eventually raised $6.5 million, most of it too late to change the course of the campaign. Kinky raised $3.8 million but was fading as the campaign closed.[16]

Fully two-thirds of campaign money goes to buy television time. Texas has twenty-seven major media markets in which serious statewide campaigns must compete. A single thirty-second ad on a major urban television station in an attractive time slot, say leading into the local news, costs about $10,000. Running such an ad statewide, just once, costs about $150,000. Campaign professionals know that a commercial must run six or eight times before its message penetrates the consciousness of a busy and distracted voter. Obviously, costs pile up quickly. A well-funded gubernatorial campaign, meaning just Perry and Strayhorn in 2006, hopes to spend $1 million a week on television from Labor Day to late-October and then dump what is left into the final week.[17]

Luckily (or not), Texas has some of the most permissive campaign finance laws in the country. The Texas Campaign Reporting and Disclosure Act of 1973, as amended over the years, allows Texans, and we really mean wealthy Texans, to give unlimited amounts of money to Texas state politicians, so long as those contributions are publicly recorded. In practice, reporting often occurs after the election and there are no enforcement provisions to insure that campaign finance reports are timely, accurate, and complete.

In 2006, Judge Mike Lynch presided over a trial in which Congressman (now former-Congressman) Tom DeLay, his political action committee, and the Texas Association of Business (TAB) were charged with illegally using corporate money in the 2002 Texas legislative elections. Judge Lynch dismissed some of the charges against TAB, describing Texas election law as an "archaic, cumbersome, confusing, poorly written document in need of a serious legislative overhaul."[18] (Note to students: If it was a little later in the semester and you had read a little further in this book, you would be smiling now. But since it is early in the semester, just ask yourself, why would elected politicians write campaign finance laws that judges find too "archaic, cumbersome, confusing, (and) poorly written" to apply?) In 2008, the TAB plead guilty to a misdemeanor charge of unlawful campaign expenditure and a slap on the wrist $10,000 fine to conclude their part of the case. One criminal indictment against DeLay is all that remains of this case.

Style and Tone

Even in a well-funded campaign, money is not in endless supply. Campaign officials must decide what kind of spending, particularly what kind of advertising, is likely to bring the greatest bang for the buck. Increasingly, American political campaigns, including those in Texas, depend on mudslinging and attack ads. While the McCain-Feingold campaign finance reforms sought to limit money in politics and control attack ads in presidential and congressional campaigns, Texas has made no attempt to clean up its politics.

While you can find a fair amount of mudslinging in most Texas elections, the 2002 gubernatorial election was particularly memorable. The Democratic challenger, Tony Sanchez, set off a real donnybrook by running a campaign commercial charging incumbent Republican Governor Rick Perry with abuse of power in trying to avoid a traffic ticket. Perry responded with thoroughly scurrilous charges that Sanchez had allowed banks under his control to launder Mexican drug money. As if that were not enough, another Perry commercial presented two former Drug Enforcement Agency (DEA) agents speculating broadly, and with no apparent evidence, that Sanchez had somehow been involved in the 1985 murder of DEA agent 'Kiki' Camarena. Perry won re-election, but both candidates were demeaned in the process.

By Texas standards, the 2006 campaign had a moderate tone, caused more by the nature of the race than by the innately gentle disposition of the candidates. Governor Perry, though he rarely polled above 40 percent, led the race throughout. Chris Bell, the Democrat, did not have enough money to get up on television until late in the race. Bell, because he was not widely known, and Carole Strayhorn, because her last name had changed from Rylander to Strayhorn since her last race, had to spend more time introducing themselves than attacking Perry. Kinky Friedman urged voters to reject traditional partisan politics to vote for a "Good Shepherd" (him) who would look after all Texans. No single challenger ever emerged to threaten Perry and the race fizzled.

TYPES OF ELECTIONS IN TEXAS

Texans participate in three types of elections—primary elections, general elections, and special elections. Primary elections select party candidates for office, general elections select officeholders from among the party nominees, and special elections decide special issues or fill vacant offices. Primary and general elections are partisan elections. Special elections are generally nonpartisan, though partisanship often intrudes.

> **Q6.** What kinds of elections do we have in Texas?

Primary Elections

Primary elections
A preliminary election in which voters select candidates to stand under their party label in a later general election.

About a dozen states nominate candidates for office in caucuses and conventions, but the rest use primary elections. **Primary elections** can be organized in different ways. Most states employ closed primaries in which only voters registered with the party may participate. Some states use open primaries in which voters get to decide on election day in which party's primary they will participate. And two states, Washington and Alaska, use a blanket primary in which voters get a single ballot and choose office-by-office in which party primary to participate.

Texas, few will be surprised to hear, uses an unusual mixed primary and caucus system. The Texas primary process occurs in two stages: the first stage is open, the second closed. Texas permits registered voters to choose the party primary in which they wish to participate on election day (so it is open at this point). As soon as the polls close on primary election day, each precinct holds a caucus which anyone who voted at that precinct earlier in the day is entitled to attend to do other party business. As we shall see more fully in Chapter 5, high turnout in 2008, especially on the Democratic side, nearly overwhelmed this usually sleepy system.

The second stage of the primary process in state elections (though not in presidential contests) is the runoff stage. Texas electoral rules require a majority to win. In a race with three or more candidates, no candidate may win a majority of the vote, in which case a runoff election between the top two vote-getters is required. Runoff primaries are held four weeks after the first primary and are supposed to be closed to persons who voted in the other party's primary (so runoff primaries are at least partially closed). Voter turnout in party primary and runoff elections often runs in the single digits.

Moreover, voters who choose to participate in a party primary may not later sign a minor party's or an independent candidate's petition to get on the general election ballot. In 2006 Kinky Friedman, an independent candidate for governor, encouraged voters to "save themselves for Kinky" by skipping the party primaries so they could sign his ballot petitions. Minor parties, defined as those receiving less than twenty percent of the vote in the last general election, are permitted to avoid the expense of a primary election by picking their candidates in a state party convention.

Since 1986, Texas has held its primary elections on the second Tuesday of March in even-numbered years. In presidential election years (2000, 2004, 2008, etc.), the presidential primary gets most of the attention though state and federal legislative races are also held. In off-year elections (even-numbered years off the presidential cycle, 2002, 2006, 2010, etc.), the gubernatorial and other statewide office primaries, along with all of the Texas and federal legislative races, are held.

General elections
A final or definitive election in which candidates representing their respective parties contend for election to office.

General Elections

General elections are held on the first Tuesday after the first Monday in November of even-numbered years. In the general election, voters choose among the winners of the major party primaries and the minor party nominees selected in convention. In the general election, a plurality of the votes cast for that office, even if less than a majority, is sufficient to win. There are no runoffs in the general election.

Finally, the general election ballot allows voters the option of casting a "straight ticket" or party ballot. The voter can mark a box at the top of the ballot to vote for all of one party's candidates. Voters are also permitted to mark the straight ticket box, but then go selectively down the ballot and vote for some candidates of other parties. About half of Texans vote a straight ticket.

Special Elections

Special elections are employed for a variety of purposes, such as to fill vacancies caused by resignation or death, or to decide on constitutional amendments, local bond issues, or other nonrecurring issues. Special elections can be scheduled at any time and are conducted on a nonpartisan basis to avoid the need for major party primaries and minor party conventions. Most special elections are low visibility, low turnout, affairs.

Special election
Special elections are held to decide constitutional amendments, local bond proposals, and other nonrecurring issues.

ELECTORAL REFORM POSSIBILITIES

How concerned should we be that most Texans do not participate in elections and that those who do tend to be led by fewer than 200 big contributors? And if we are concerned, what might we consider doing to broaden participation and insure that votes count for at least as much as dollars?

First, while turnout is low among all Texans, it is especially low among Hispanics. That will change over time, but it will not change very fast unless policymakers enact programs to encourage non-citizens to become citizens, then to register to vote, and finally to turn out on election day. Turnout for all Texans, including new citizens, has improved slightly since early voting was initiated in the late-1980s, but clustering elections so voters thought of them as more important and allowing citizens to register to vote right up to and on election day might help as well.

Second, the wild west approach to campaign finance in Texas may convince many citizens that their little contribution and perhaps even their vote is of little consequence. Federal law limits contributors to $2300 per candidate per election. Texas law allows unlimited campaign contributions. "In 2006, according to watchdog group Texans for Public Justice, 140 Texans gave $100,000 or more, for a total of $52 million: more than one of every four dollars reported by campaigns."[19] Proponents of the current system say that money is political expression and should not be limited while critics argue that big money can sometimes buy elections and can often rent politicians.

Finally, the tremendous turnout in the 2008 Democratic primary and caucus highlighted the unusual character of that system. Do you think the primary alone should determine who wins Texas delegates to the Democratic National Convention, or should those willing to caucus later in the evening have special influence?

CHAPTER SUMMARY

Political participation encompasses all of the actions that citizens undertake to influence politics. The most common forms of political participation include talking and reading about politics and voting. Fewer citizens make the deeper commitment to work in a campaign, contribute money, serve on an advisory committee, or stand for office. In general, U.S. political participation rates are lower than European rates, and Texans participate at rates well below the U.S. average.

Historically, Texas actively restricted political participation by minorities and poor whites. In recent decades, most formal restrictions have been removed, but voter turnout in Texas remains six to eight percent below U.S. averages. In modern Texas, citizens with good educations and incomes and strong ties to their community vote in significantly higher rates than those without these advantages and attributes. Anglos and blacks turn out at approximately equal rates, while Hispanics turn out at about half their rates.

Texas selects its political leaders through partisan primaries and party conventions. Party nominees face off in general elections. Local races still involve door-to-door campaigning, talks at the local civics clubs, and weekend barbecues. Statewide elections, especially for high profile offices like governor, are expensive, often raucous, affairs. Campaign professionals manage these contests and the mud flies thick and fast.

KEY TERMS

General elections	Poll tax	Suffrage
Grovey v. Townsend	Preclearance	*U.S. v. Texas*
Motor Voter	Primary elections	Voter turnout
Nixon v. Herndon	*Smith v. Allwright*	White primary
Political participation	Special election	

SUGGESTED READINGS

Ben Barnes, *Barn Burning, Barn Building: Tales of a Political Life from LBJ to George W. Bush* (Albany, TX: Bright Sky Press, 2006).

George N. Green, *The Establishment in Texas Politics: The Primitive Years, 1938–1957* (Norman: University of Oklahoma Press, 1984).

Darlene Clark Hine, *Black Victory: The Rise and Fall of the White Primary in Texas* (Columbia, MO: University of Missouri Press, 2003).

Michael Lind, *Made In Texas: George W. Bush and the Southern Takeover of American Politics* (New York: Basic Books, 2003).

Sue Tolleson Rinehart, *Claytie and the Lady: Ann Richards, Gender, and Politics in Texas* (Austin, TX: University of Texas Press, 1994).

WEB RESOURCES

http://www.texas.gov Texas Online is the state's general web portal. It provides access to many online services and helpful links.

http://www.tsha.utexas.edu/handbook/online The Handbook of Texas Online is sponsored by the Texas State Historical Association and UT Austin. It is an encyclopedia of Texas history, geography, and culture.

http://www.sos.state.tx.us The Texas Secretary of State's website contains extensive information on voter registration, turnout, and election results.

http://www.followthemoney.org The Institute on Money in State Politics is a nonpartisan organization that tracks fundraising and spending in state elections.

http://www.lwv.org The League of Women Voters focuses on voter information and education.

END NOTES

1. Donald S. Strong, "The Poll Tax: The Case of Texas," *American Political Science Review,* August 1944, vol. 38, no. 4, pp. 693–709.
2. Darlene Clark Hine, *The Rise and Fall of the White Primary in Texas* (Millwood, NY: KTO Press, 1979).
3. Charles L. Zelden, *The Battle for the Black Ballot:* Smith v. Allwright *and the Defeat of the Texas All-White Primary* (Lawrence, KS: University of Kansas Press, 2004).
4. Gray and Hanson, *Politics in the American States,* 9th ed., pp. 78–81.
5. See the Texas Secretary of State's HAVA website. http://www.sos.state.texas.us/elections/hava/index.shtml.
6. See http://www.sos.state.tx.us/elections/historical/index.shtml. This is the Texas Secretary of State's website.
7. See http://www.census.gov/population/socdemo/voting/cps2006/table04b.xls. This is the website of the U.S. Census Bureau.
8. Paul Burka, "Minority Report," *Texas Monthly,* January 2007, pp. 10–14.
9. Dave Mann, "Voto Por Voto: Will Hispanic Voters Stand and Be Counted?, *The Texas Observer,* February 22, 2008.
10. http://elections.gmu.edu/turnout%201980-2008.xls. This is Professor Michael McDonald's website.
11. John Spong, "You're Rick Noriega, Do You Approve This Message?" *Texas Monthly,* July 2008, pp. 132–137, 166–171.
12. Christy Hoppe, "Getting to Know You: Perry Camp Studying Up On Voters," *Dallas Morning News,* July 26, 2006, A1, A4.
13. Texans for Public Justice, "Money in PoliTex: A Guide to Money in the 2006 Texas Elections," September 2007. http://www.tpj.org/reports/politex2006. See also *Texas Almanac* 2008–2009, pp. 444–450.
14. W. Gardner Selby, "Final Governor's Race Tally," *Austin American-Statesman,* January 19, 2007, 3A.
15. Wayne Slater, "$10M From Perry's Elite: Number of Big Donors Tops Rivals, Predecessors," *Dallas Morning News,* August 17, 2006, 1A, 15A.
16. Paul Burka, "Capture the Flag," *Texas Monthly,* July 2006, pp. 95–101, 172–175.
17. Kelley Shannon, AP, "Unusual Texas Governor's Race Accelerates on Labor Day," *Austin American-Statesman,* September 6, 2006.
18. Editorial Board, "Legislature should close TAB's loophole," *Austin American-Statesman,* July 1, 2006.
19. Laylan Copelin, "Campaign Finance Legislation Doesn't Seem to Have Much Support This Session," *Austin American-Statesman,* April 22, 2007, A1.

CHAPTER 4

Interest Groups in Texas

Focus Questions

Q1. Why do the U.S. and Texas Constitutions protect interest groups?

Q2. Which Texas interest groups tend to be best organized?

Q3. How do interest groups try to influence the political process?

Q4. What roles do interest groups play in political campaigns?

Q5. Have we done enough to regulate interest groups in Texas?

Americans have always been concerned that narrow private interests, whether based in religion, ideology, partisanship, or profit, might overcome the broad public interest. The founding generation, led by James Madison, worried that highly motivated groups of citizens, like the commercial elites in the cities, or the holders of government debt, might work to skew government policy to their benefit and to the detriment of the broader public. Madison famously defined "factions," what we would call interest groups today, as "a number of citizens, whether amounting to a majority or minority of the whole, who are united by . . . some common impulse of passion, or of interest, adverse to . . . the permanent and aggregate interests of the community."[1]

James Madison was not alone in his concern about the impact of clashing interests on the common good. Sam Houston warned his fellow Texans and the nation of the dangers posed by sectionalism. Speaking in Tremont Hall, Boston, on Washington's birthday, 1855, he urged his listeners to send to Congress and the presidency "men who will care for the whole people, who will . . . reconcile conflicting interests. This can be done, and let us not despair and break up the Union."[2] Despite Houston's best efforts, conflicting interests became more strident, party conflict deepened, and civil war came. But despite the potential hazards of factions and interests in democratic politics, Madison, Houston and most Americans with them have recognized that free people must have the right to join together, express their views, and press those views on government.

> **Q1.** Why do the U.S. and Texas Constitutions protect interest groups?

Both the United States and Texas Constitutions protect the right of citizens to join together, discuss their views, and press their interests on government. The first amendment to the U.S. Constitution declares that, "congress shall make no law . . . abridging . . . the right of the people peaceably to assemble, and to petition the Government for a redress of grievances." Similarly, Article 1, section 27, of the Texas Constitution declares that, "citizens shall have the right, in a peaceable manner, to assemble together for their common good and to apply to those invested with the powers of government for redress of grievances or other purposes, by petition, address, or remonstrance."

Interest groups
Organizations that attempt to influence society and government to act in ways consonant with their interests.

The most prominent contemporary definition of **interest groups** comes from David B. Truman's classic study of the governmental process. In terms similar to Madison's, Truman defined an interest group as "any group that, on the basis of one or more shared attitudes, makes certain claims upon other groups in society."[3] Others highlight the interplay of interest groups and government. Graham Wilson noted that "interest groups are generally defined as organizations, separate from government though often in close partnership with government, which attempt to influence public policy."[4]

Despite the prominence of modern interest groups, politicians and scholars continue to ask whether they strengthen or weaken democracy. Two general answers have been offered. **Pluralism** suggests that groups arise to represent most interests in society and that the struggle between groups produces a reasonable policy balance. In this view, interest groups play a positive, even necessary, role in democratic politics. **Elitism** contends that effective, well-funded interest groups are much more likely to form, win access, and exercise influence on behalf of the wealthy and prominent than the poor and humble. In this view, the playing field is tilted in favor of the wealthy and powerful and, hence, democracy is at risk.

Pluralism   The belief that the interest group system produces a reasonable policy balance.

Elitism   The belief that the interest group system is skewed toward the interests of the wealthy.

In this chapter we evaluate the organization, activities, and effectiveness of interest groups in Texas. We describe the kinds of interest groups active in Texas and how they seek to influence the political process. We ask what legal restraints are in place to regulate and control their activities and what additional reforms might be advisable. As we shall see, interest groups and their lobbyists play an influential, even dominant, role in Texas government and politics.

INTEREST GROUPS IN TEXAS

Both nationally and in Texas, the interest group world is tilted toward occupational or economic groups that represent corporate, business, and professional interests. In the traditional political culture of Texas, these interests tend to be especially well-organized, well-funded, and influential. They play offense. Labor, public interest groups, and social equity groups tend to be less well-organized, less well-funded, and much less influential. They play defense.[5] As we explore the world of Texas interest groups, we will find that elitism is a better guide than pluralism.

Business Interests

Groups that represent business come in many shapes and sizes, but together they are the dominant force in Texas politics. They work to promote a strong business environment—which usually means protecting the competitive position of the state's largest businesses, encouraging support for new and expanding businesses, and discouraging business taxation and regulation. A few very prominent groups represent business in general, while most represent narrower sectors or types of businesses.

Peak associations, like the Chamber of Commerce and the Texas Association of Business (TAB), represent the interests of business throughout the state. **Trade associations,** such as the Texas Oil and Gas Association, Texas Hotel and Lodging Association, and the Texas Good Roads and Transportation Association, represent particular business sectors. Finally, most major corporations, including ExxonMobil, Texas Instruments (TI), and Electronic Data Systems (EDS), lobby the Texas state government. These companies and their employees pay taxes into the state's coffers, support or oppose candidates and officeholders, and have information that state officials need to do their jobs. The associations and their representatives have no trouble getting the attention of Texas officials.

Professional Interests

Like business, Texas professions are well-organized and influential. While there are no peak associations representing all of the professions, the most prominent **professional associations,** including the Texas Medical

Q2. Which Texas interest groups tend to be best organized?

Peak associations
Peak associations, like the U.S. Chamber of Commerce, represent the general interests of business.

Trade associations
Associations formed by businesses and related interests involved in the same commercial, trade, or industrial sector.

Professional associations
Organizations formed to represent the interests of professionals in occupations like medicine, law, accounting and cosmetology.

Bill Hammond was named President and Chief Executive Officer of Texas Association of Business & Chambers of Commerce (TABCC) on the first of April, 1998. *Texas Association of Business*

Association, the Texas Bar Association, the Texas Association of Realtors, and the Texas Federation of Teachers, are well represented in Austin. Only occasionally, as in the case of medical malpractice reform, do the professional associations—in this case, the associations representing doctors and lawyers—go toe-to-toe. Usually, each quietly and effectively works its own side of the street.

In addition to the prominent and well-funded associations representing the doctors, lawyers, realtors, and teachers, there are dozens of other professional associations. They represent the accountants, architects, engineers, dentists, nurses and pharmacists, barbers, hair dressers and cosmetologists, surveyors, plumbers, and many more. The goal of interest groups representing professions is to keep incomes up by limiting entry into the profession, usually through some sort of licensing procedure, in exchange for modest state regulation and oversight. These groups generally dominate state policy that affects them because they care more than anyone else, they know the issues better than anyone else, and they are eager to serve on the state boards that regulate their professional activities.[6]

TABLE 4.1
Texas 2007 Lobby Contracts by Interest Represented

Interest Group	Max. Value of Contracts	Min. Value of Contracts	No. of Contracts	Percentage of Max. Value
Energy/Natural Resources	$59,980,013	$33,330,000	1,101	17%
Ideological/Single Issue	$49,148,003	$21,173,000	1,549	14%
Health	$42,890,000	$19,830,000	1,013	12%
Miscellaneous Business	$37,315,002	$17,830,000	930	11%
Lawyers & Lobbyists	$27,085,027	$20,080,000	360	8%
Communications	$22,705,000	$11,440,000	416	7%
Finance	$18,445,002	$9,015,000	463	5%
Real Estate	$17,430,002	$8,525,000	433	5%
Insurance	$15,395,000	$7,035,000	428	4%
Transportation	$12,490,001	$5,680,000	348	4%
Computers & Electronics	$12,185,001	$5,910,000	296	3%
Construction	$11,905,002	$5,975,000	273	3%
Agriculture	$8,240,000	$3,745,000	235	2%
Other	$7,125,001	$3,585,000	163	2%
Labor	$4,775,000	$2,155,000	126	1%
Unknown	$1,150,000	$515,000	32	<1%
TOTAL	**$348,263,054**	**$175,823,000**	**8,166**	**100%**

Source: Texans for Public Justice, *"Austin's Oldest Profession: Texas's Top Lobby Clients and Those Who Serve Them,"* 2008 edition, III, Lobbyists. *http://www.tpj.org/reports/austinsoldest07/lobbyists.html.*

Agricultural Interests

Farming and ranching are still important parts of the Texas economy, but not nearly as important as they once were. While they have to fight harder for attention, when issues that matter to rural Texans come before state government, the Texas Farm Bureau speaks for the bigger producers and the Texas Farmers Union speaks for the smaller family farms and ranches. Commodity producers, including cattle, cotton, grain, poultry, sheep, and timber, have their own associations ready to act when their interests come into play.

Organized Labor

In states like Michigan, Pennsylvania, and New York, organized labor shapes state policy on workplace safety, employment security, and workers' rights. Not so in Texas. In Texas, business shapes labor policy. Texas is one of twenty-two mostly southern and southwestern **right-to-work** states. These states prohibit the closed or union shop, in which a majority vote of a business' workers to join a union requires every worker in the business to join the union, pay dues, and abide by union rules. Right-to-work laws weaken unions in relation to management and owners. They allow individual workers to decide whether to join the union. Some do, and some—wanting to save the union dues—do not, and the union is weakened as a bargaining unit. In 2006, only 4.9 percent of the Texas's 10.6 million workers (compared to 12 percent nationally) were members of a labor union.

Right-to-work Legal principle prohibiting mandatory union membership.

There are pockets of union strength in Texas. The Texas chapter of the American Federation of Labor and Congress of Industrial Organizations (AFL-CIO) and the Oil, Chemical, and Atomic Workers of Texas are strong in the Houston-Beaumont-Port Arthur area. The Service Employees International Union (SEIU) had some success in organizing janitors and health care workers in Houston in 2006 and 2007. Texas unions can affect local and regional issues and elections, but they usually struggle when they attempt to operate in Austin. They lose most direct confrontations with business interests.

Ethnic Groups

Texas is a majority-minority state, but the state's interest group structure is still very much dominated by its Anglo minority. While prominent minority interest groups have operated in Texas for nearly a century, they have generally not prevailed in the Texas legislature and courts. Their successes usually came when Congress and the federal courts weighed in. The National Association for the Advancement of Colored People (NAACP) and the League of United Latin American Citizens (LULAC) have operated in Texas since 1915 and 1929 respectively. The NAACP initially focused on voting and political access while LULAC focused on equal educational opportunity.

The period of greatest success for the NAACP, LULAC, and related groups came from the mid-1940s through the mid-1960s. The national

"I hope people will give me a chance," said Joy Fenner, the new president of the Baptist General Convention of Texas. The group's annual meeting was in Amarillo. *MICHAEL SCHUMACHER/* Amarillo Globe-News

NAACP and its Texas chapter won a series of voting rights victories, including *Smith v. Allwright* (1944), which opened up the Democratic party primary to blacks. LULAC and the newly formed G.I. Forum (composed of Mexican-American G.I.s who had recently returned from World War II and were insisting upon equality) prevailed in a case, *Delgado v. Bastrop ISD* (1948), which declared that Mexicans could not be segregated in public schools. LULAC prevailed again in *Edgewood ISD v. Kirby* (1989), which mandated equalization of school funding between rich and poor districts.

Neither the NAACP nor LULAC have been particularly effective in recent years. In fact, LULAC has been challenged by two newer and more aggressive organizations, La Rasa and the Mexican American Legal Defense and Education Fund (MALDEF). Like the unions, interest groups representing minorities have been most effective in areas where their numbers are concentrated. The NAACP has been most effective in the state's urban centers, especially Houston and Dallas, while LULAC, La Rasa, and MALDEF have been most effective in South Texas, especially San Antonio and the Rio Grande Valley. At the capitol, they strain to be heard over the louder voices of business and the professions.

Religious Groups

For most of the 20th century, religion was important to many Americans, but it was not an organized political force. A series of Supreme Court rulings prohibiting state-sanctioned prayer and religious symbolism in the public schools seemed to many religious people to threaten the complete exclusion of religion from public life. By the late 1970s, Christian conservatives had begun to organize and push back.

Religious groups have been strongest in the Midwest and South and very strong in Texas. Since 1994, Christian conservatives have controlled the state's Republican Party and are central to Governor Rick Perry's support coalition. Governor Perry has met several times for "policy briefings" with a group of conservative Texas ministers called the Texas Restoration Project. Christian conservatives campaign for prayer in the public schools, faith-based social policy initiatives, abstinence-based sex education, strict limits on access to abortion services, home schooling, charter schools, private school vouchers, and defense of traditional marriage.

Religious conservatives are not unchallenged in Texas. The moderate Baptist General Convention of Texas elected an Hispanic president in 2004, a black president in 2005, and a female president, Joy Fenner of Garland, in 2007. The Catholic Church and the Interfaith Alliance have worked extensively in local communities to improve education, alleviate poverty, act as a liaison between those in need and social service agencies, and help with employment, language training, and health care. The Texas Freedom Network stands for separation of church and state and worries about prayer in the schools and faith-based social programs. But in Texas, religious conservatives are close to power, whispering in the Governor's ear, while religious moderates and secularists whisper earnestly to the Democrats about the dangers of mixing religion and politics.[7]

Single Issue Groups

Some groups are tightly focused on one or a few related issues. The best example of a prominent single issue group is the National Rifle Association (NRA). While a national group, the NRA is powerful in Texas. The NRA favors a broad understanding of the gun owner's rights and opposes government restrictions on those rights. The Texas Constitution protects the right to bear arms but allows the legislature to regulate the right to prevent crime. In Texas, this means arming honest citizens so they can better resist the criminals.

Texas' strong support for the right to bear arms came under close scrutiny in the 2000 presidential campaign. In 1995, Governor George W. Bush signed a bill that gave Texans the right to carry concealed weapons. In 1997, he signed an amendment to the concealed-carry law that stripped out provisions forbidding concealed weapons in churches. The amendment required churches to post signs if they wanted to exclude guns. On September 16, 1999, seven people were shot and killed in a Fort Worth church. Vice President Al Gore, soon to be the Democratic nominee for president, criticized George W. Bush, soon to be the Republican nominee for president, for supporting the 1995 law and the 1997 amendments.[8]

Abortion is another highly contentious issue that has spawned single issue groups on both sides. The Texas chapter of the National Abortion Rights Action League favors "a woman's right to choose," or simply "choice." Supporters of the pro-choice position envision a situation in which abortion is legal and women and their doctors decide when it is appropriate. The Texas Right to Life Committee lobbies the Texas legislature to regulate the timing and circumstances under which abortions are available. Pro-life interest groups play an influential role in Texas politics while pro-choice groups have a very rough time. In 2005, Texas passed a law requiring written parental approval for unmarried women under 18 to secure an abortion.

Public Interest Groups

Many groups claim to pursue the public interest, rather than partisan, ideological, or economic interests. Like the single issue groups, the most prominent public interest groups are national groups with Texas chapters. The best example of a non-partisan public interest group is the Texas League of Women Voters. The League of Women Voters works to enhance voter awareness and participation. Despite their claims to the contrary, most public interest groups lean to the right or the left. Examples on the left, in the sense that they support an activist government, are Texans for Public Justice, Common Cause, and Public Citizen. These and similar groups work for consumer safety, environmental protection, and open government. The "good government" groups are often patronized and, more often, ignored by the powers that be in Texas politics.

On the right is the Texas Eagle Forum. The Texas Eagle Forum works for traditional values, law and order, small government, and low taxes. Leaders of the Eagle Forum are more likely to growl than to plead if they feel public officials are drifting from the approved path. In the summer of 2006, Lt. Governor David Dewhurst and Senator Kay Bailey Hutchison both suggested the need for a guest worker program as part of their re-election campaigns. Cathie Adams of the Texas Eagle Forum told Gardiner Selby of the *Austin American-Statesman* that "Dewhurst and Hutchison seem to speak for corporations. 'What we are up against [Adams said] is the taxpaying citizen versus the elites who are only looking out for the cost of doing their own business. . . . This is hurting. I'm sorry that maybe our voices haven't been loud or clear enough.' "[9]

INTEREST GROUP ACTIVITIES AND RESOURCES

Q3. How do interest groups try to influence the political process?

Texas state governments, with the singular exception of the strong state government created by the post-Civil War Reconstruction Constitution of 1869, were designed to be weak and diffuse so that they could not dictate to private individuals and interests. This is particularly true of the Texas Constitution of 1876, the current constitution, with its weak governor, part-time legislature, elected judges, and diffuse and under-funded bureaucracy. Interest groups wield great influence in Texas because, oftentimes, they are better organized, better informed, and better funded than Texas state government.

Interest groups use a variety of tools in their attempts to influence the elected and appointed officials of state government. Most groups have knowledge and expertise that the public officials need. Some groups have deep pockets, some have many members, and some have a small number of influential and well-connected members. Other groups have influential leaders or well-established ties to important economic and ideological networks. Interest groups and their lobbyists deploy their resources to influence the making and implementation of public policy in Texas.

Lobbying Government Officials

Most major interest groups hire one or more **lobbyists** to defend their interests in Austin. Nearly 1800 lobbyists registered with the **Texas Ethics Commission** (TEC) prior to the 2007 legislative session.[10] TEC records (which record ranges rather than precise dollar amounts) indicate that lobbyists earned between $348 and $176 million representing clients before the Texas legislature.[11]

Most of the top professional lobbyists have a detailed knowledge of Texas government and policy. They are often former members of the legislature, like Stan Schlueter former Chair of the House Calendars Committee, or former senior staff to the legislature, like ex-Speaker's aide Rusty Kelley. Others cut their teeth in the governor's office or in a key element of the bureaucracy. Former officials know the legislative and bureaucratic process and they have networks of former colleagues and friends who will assure them a respectful hearing.

One major interest group, the Texas Cable and Telecommunications Association (TCTA), learned a costly lesson in Texas "pay to play" politics in 2005. Texas phone companies, led by SBC Communications and Verizon Communications, pushed for legislation allowing them to offer statewide internet-based television services without negotiating separate agreements with Texas cities as the cable companies are required to do. The cable companies opposed the bill, arguing that it would give the phone companies an unfair competitive advantage.

Lobbyists   Hired agents who seek to influence government decision making in ways that benefit or limit harm to their clients.

Texas Ethics Commission   Created in 1991, the TEC administers the state's ethics, campaign finance, and lobbying laws.

TABLE 4.2
The "Rainmakers" of the Texas Lobby

Lobbyist	Contracts Max. Value	Contracts Min. Value	# Contracts	Lobbyist's Background
Todd M. Smith	$3,875,003	$2,885,000	26	Impact TX Communications
Carol McGarah	$3,405,000	$1,665,000	64	Ex-Senate Aide; Blackridge, Inc.
Russell T. Kelley	$3,295,000	$1,685,000	63	Ex-Speaker Aide; Blackridge, Inc.
Robert D. Miller	$3,080,002	$2,070,000	28	Ex-Senate Aide
W. James Jonas III	$3,050,003	$2,495,000	16	Holland & Knight
Randall H. Erben	$3,025,000	$1,605,000	33	Ex-Asst. Sec. of State
Arthur V. Perkins	$2,875,000	$1,435,000	57	Coats Rose Law Firm
Amy Tankersley	$2,875,000	$1,435,000	57	Coats Rose Law Firm
Andrea McWilliams	$2,865,000	$1,455,000	41	Ex-Legislative Aide
Stan Schlueter	$2,760,000	$1,725,000	23	Ex-Legislator
Michael Toomey	$2,710,000	$1,510,000	37	Ex-Governor's Aide; Ex-Legislator
David Sibley	$2,675,000	$1,500,000	45	Ex-Senator
Frank R. Santos	$2,600,000	$1,470,000	29	Ex-House Aide; Santos Alliances
Laura M. Matz	$2,550,000	$1,445,000	29	At Santos Alliances

Source: Texans for Public Justice, *"Austin's Oldest Profession," III, Lobbyists.*

The phone companies fertilized the legislative process by contributing $156,000 to Governor Perry and spending as much as $10.2 million on lobbying. The cable companies gave Governor Perry only $25,000 and spent $1.7 million on lobbying. The phone company's bill passed in the second special session of 2005 and the responses of interested observers and participants were instructive. Andrew Wheat, research director for Texans for Public Justice (a left-leaning public interest group), said "Nobody is shocked to learn that moneyed interests call the shots in Austin. Yet it is truly boggling that a single special interest has the 'stroke' to push its legislation through the special session . . . The only way to adequately recognize this feat is to rename the Capitol 'SBC Arena.' "

Wheat was right to point to SBC's impressive "stroke" with the governor and the legislature, but he was wrong to say that nobody was "shocked to learn that moneyed interests call the shots in Austin"—the cable companies certainly were shocked. Tom Kinney, chairman of the TCTA, said "The cable industry chose to stand by the merits of our position—namely, create regulations that treat each player in the telecom market equitably—rather than spend huge amounts of money on lobbyists and political contributions." It did not take the cable lobby long to rethink its strategy. A little more than two months later, Representative Todd Baxter (R-Austin) resigned his seat in the Texas House and on the House Regulated Industries Committee to become the top lobbyist for the Texas cable industry. Kinney observed that Baxter's "experience at the Capital will serve TCTA well."[12] Lesson learned.

In 2007, a similar fight broke out between Texas liquor wholesalers and package store distributors. Since Texas legalized liquor by the drink in 1971, liquor wholesalers have sold to package stores and package stores have enjoyed a monopoly on selling liquor to bars and restaurants. In the ten weeks prior to the 2007 regular session, the wholesalers lubricated the Texas political establishment with $1.7 million, $100,000 apiece to Governor Perry and Speaker Craddick, $75,000 to Lieutenant Governor Dewhurst, and amounts ranging from $40,000 to $1,500 to a majority of the House and Senate, to get the law changed. The wholesalers also spent $1.1 million on lobbyists, while the package store owners responded with $635,000 on lobbying contracts.

Despite outspending the package store distributors, the wholesalers lost when Rep. Kino Flores (D-Mission) refused to bring the bill up in his Licensing and Administrative Procedures Committee. Does this mean that Texas politicians cannot be bought, or just that sometimes the deep-pocketed special interests have to pay more than once before getting their way? Suzy Woodford of Common Cause Texas observed that the fight "shows that in Texas, we have a pay-to-play system. We have no limits on the amount of money that . . . individuals, their PACs, and their officers can contribute. So it clearly demonstrates to the average Joe that if you don't have the big bucks . . . the item you care about is not even going to be considered."[13]

Unlike the highly visible and well-funded fight between the phone and cable companies, or the liquor wholesalers and package stores, most lobbying is low profile, even behind-the-scenes. The most potent resource that most lobbyists have, especially during the crush of the legislative session, is information. A lobbyist representing an interest group will have all of the information that is available to that group. They may offer the legislator only, or at least mostly, that information that supports the group's policy position, but the interested legislator can get the rest of the information from a competing lobbyist. Lobbyists also testify before legislative committees and often participate directly in the discussions and negotiations that lead to the final legislative product.

Lobbyists also work to establish a personal, as well as a professional, relationship with legislators. Lobbyists hold an endless series of receptions, lunches, and dinners for legislators throughout the session. At the end of the session, they host parties and contribute to the purchase of gifts for the legislative leaders and committees with whom they worked most closely. There are state laws governing lobbyist expenditures, but they are weak and their weakness is no accident.

Lobbyists and other interest group representatives are integral to the consultative, deal-making, legislative process, but their work does not end when the legislature adjourns. Laws have to be implemented and bureaucratic decisions about rules, regulations, and procedures that govern implementation can be critical. A group that opposed a particular piece of legislation might gain back some of what it lost in the legislature if its representatives can shape the way the bureaucracy administers the law. Alternatively, a group that supported the legislation, seeing it administered in unintended ways, might appeal to the courts for a judgment on the law's real meaning.

Lobbying the Public

While most interest groups and all lobbyists prefer to make their case directly to politicians and decision makers, groups also lobby the public. They do this through newspaper and television advertising, direct mail, and public meetings intended to educate, inform, and rally citizens to the group's issue positions and legislative proposals.

Once citizens are informed and engaged, they can be organized in mail, phone, and e-mail campaigns. They might also be taken to Austin to meet with their legislators, address committees where appropriate, and even rally and demonstrate on the capitol steps. If television cameras can be attracted, all the better. Lobbying the public is intended to encourage citizens to supplement the efforts of professional lobbyists, or, where professional help is too expensive, to bring the pressure of public opinion directly to bear against elected officials and bureaucrats.

Campaign Support

Wealthy individuals, interest groups, and their lobbyists know that if they contribute to a candidate's campaign or political committee, that candidate will meet with them and listen to them once elected.[14] On the other hand, statewide elected officials, legislative leaders, committee chairs, and many others take contributions from interests on all sides of major public issues.

Q4. What roles do interest groups play in political campaigns?

Political action committee Legal entity, often associated with interest groups, through which campaign contributions and other forms of support can be given to parties and candidates.

Contributors know that while making a contribution gets them a hearing, it does not necessarily buy them a vote.

Most interest groups make their contributions through a **political action committee** or PAC. Regulation of PACs in Texas is far looser than are federal regulations or regulations in most other states. Texas PACs (there were 1,576 in 2007) are required to register with the TEC, name a treasurer, and file regular reports. Those reports must identify persons who give more than $50 to a Texas campaign, but unlike federal campaigns, where contributions are limited to $2,300, there are no limits on the amount that an individual or PAC can contribute in Texas.[15]

Some PACs also have the resources to try to shape elections more generally, by participating in candidate recruitment, voter registration and mobilization, polling, and advertising. One prominent Texas PAC, Tom DeLay's Texans for a Republican Majority (TRMPAC), raised more than $532,000 to target 23 Texas House districts in 2002.[16] Most of their preferred candidates won, giving the Texas House a Republican majority for the first time since the early 1870s. Subsequent charges that TRMPAC had accepted illegal corporate contributions led to the indictment and conviction of some TRMPAC officials, the demise of TRMPAC itself, and Tom DeLay's resignation from Congress—but the election results stood.

Not surprisingly, the largest political donor in 2006 was a Texan. Houston home builder Bob Perry gave $16 million, 92 percent to Republican candidates and causes; $6.7 million in Texas contests and $9.3 million in other state and national contests. Bob Perry gave $380,000 to Governor Rick Perry, $320,265 to incumbent Republican Attorney General Greg Abbott, $285,000 to incumbent Lieutenant Governor David Dewhurst, and more than $100,000 in half a dozen other Texas elections. Most of Bob Perry's national contributions were not to candidates, where Federal law limits contributions to $2,300, but to groups called 527s which are independent expenditure groups that can support causes and candidates without expenditure limits. Little wonder that Texas politicians show so little interest in limiting contributions to state contests.[17]

Litigation

Interest groups are nothing if not tenacious. If they lose on an important issue before the legislature and executive branch, they often look to the courts. Bureaucrats make policy by deciding precisely how to implement legislation, and courts make policy by judging whether legislative intent was constitutional and, if so, whether it has been followed.

Powerful interest groups attempt to shape the judiciary by recruiting favorable candidates for judicial office, contributing to their campaigns, and supporting them for re-election. Weaker interest groups have to take the judiciary as it is, but they can sometimes prevail by suing to insure that the letter of the law in applied. The NAACP, LULAC, and MALDEF have all won major victories in the Texas courts over the years. While victories expanding civil liberties, political access, and equal opportunity have not

TABLE 4.3
Let's Compare: State Ethics Agencies: Jurisdiction Subject Areas

The *Book of the States* is a publication of the Conference on State Legislatures and compares state government institutions, policies, and procedures across literally hundreds of dimensions. One dimension upon which the states are compared is the jurisdictional range and breadth of their ethics agencies. Texas does not fare well.

States	Campaign Finance	Conflict of Interest	Ethics	Financial Disclosure	Gift Restriction	Lobbying
California	Y	Y	Y	Y	Y	Y
Texas	Y	N	N	N	Y	Y
New York	Y	Y	Y	Y	Y	Y
Florida	Y	Y	Y	Y	Y	Y
Pennsylvania	N	Y	Y	Y	N	N
Ohio	N	Y	Y	Y	Y	Y
Michigan	Y	N	Y	Y	Y	Y
North Carolina	N	Y	Y	Y	N	N
Georgia	Y	N	N	Y	Y	Y
Oklahoma	Y	Y	Y	Y	Y	Y

Source: Book of the States 2005, (Lexington, KY: Council of State Governments, 2005), Vol. 37, Table 6.9, pp. 374–375.

been frequent, they have been important, and sometimes the courts are the only means that the politically weak have to move a system that usually gives them little heed.

INTEREST GROUPS AND LOBBY REFORM

Texas has had laws on the books to regulate the activities of interest groups and lobbyists for at least a century. The first law, passed in 1907, instructed lobbyists to use no inducements other than sweet reason to influence legislation. New laws requiring interest groups and their lobbyists to register with the legislature and report on various aspects of their activities were passed in 1957, 1973, and again in 1983. Each was riddled with loopholes, lacked enforcement provisions, and was generally ineffective. New laws were passed in 1991 and updated in 1997 and 2003, but Texas remains the wild west as far as effective regulation of interest groups, lobbyists, and campaign contributions are concerned.

> **Q5.** Have we done enough to regulate interest groups in Texas?

Generally, ethics laws try to control, or at least record, the benefits, gifts, and contributions that lobbyists shower on legislators and, to a lesser extent, on bureaucrats and judges. Lobbyists buy meals and drinks for legislators, direct benefits and gifts their way, and make campaign contributions to them. Texas law does not forbid gifts, gratuities, and contributions, it merely requires that a public record of them be kept. In fact, as we shall see below, it barely requires that.

The Lobby Registration Act of 1973 and the Ethics Law of 1991 form the basis of Texas's modern regulatory structure. The 1973 **Lobby Registration Act** required groups and individuals attempting to influence state government to register and file reports on their activities. The 1991 Ethics Law created the eight-member TEC. It required any person who spends

Lobby Registration Act A 1973 Texas law requiring groups and individuals attempting to influence state government to register and report on certain of their activities.

more than $500 or receives more than $1,000 in a calendar quarter for activities designed to influence legislative or executive branch activities to register with the TEC. The law further required lobbyists who spend more than $50 on a legislator to name the legislator and detail the expenditures.

Perhaps most importantly, the 1991 Ethics Law charged the TEC to receive complaints about violations of the ethics rules, conduct investigations, and issue findings. Nonetheless, the 1991 act left some gaping loopholes. First, members of the TEC are appointed by the governor, lieutenant governor, and speaker of the house from a list of candidates declared acceptable by the legislature. Hence, TEC members are, almost by definition, friendly with the politicians they are appointed to scrutinize. Second, the TEC requires a super-majority of three quarters to initiate important actions. Complaints that are not upheld are kept secret; neither the charge nor the Commission's findings are ever made public.

Third, because Texas legislators receive only $7,200 a year, plus a modest *per diem* when the legislature is actually in session or they are engaged in official legislative business, they search for money to meet their living expenses while in Austin. Current law permits legislators to accept unlimited amounts of money from lobbyists and others, deposit it into their campaign accounts and then to draw on those accounts to cover living expenses in Austin. Clearly, accepting money for these expenses from lobbyists guarantees that legislators will be beholden to them.

It gets worse. In 2004 and 2005, Bill Ceverha, a former official of TRMPAC and current member of the State Employees Retirement System board, accepted two checks from Houston real estate developer Bob Perry (no blood relation to Gov. Rick Perry, but the top Republican donor in Texas). Ceverha incurred more than $1 million in legal fees and civil penalties for his role in TRMPAC's illegal fund raising for the 2002 state legislative races. Ceverha was forced to declare personal bankruptcy and to appeal to friends and associates for assistance. Perry felt sorry for Ceverha and made charitable gifts to him to help defer legal expenses.

Ceverha, as required by Texas law, filed reports with the TEC on which he listed the first of these gifts as a "check." When public advocacy groups demanded more information—for example, how much the "check" was for—the TEC ruled that state disclosure laws do not require that the amount of cash gifts be disclosed. Clean-government types howled and eventually Perry and Ceverha announced that two checks, totaling $100,000, had passed from Perry to Ceverha.[18] Sage old veterans of Texas politics just smiled and shook their heads. "Let the big dogs hunt."

CHAPTER SUMMARY

Interest groups and their lobbyists are an integral part of American and Texan political life. The U.S. and Texas constitutions explicitly assure citizens that they have the right to assemble, share their views in speech and writing, and petition their government for redress of grievances. Nonetheless, Americans and Texans worry that powerful interest groups and effective lobbyists may skew public policy toward narrow private interests rather than toward the broader public interest.

In Texas, this concern is particularly acute. Organized interests, along with their PACs and lobbyists, are particularly numerous, well-funded, aggressive, and effective. Business and professional groups, like the Texas Association of Business, the Texas Oil and Gas Association, and the Texas Medical Association, wield decisive influence. Labor, civil rights, and environmental groups do the best they can, but they are at distinct disadvantages when it comes to numbers, money, talent, and relevant expertise.

The dominant interest groups tend to lobby government officials directly and to come to the support of elected officials in their campaigns. Less effective groups are left to demonstrate, lobby the public, and appeal to the courts. Texas's very permissive campaign finance system, which allows unlimited contributions and demands only modest reporting requirements, gives the established interests and their agents a formidable role in Texas politics.

KEY TERMS

Elitism
Interest groups
Lobby Registration Act
Lobbyists
Peak associations

Pluralism
Political action committee
Professional associations

Right-to-work
Texas Ethics Commission
Trade associations

SUGGESTED READINGS

Benjamin Marquez, *LULAC: The Evolution of a Mexican American Political Organization* (Austin, TX: University of Texas Press, 1993).
H. C. Pittman, *Inside the Third House: A Veteran Lobbyist Takes a 50-Year Frolic Through Texas Politics* (Austin, TX: Eakin Press, 1992).
Guadalupe San Miguel, Jr., *Let Them All Take Heed: Mexican Americans and the Campaign for Educational Equality in Texas, 1910–1981* (Austin, TX: University of Texas Press, 1987).
Dennis Shirley, *Valley Interfaith and School Reform: Organizing for Power in South Texas* (Austin, TX: University of Texas Press, 2002).

WEB RESOURCES

http://www.ethics.state.tx.us Website of the Texas Ethics Commission.
http://www.tpj.org Website of Texans for Public Justice.
http://www.texasaflcio.org The Texas AFL-CIO, top labor organization in the state.
http://www.texmed.org The Texas Medical Association.
http://www.lulac.org The League of United Latin American Citizens.
http://www.txoga.org The Texas Oil and Gas Association.

END NOTES

1. James Madison, *The Federalist* (New York: Modern College Library Edition, 1937), no. 10, 54.
2. James L. Haley, *Passionate Nation: The Epic History of Texas* (New York: Free Press, 2006), 289.
3. David B. Truman, *The Governmental Process: Political Interests and Public Opinion* (New York: Knopf, 1958), 33.
4. Graham Wilson, *Interest Groups* (Cambridge, MA: Blackwell, 1990), 1.
5. L. M. Sixel, "Unions Vie for Health Care Workers," *Houston Chronicle,* July 18, 2007, A1.
6. Robert T. Garrett, "Lobbyists Revision Would Help Client," *Dallas Morning News,* April 30, 2007, A1, A8.
7. See Texas Lyceum poll on religion, ethics, and public morality. http://www.texaslyceum.org/pollpage.aspx
8. Adam Clymer, "Gore Assails Bush on Texas Law that Permits Guns in Church," *New York Times,* September 18, 1999.
9. W. Gardiner Selby, "Dewhurst, Hutchison Speak Out on Immigration," *Austin American-Statesman,* July 26, 2006.
10. Texas Ethics Commission. http://www.ethics.state.us.tx/tedd/subbb2005b.htm. 2007 figure supplied by TEC.
11. Texans for Public Justice, "Austin's Oldest Profession: Texas' Top Lobby Clients and Those Who Serve Them," 2008 edition, p. 4. http://www.tpj.org/reports/austinsoldest07.
12. Claudia Grisales, "Phone Industry Outlobbied, Outspent Cable Rivals in Legislative Fight," *Austin American Statesman,* August 18, 2005; and Grisales, "Former State Rep Becomes Top Cable Industry Lobbyist," *Austin American Statesman,* November 15, 2005.
13. Robert T. Garrett, "Liquor Wholesalers Ply Legislator with Cash," *Dallas Morning News,* January 24, 2007, A1, A2.
14. Richard S. Dunham and Kathrine Schmidt, "Texas' Top Corporations Stay Loyal to GOP," *Houston Chronicle,* November 26, 2007.
15. See National Conference of State Legislatures at http://www.ncsl.org/programs/legismgt/about/IndCond.htm
16. Scott Gold, "Ruling Targets DeLay Fund-raising Arm," *Los Angeles Times,* May 27, 2005.
17. Wayne Slater, "Texas Was Largest Donor to Campaigns," *Dallas Morning News,* December 6, 2006, 3A.
18. Christy Hoppe, "Cash Gift Sums Can Stay Secret," *Dallas Morning News,* November 28, 2006, 3A.

CHAPTER 5

Political Parties in Texas

Focus Questions

Q1. How are the Texas Democratic and Republican parties organized?

Q2. How does Texas law treat minor-party and independent candidates?

Q3. Why was Texas a one-party Democratic state for so long?

Q4. What led to the rise of the Republican Party in the late 20th century?

Q5. Is the shift of power from Democrats to Republicans in Texas permanent?

Political parties, like interest groups, are sets of like-minded individuals who work to make their government more supportive of their values, goals, and policy preferences. But political parties and interest groups differ in how they organize and act to affect politics. As we saw in the previous chapter, interest groups usually focus on a narrow range of issues that are of particular interest to their members and try to influence officeholders to act favorably on those issues. **Political parties** adopt attractive policy positions, recruit and train talented candidates, and support those candidates in elections. Their ultimate goal is to win majority control of government so that they can appoint senior officials and influence all of the issues that come before the government.[1]

Many scholars argue that political parties should articulate clear policy positions, campaign on them during elections, and then seek to implement those positions once elected. In this **responsible party model,** parties are expected to campaign on ideologically coherent platforms so voters know what they will get if they vote for the party and it wins control of the government. Other scholars and most politicians believe that a **big tent model** is more realistic and more effective. The big tent model encourages parties to blur contentious issues and present themselves as a comfortable home for most, if not all, voters. If the goal of political parties is to win elections (and it is), it usually makes sense to frame the party's appeal broadly.

Political parties
Organizations designed to elect government officeholders under a given label.

Responsible party model Sees political parties as organizations that campaign on coherent ideological platforms and then seek to implement their policies if elected.

Big tent model Sees political parties as organizations that appeal to the broadest range of potential voters rather than seeking to implement a coherent ideological program.

Few readers will be surprised to hear that once political parties win power, they seek to retain it. As "Mr. Dooley," the Chicago saloon-keeper and political sage, once observed, "politics ain't beanbag." The stakes are too high and the fruits of victory are too sweet to treat the rules governing the electoral process as anything but flexible. Officeholders seek to tilt the electoral process in their favor in two principal ways. Both have been on clear display in recent Texas politics. First, the major parties team up to deny potential competitors—third parties, independents, and write-in candidates—access to the fight. And second, if either major party wins control of state government, they seek to shape the electoral districts so that future fights will be conducted to their advantage.

In this chapter, we evaluate the organization, activities, and effectiveness of political parties in Texas. We describe the structure of political parties in Texas, the history of party competition in the state, the rules governing ballot access and redistricting, and the likely balance of power between Democrats and Republicans in the coming decades.

MAJOR PARTY ORGANIZATION IN TEXAS

Q1. How are the Texas Democratic and Republican parties organized?

The Democratic and Republican parties in Texas are broad and amorphous organizations. They spring to life for elections and then fade into the political background between elections. They are composed of full-time officers, part-time activists, and the voters who stand with them on election day. The full-time officers hold official positions in the party bureaucracy. Their job is to lay the groundwork for the successful election of the party's candidates. The temporary party organization is a series of party caucuses and conventions in which the activists chose party leaders and hash out the party platform. Texas has no party registration, so the party's members are those voters who present themselves to vote in the party's primary election.

Precinct-Level Organization

Precinct Geographical area within which voters go to a polling place to cast their ballots on election day.

The precinct level is the foundation of Texas politics. A **precinct** is the geographical area surrounding the local polling place where voters go on election day to cast their ballots. There are about 9,000 precincts in Texas.

The major parties hold party primary elections in March of even-numbered years. Voters in the party primary elections select the party's candidates for the general election, as well as party precinct and county chairs. The precinct chair's job is to organize the precinct so that the party carries it on election day. The precinct chair registers new voters, raises money, secures a volunteer workforce for election day, insures that voters get to the polls, and reports the precinct vote totals to the county office when the election is over. The precinct chair draws no salary.

Any voter that voted in the party primary is entitled to participate in the precinct convention (commonly referred to as the precinct caucus) that evening. The precinct caucus begins with the election of a caucus chair (usually the precinct chair, though it may be the outgoing precinct chair if the position is changing hands) and secretary. The caucus then selects delegates, one for every twenty-five votes cast in the precinct earlier that day, to later attend the county or district-level convention. Finally, the floor is opened to resolutions offered by participants. These resolutions are debated and those adopted are forwarded to the county convention for consideration.

Normally, voter turnout in primaries is light, often around 10 percent of eligible voters, and precinct turnout is very light, usually attracting only a handful of party activists to each precinct. 2008 was dramatically different, especially on the Democratic side. 4.24 million Texans, 2.87 million Democrats, and 1.36 million

Texas Democrats were in high spirits when they met in Austin, June 5–7, for the 2008 Texas Democratic Convention. *Source:* Photo by Barbara Schlief, courtesy of the Texas Democratic Party.

Republicans, 24 percent of the voting age population, voted in the 2008 primary. The previous record was 2.7 million, set in 1988. Even more remarkably, nearly a million voters, including 750,000 Democrats, returned in the evening to participate in the precinct caucuses. The caucus organization and infrastructure was nearly overwhelmed and talk of reform began almost immediately.

County and District-Level Organization

Parties organize by county in rural areas and by state senatorial districts in the more populous urban areas. The county and district conventions occur three weeks after the primary. Turnout was up again, but parties were forewarned and better organized to handle it. The convention process closely mirrors the precinct level, beginning with the election of a convention chair and secretary. The delegates select representatives to the state convention, usually one for every 300 votes cast in the party primary. Precinct resolutions that have been vetted and approved by the county convention's resolutions committee are then debated and voted upon. Approved resolutions are sent forward to the state convention.

County and district chairs are elected by voters in the party primary. They serve for two years and may be re-elected as often as the party's voters wish. There is no salary. County chairs preside over a county executive committee made up of all of the precinct chairs in the county. The county chair's job is to coordinate the precinct chairs and serve as liaison with statewide candidates that come to campaign and with the state party. County chairs are also spokespersons and fundraisers for the county party.

FIGURE 5.1   Texas Democratic Party Structure

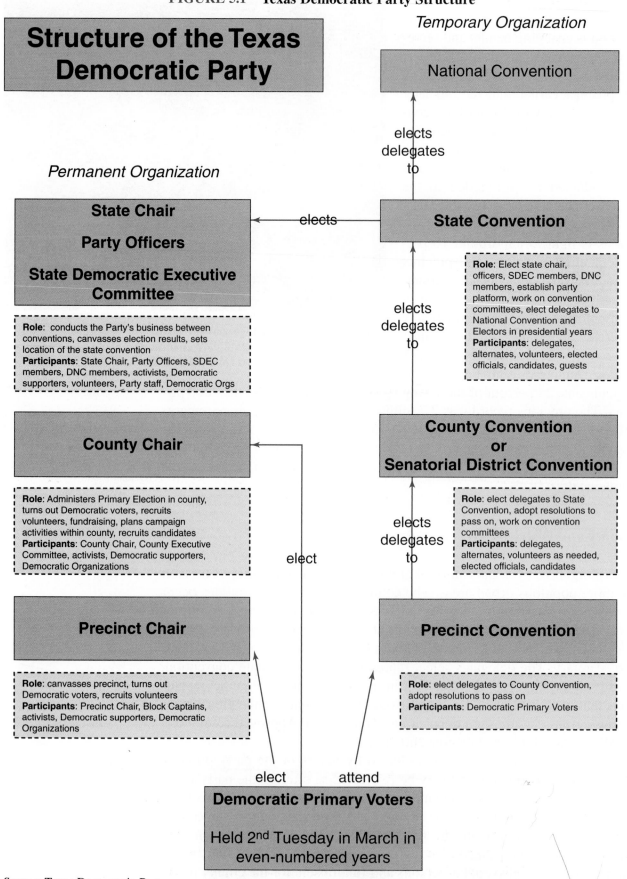

Source: Texas Democratic Party

State-Level Organization

State party conventions are held in June of even-numbered years. The convention selects a chair and secretary to guide the delegates through several critical tasks. First, delegates discuss and approve the party platform. Second, delegates elect a party chair and vice chair. Third, the delegates separate into state senatorial districts and each of the 31 groups elect a man and a woman to serve on the state party executive committee. Finally, in presidential election years, they elect delegates to the national party convention and select presidential electors in case their party's presidential candidate carries Texas in November.

The party chair, vice chair, and executive committee are unpaid and all serve two-year terms. The party chair serves essentially full-time. He or she is the party's statewide spokesman, organizer, problem solver, and fundraiser. With the vice chair and the executive committee, the party chair organizes the next state convention, prepares the party for the next election, and directs the party's professional staff. Tina Benkiser, a Houston lawyer, has been the Republican party chair since 2003. Boyd Richie, a lawyer from West Texas, has been Democratic party chair since 2006.

MINOR PARTIES, INDEPENDENTS, AND WRITE-INS

The Republicans and Democrats see minor-party, independent, and write-in candidates as distractions and irritants. Major parties cannot exclude them completely without insulting constitutional principles and popular expectations, but they do all they can to make life difficult for them.[2] Minor-party, independent, and write-in candidates almost never win state office, though they occasionally win county and local office.

> **Q2.** How does Texas law treat minor-party and independent candidates?

Two minor parties, the Libertarian Party and the Green Party, are particularly active in Texas. The Libertarian Party was founded in Texas in 1971 and stands for maximizing individual autonomy and minimizing the size and cost of government. The Green Party was founded in Texas in 1999 and stands for environmental awareness, corporate regulation, and local democracy. Texas allows minor parties to select their candidates in state conventions, rather than in statewide primary elections like the major parties do.

Texas law requires that minor parties gather signatures equivalent to one percent of the votes cast in the last gubernatorial election to gain access to the ballot. These signatures must be gathered in the 75 days after the Republican and Democratic primaries from registered voters that did not participate in the primaries. In 2008, minor parties were required to collect 43,991 valid signatures each. To maintain ballot access from one election to the next, at least one of the party's nominees must win two percent of the vote in the last governor's race or five percent of the vote in any other statewide race. Libertarians secured automatic ballot access by winning more than five percent of the vote in several 2006 statewide judicial contests. Greens failed to collect the required signatures so their candidates will not appear on the 2008 ballot.

TABLE 5.1
Let's Compare: 2008 Petition Requirements for Presidential Ballot Access

The major parties, Democrats and Republicans, dominate the politics of all 50 states, including Texas. They use their control of state government to enact and enforce laws that make it very difficult for minor-party, independent, and write-in candidates to get on the ballot. The greater the number of signatures required and the earlier the deadline for submitting the signatures, the greater the difficulty. Texas requires a large, though not extraordinary, number of signatures, but its deadline for turning in the signatures is very early.

State	Signatures for Minor Party	Signatures for Independent Candidate	Libertarian Success in 2008	Green Party Success in 2008	Deadline for Signatures
California	88,991	158,372	Yes	Yes	August 8
Texas	**43,991**	**74,108**	**Yes**	**Write-in**	**May 12**
New York	No procedure	15,000	Yes	Yes	August 19
Florida	Be organized	104,334	Yes	Yes	July 15
Pennsylvania	No procedure	24,666	Yes	Write-in	August 1
Illinois	No procedure	25,000	Yes	Yes	June 23
Ohio	Have support	5,000	Yes	Yes	August 21
Michigan	38,024	38,034	Yes	Yes	July 17
North Carolina	69,734	69,734	Yes	Write-in	June 12
Georgia	44,089	42,489	Yes	Write-in	July 8

Source: Derived from *Ballot Access News*, September 2008. *http://www.ballot-access.org/2008/090108.html.*

The hurdles facing most independent candidates for political office in Texas are even higher than those facing minor parties. Each independent candidate has to gather the same number of signatures as minor-party candidates, one percent of the vote in the last governor's race. Moreover, they have to do it in 60 days after the primary, rather than the 75 days allowed to minor parties. Independent candidates for statewide office in Texas are rare, though two, Carole Strayhorn and Kinky Friedman, were on the ballot for governor in 2006. Independent candidates for president have to gather signatures equivalent to one percent of the votes cast in the last presidential election, or 74,108 signatures in 2008.

Finally, voters that do not wish to vote for any of the candidates that appear on the ballot for a particular office may not simply write-in another name. To be a certified write-in candidate in Texas, one must file a declaration of intent, along with a filing fee or designated number of signatures, with the appropriate authorities at least 70 days before the general election. If these requirements are met, the candidate's name appears on an approved list of write-in candidates posted in polling places. Write-in votes for persons not on the list are not counted.

THE EVOLUTION OF PARTISAN CONFLICT IN TEXAS

Texas has long been a conservative state, favoring small government, low taxes, and pro-business policies as the best paths to social order and economic growth. Once these commitments drove most Texans to the

Democratic Party; now they drive them to the Republican Party. As with most southern states, the evolution of party competition in Texas pivots on two events—the Civil War and the civil rights struggle of the mid 20th century.

> Q3. Why was Texas a one-party Democratic state for so long?

In the agricultural economy of the 19th and early 20th century, looking after the interests of white men and their families meant a firm commitment to the Democratic Party. No Republican won statewide elective office in Texas between 1874 and 1961. However, as the American society and economy evolved, particularly in the post World War II period, many Texans came to see the Republican Party as the more dependable vehicle to pursue social conservatism and economic development. The movement of Texas from one-party Democrat to one-party Republican took decades. It is now, at least for a time, complete. No Democrat has held statewide office in Texas for more than a decade. Still, Democrats are stirring and formerly complacent Republicans are alert to approaching danger.[3]

The Democratic Ascendancy

Texas was a Democratic state before it was a state. Most white settlers entered Texas from the American South. Sam Houston, for example, was born in Virginia, went to Tennessee as a young man, and rose through the ranks of the state's Jacksonian Democratic machine to become a general, congressman, senator, and governor. When a new marriage collapsed, Houston fled into the wilderness and eventually ended up in Texas. He and Texas made brilliant use of his military and political skills. Houston commanded the victorious Texans at San Jacinto and then served as Texas' leading political figure for a quarter century.

When Texas seceded from the Union in February 1861 (over then-Governor Houston's vehement objection), most officeholders were Democrats. Most of those elected to serve in state government and those appointed to high military positions during the Confederacy also were Democrats. In the wake of the Civil War, the U.S. Congress barred senior Confederate political and military officials from voting or holding office. The Republican Party—the party of northern carpetbaggers, southern scalawags, former slaves, Lincoln, the Union Army, and Reconstruction (you get the point)—dominated Texas politics between the end of the war in 1865 and the end of Reconstruction a decade later. By the early 1870s, former Confederates were allowed back into the electorate, and by 1875, they had resumed control of state politics.

For the next seventy-five years, the dominant Democratic Party stood for white supremacy, racial segregation, and minority disenfranchisement. Poll taxes, the white primary, and political and economic intimidation kept minorities from the polls, except where their votes were managed by white power brokers. Agricultural interests and rural issues dominated Texas politics. They controlled the Constitutional Convention of 1875, provided the basis for Governor James Stephen Hogg's influence between 1890 and 1910, and then for Jim and Miriam (Pa and Ma) Ferguson's influence between 1914 and 1935.

The Democratic ascendancy in Texas began to crack when the national Democratic Party departed from the traditional orthodoxy of small government, low taxes, states rights, and local control. Franklin Roosevelt's "New Deal" signaled an era of bigger, more expensive, intrusive government that concerned many Texans. FDR's Vice President, John Nance (Cactus Jack) Garner, longtime leader of the Texas congressional delegation and former Speaker of the House, ultimately broke with Roosevelt over his desire to stand for a third term. Garner challenged FDR for the Democratic nomination for president in 1940. A few Texans, including a young LBJ, stayed with FDR, but many, led by Speaker Sam Rayburn, went with Garner. That breach in the Texas Democratic Party, between the liberals who sided with FDR and the conservatives who sided with Garner, never fully healed.[4]

Democrats of Texas
Liberal faction of the mid-20th century Democratic party, led by elected officials like Lyndon Johnson and Ralph Yarborough.

Texas regulars
Conservative faction of the mid-20th century Democratic party, led by elected officials like Coke Stevenson and Allan Shivers.

When the national Democratic Party approved a strong civil rights plank for the 1948 campaign, the split within the Texas Democratic Party deepened. These divisions hardened into a factional split within the party between the liberals, led by Lyndon Johnson, Ralph Yarborough, and former Governor James Allred, who called themselves the **Democrats of Texas,** and conservatives, led by John Garner, former Governor Coke Stevenson, and Governor Allan Shivers, who called themselves the **Texas Regulars.** Governor Shivers led the Texas state Democratic Convention away from Adlai Stevenson and to the Republican presidential candidate, Dwight D. Eisenhower, in both 1952 and 1956. Texas voted for Eisenhower both times. Despite this presidential Republicanism, Democrats retained near total dominance in Texas.[5]

The Rise of the Republican Party

Q4. What led to the rise of the Republican Party in the late 20th century?

The Republican Party had no meaningful presence in Texas between 1875 and 1950. Black votes kept a few Republicans in the state legislature until 1900, by which time most blacks were disenfranchised, and a few wealthy precincts in Houston and Dallas voted defiantly Republican through the first half of the 20th century. But in 1950, there were no Republicans in the Texas state legislature, in statewide office, or in the state's congressional delegation. The first notable Republican victory in Texas was the election of Bruce Alger of Dallas to the U.S. House in 1954. Alger, a fierce anticommunist and conservative firebrand, was re-elected four more times. The next three decades saw isolated Republican success, but little that suggested permanent change.

One Republican, though not yet the party, got a big break in 1960. Lyndon Johnson campaigned for the Democratic nomination for president in 1960, but John F. Kennedy defeated him. When Kennedy offered LBJ the vice-presidential nomination, he accepted. But Johnson was majority leader of the U.S. Senate and was unwilling to risk this powerful position for the chance of becoming vice president. So he pressured the Texas legislature to pass a bill allowing him to run for vice president on the Democratic ticket with Kennedy and re-election to the Senate at the same time.

In the spring of 1960, Johnson won the Democratic primary for the U.S. Senate and a little known political-science professor, John G. Tower, from Midwestern State University in Wichita Falls, won the Republican nomination. In the November general election, LBJ retained his Senate seat with nearly 60 percent of the vote, but he was also elected vice president on the Democratic ticket with Kennedy. Hence, LBJ resigned his senate seat to become Vice President of the United States. Governor Price Daniel Jr., a conservative Democrat, appointed Dallas' staunchly conservative William Blakley, also a Democrat, to fill Johnson's senate seat until a special election could be held.

Seventy-one candidates declared for the special election. Several prominent Democrats, including San Antonio's Congressman Henry B. Gonzales, Fort Worth's Congressman Jim Wright, and Senator William Blakley, entered the race. John Tower was the only prominent Republican. In this crowded field, Tower ran first with 31.5 percent, and the conservative Democrat William Blakley edged the more liberal Democrat, Jim Wright, 18.3 percent to 16.4 percent. Texas Democrats were flummoxed; two conservatives, Tower and Blakley, were in the runoff. Liberal Democrats saw little to choose between them. In fact, many liberals simply stayed home while some voted for John Tower to send Blakley and Daniel

TABLE 5.2
Growth of Republican Officeholders in Texas, 1974–2008

Year	U.S. Senate	Other Statewide Offices	U.S. House	Texas Senate	Texas House	Local Offices	Total
1974	1	0	2	3	16	53	75
1976	1	0	2	3	19	67	92
1978	1	1	4	4	22	87	119
1980	1	1	5	7	35	166	215
1982	1	0	5	5	36	270	317
1984	1	0	10	6	52	377	446
1986	1	1	10	6	56	504	578
1988	1	5	8	8	57	613	692
1990	1	6	8	8	57	722	802
1992	1	8	9	13	58	822	911
1994	2	13	11	14	61	958	1059
1996	2	18	13	17	68	1225	1343
1998	2	27	13	16	72	1397	1527
2000	2	27	13	16	72	1579	1709
2002	2	27	15	19	88	1815	1966
2004	2	27	21	19	87	2010	2166
2006	2	27	19	20	82	2203	2353
2008	2	27	20	19	76	*	*

Source: Political Department, Republican Party of Texas. *Not available from early data.

a message. Tower squeaked through to win the Senate seat by about 10,000 votes out of almost 900,000 votes cast.[6]

John Tower's stunning victory made him the first Republican to win a statewide race in Texas since 1870. In fact, though Tower held his U.S. Senate seat with statewide wins in 1966, 1972, and 1978, few other Republicans were able to join the ranks of Texas officeholders during these years.

To the surprise of most, 1978 was a watershed year for the Republican Party in Texas. Senator Tower held his U.S. Senate seat by just 12,000 votes, and Republican gubernatorial candidate, William P. Clements, defeated the Democratic favorite, John Hill, by 17,000 votes. Though Clements was defeated for re-election in 1982, he came back to win again in 1986.[7] Clements' governorship, far more than Tower's elections to the Senate, marked the arrival of competitive two-party politics in Texas. Clements systematically used his appointment powers to build a Republican presence in the bureaucracy and the courts.

Texas Republicans slowly gathered strength and momentum during the 1980s as lifelong Democrats edged nervously toward and eventually into the Republican Party.[8] Republican President Ronald Reagan helped to draw some high-powered Democrats into the Republican party, including Congressman Phil Gramm in 1983. Gramm resigned his House seat, won it as a Republican, and then in 1984 won the U.S. Senate seat being vacated by John Tower. Six new Republicans, dubbed the "Texas six-pack," won seats in the U.S. House. Republican strength in the 150-member Texas House grew from 35 in 1980 to 52 in 1984 and 57 in 1988; a big improvement, but still barely a third of the membership. The Republican presence in the Texas Senate inched ahead from 7 to 8 from 1980 to 1988.

In 1988, Texas Republican George H.W. Bush, Reagan's vice president during the previous eight years, won the presidency, and Texas Republicans showed deeper strength in statewide races. Republicans won three seats on the Texas Supreme Court and one of the three seats on the Texas Railroad Commission. In 1990, Phil Gramm easily retained his Senate seat, despite Democrat Ann Richards' victory over gaffe-plagued millionaire Clayton Williams for governor. Two new Republican faces, Kay Bailey Hutchison and Rick Perry, a recent convert from Democrat to Republican, won statewide election to the positions of treasurer and agriculture commissioner, respectively.

The changing shape of Texas politics became even more clear in 1993 when Democratic Senator Lloyd Bentsen resigned to become Secretary of the Treasury in the Clinton administration. Democratic Governor Ann Richards appointed a Democrat, Bob Krueger, to fill the vacant Senate seat until a special election could be held. An even two-dozen candidates, including Krueger, as well as two U.S. congressmen, Democrat Jack Fields and Republican Joe Barton, and Republican state Treasurer Kay Bailey Hutchison, contested the election. Hutchison and Krueger ran first and second and Hutchison prevailed in the runoff with an impressive two-to-one majority.

The Republican Ascendancy

In 1994, George W. Bush, son of the former president and managing partner of the Texas Rangers baseball team, challenged the popular Democratic incumbent governor Ann Richards. Initially given little chance of winning, Bush ran a careful, competent, controlled, and, ultimately convincing campaign to win comfortably. Rick Perry retained his position as commissioner of agriculture and Republicans picked up seats to take majority control of the Supreme Court, the Railroad Commission, and the State Board of Education. Meanwhile five Democratic incumbents, including the powerful lieutenant governor, Bob Bullock, retained their positions. In fact, Bullock, the wily Democratic veteran, took Bush under his wing and Bush was smart enough to let him do it.

By 1996, George W. Bush was secure in his role as governor and the Republican Party was ready to assume the majority-party mantle in Texas. In 1996, Republicans took majority control of the Texas Senate, 17 seats to 14 seats. In 1998, George W. Bush won re-election as governor with 68 percent of the vote, Rick Perry moved up to lieutenant governor, and Republicans carried all of the statewide executive offices, as well as every seat on the Texas Supreme Court, the Texas Court of Criminal Appeals, and the Railroad Commission.

When George W. Bush resigned as governor in 2000 to run for president of the United States, Lieutenant Governor Rick Perry assumed the governorship and the Republican juggernaut never missed a beat. In 2002, Perry easily retained the governorship and Republicans won every statewide office on the ballot and took majority control of the Texas House, 88 seats to 62. Though Republican fundraising and campaign tactics in the 2002 state races have been widely criticized, no one can argue with the results.[9] Once the Texas House fell to the Republicans, they turned to address the last bastion of Democratic power, the U.S. House delegation, where Democrats clung to a 17 to 15 majority.

THE GREAT TEXAS REDISTRICTING BATTLE, 2001–2006

The U.S. Constitution gives each state the responsibility to draw the districts within which its state and federal elections will be conducted. After each census, the districts must be redrawn to reflect population growth and change. **Redistricting** provides the dominant party in a state the opportunity to draw district boundaries that favor them and limit the electoral prospects of their opponents. Partisan redistricting, also known as "gerrymandering," is as old as the republic.

The term "gerrymander" derives from the early 19th century. Elbridge Gerry was a prominent founding father; signer of the Declaration of Independence, delegate to the Constitutional Convention, Governor of Massachusetts, and vice president in the Madison administration. As governor of

Redistricting The political process by which electoral district boundaries are redrawn to reflect changes in population and party power.

Massachusetts, Gerry oversaw a particularly creative redistricting process in which one district was said to look like a salamander, hence the term "gerrymander."

For most of Texas history, Democrats drew electoral boundaries at will. In 2003, when the 78th Texas legislature convened with Republican majorities in both houses for the first time since the 1870s, redistricting was high on their agenda. Republican leaders believed that previous Democratic maps had treated them unfairly and they meant to redress those grievances. Republicans set out to grieve the Democrats for a change.

The Texas legislature has the initial responsibility for redistricting, but they are at something of a disadvantage. The legislature meets in regular session from January to May of odd-numbered years. The census, carried out at the beginning of each decade (1990, 2000, and 2010, for example), delivers preliminary data to the states in December and final data in March of the following year. By March, the Texas legislature is halfway through its regular session and little time is left for the complicated and contentious process of redistricting.

In 1951, Texas adopted a new redistricting process. If the legislature fails to approve a plan, a Legislative Redistricting Board (LRB), made up of the speaker, lieutenant governor, comptroller, land commissioner, and attorney general, is charged to adopt a plan within 150 days of the end of the legislative session. Whether or not the legislature or the LRB passes a plan, state and federal courts inevitably become involved. With so much at stake, the minority party, interest groups, and individuals head to court if they think they have been treated unfairly—and they always think they have been treated unfairly.

Democrats still controlled state government following the 1990 census, though Republican fortunes were on the rise. Martin Frost, a senior Democratic congressman from the Dallas-Fort Worth area, oversaw the redistricting process. Lines were drawn to protect Democratic incumbents and check the rise of Republican challengers. Though Texas Democrats won just 51 percent of the vote in the 1992 congressional races, Frost's carefully drawn congressional districts helped Democrats win 70 percent (21 of 30) of house seats. Though the Republican vote share rose to 55 percent by 1998, they won only 43 percent (13 of 30) seats.

The 2000 census recorded population growth in Texas that resulted in two new congressional seats, moving the state's total from 30 to 32. All of the state's congressional districts had to be redrawn to accommodate the two new districts and to insure that each district contained an equal number of residents. But control of the Texas legislature remained split; Republicans controlled the Senate 16 to 15, while Democrats controlled the House 78 to 72. Partisan divisions blocked action in the legislature. The five-member, all-Republican, LRB moved quickly to adopt new district lines for the Texas House and Senate, but the proposed congressional-district boundaries were challenged in the federal courts.

A three-judge panel, composed of Judge Patrick Higginbotham of the U.S. Fifth Circuit Court of Appeals, District Judge Lee Rosenthal of Houston, and District Judge T. John Ward of Marshall, produced a congressional map that accommodated the two new districts, preserved 8 majority-minority districts as required by the Voting Rights Act, and protected incumbents wishing to stand for re-election. Democrats were generally pleased with the court's map, Republicans were not. In the 2002 Texas elections, Republicans won 55 percent of the total congressional vote, but only 47 percent (15 of 32) seats. On the other hand, Republicans completed their takeover of state government by winning control of the Texas House (88 to 62) for the first time since Reconstruction.

Texas Republicans soon began arguing that redistricting was a state legislative responsibility and, while the courts had reasonably stepped in when the legislature was unable to complete the task in 2001, they were now both ready and entitled to revisit the issue. And so a new Republican map was proposed in the 78th regular session of the legislature. Fifty Texas House Democrats fled to Ardmore, Oklahoma, thus denying a quorum and halting business until the session ended. It took three special sessions during the summer of 2003, punctuated by Texas Senate Democrats fleeing to Albuquerque, New Mexico, to push through the Republican congressional map. With the new map in place, Republicans won 60 percent of the 2004 congressional vote and six new Republican seats.

Democrats and minority interest groups remained convinced that at least three aspects of the new plan were unconstitutional or otherwise illegal. They argued that redistricting could only be done once per decade, that it could not be done strictly for partisan gain, and it could not be done to the detriment of

minority voters. The Civil Rights Division of the U.S. Justice Department and the three-judge panel headed by Judge Higginbotham upheld the Republican map. Democratic challenges in *LULAC v. Perry* reached the U.S. Supreme Court twice, with the final ruling coming on June 28, 2006.

The Supreme Court generally supported the Republican view of redistricting. First, Democratic claims that redistricting could be done only once a decade were rejected. Texas Solicitor Tony Cruz argued that Democrats had gerrymandered the state's congressional districts for decades and, when the Republicans came to power, they had the right to bend the political and electoral systems to their advantage. Justice Anthony Kennedy, who wrote the lead opinion for the court, said "There is nothing inherently suspect about a legislature's decision to replace mid-decade a court-ordered plan with one of its own."

Second, the court reiterated its earlier findings in *Davis v. Bandemer* (Indiana, 1986) and *Vieth v. Jubilier* (Pennsylvania, 2003) that redistricting is an inherently partisan process. Though they left open the possibility that some future gerrymander might be so harshly partisan as to be unconstitutional, no rules for separating acceptable from unacceptable partisanship currently exist.

Finally, the League of United Latin American Citizens (LULAC) and the Texas Democratic Party claimed partial vindication when the Supreme Court struck down one part of the Republican map. Republicans had moved about 100,000 Hispanic voters out of Congressman Henry Bonilla's 23rd district to improve his chances of holding his seat. Though Bonilla is the only Hispanic Republican in the Texas congressional delegation, Hispanic voters tend to support Democrats two-thirds of the time. The court held that making Bonilla's district less Hispanic illegally "diluted the voting rights of Latinos who remain in the district." Five districts had to be adjusted to return the 23rd to its previous ethnic make-up.

As the 2006 election approached, Republican gains began to erode. Congressman Tom DeLay's legal problems, some stemming from aggressive fund-raising for 2002 state house races, led to his resignation from Congress. In a particularly galling development for Republicans, former Democratic Congressman Nick Lampson, a victim of the 2003 redistricting plan, won DeLay's seat in a special election. In November 2006, scandals and declining support for the Iraq war led to a drop in the Republican Congressional vote to 54.4 percent of votes cast. Lampson held the DeLay seat and Republican Congressman Henry Bonilla was forced into a runoff and was eventually defeated by Democrat Ciro Rodriguez. Republicans retained 19 of 32 seats in the congressional delegation. Democrats also picked up six seats in the Texas House in 2006.

The 2008 elections provided few surprises and served generally to consolidate the positions of the parties. The Republican share of the congressional vote edged up to 54.7 percent and Republican challenger Pete Olson defeated Nick Lampson to take back Tom DeLay's old seat. Republicans enjoy a 20 to 12 advantage in the congressional delegation, though Democrats again made modest gains in the Texas House and Senate. Both parties

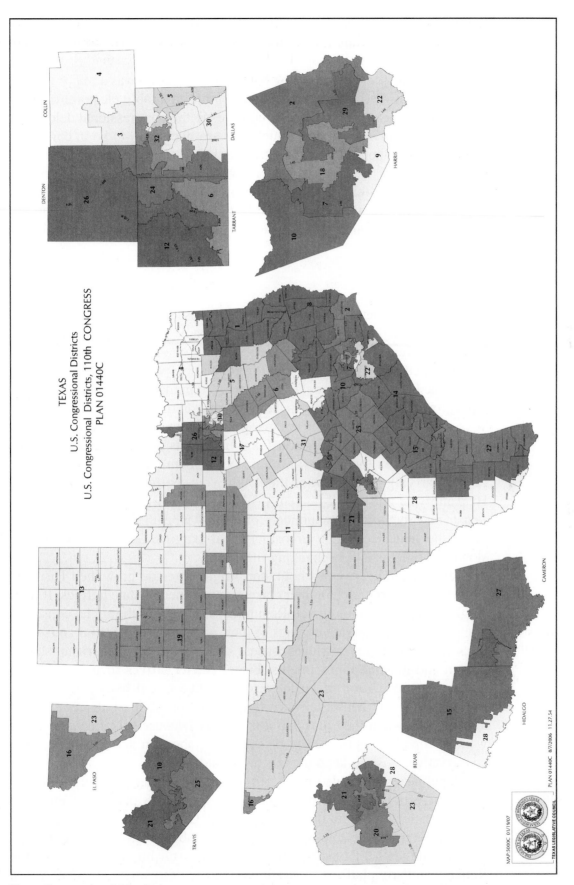

Texas Congressional Districts
Source: Texas Legislative Council, http://www.tlc.state.tx.us/redist/congress.htm

will throw all they have into the 2010 elections for the Texas legislature in order to be in as strong a position as they can be when redistricting again rolls around in 2011.

Clearly, the great redistricting battle of 2001–2006 was a major win for the Republican Party. Republicans drew more favorable electoral districts that produced new and enhanced majorities in the congressional delegation and in the Texas legislature. Republicans are likely still to be in control of Texas politics when the next redistricting battle occurs following the 2010 census. However, as we shall see below, Democrats do seem to be on the comeback trail in Texas politics. Over time a burgeoning Hispanic population and rising Democratic vote totals will push up against, if they do not wash away, the advantages produced by Republican map-makers.

THE FUTURE

Q5. Is the shift of power from Democrats to Republicans in Texas permanent?

Republican dominance since 1994 has been based on winning at least two-thirds of the Anglo vote, one-third of the Hispanic vote, and one-tenth of the black vote. Texas Democrats, limited to about one-third of the Anglo vote, have required overwhelming support from minority voters just to be competitive.[10] The Democratic formula has not worked in more than a decade, but the rapid growth of the Hispanic population suggest to many political analysts that Texas will again be a competitive two-party state in the next decade.[11]

The 2008 presidential race in Texas highlights the racial and ethnic differences between the parties. McCain beat Obama in Texas by almost 12 points, carrying 73 percent of the Anglo vote, but only 35 percent of the Hispanic vote and just 2 percent of the black vote. Similarly, in the U.S. Senate race incumbent Republican John Cornyn beat Rick Noriega, a member of the Texas House, by almost identical margins. Demography changes slowly, but in Texas it is changing inexorably.

Texas Republicans must hold their Anglo base and grow their Hispanic vote if they are to maintain their current dominance of state politics. If their Anglo base is to remain intact, Republicans must hold the social conservative and fiscal conservative wings of their party together. **Social conservatives** focus on moral or values issues, such as abortion, marriage, school prayer, and judicial appointments. **Fiscal conservatives** focus on limiting government regulation of business, cutting taxes, and balancing budgets. Social and fiscal conservatives often agree, or at least agree to work together, but when they disagree it is usually because social conservatives want to foreclose options, say on access to abortion services, that fiscal conservatives wish to keep in their own hands.

Social conservatives
Conservative faction that focuses on social issues such as abortion, school prayer, and gay marriage.

Fiscal conservatives
Conservative faction that focused on fiscal and economic issues such as taxation, spending, and business regulation.

Republicans must also reach out to minority voters. Governor Bush's 1998 re-election, a blowout in which he received 68 percent of the vote, drew high levels of minority support. But Governor Perry's election in 2002, while a comfortable win, attracted only about one-quarter of Hispanics and one-tenth of blacks. The strong focus on border security of the Republican Party platform makes it more difficult to attract Hispanic votes. With the Hispanic population of Texas growing rapidly, Republicans simply cannot give up on the Hispanic vote and still expect to dominate the electoral politics of the state. How Texas Republicans handle the immigration debate will be critical.[12]

Still, Texas Democrats cannot expect Republicans to fumble away their majority status, they must develop a strategy for taking it from them. Democrats must continue to hold their minority, union, and working-class support. They must work to stop the erosion in rural support, especially among the "Yellow Dog" Democrats of East Texas. At the same time, they must build new connections to Anglo, middle-class, suburban voters. These voters worry about taxes, but they also worry about good public schools, affordable health care, and skyrocketing college tuition.

Republicans must, of course, resist Democratic inroads on their suburban base and fight to enlarge their share of the Hispanic vote. Republicans contend that Hispanics are less focused on government support than blacks and more conservative on social issues. They point particularly to Hispanic commitment to family and opposition to abortion and gay marriage as shared values to which they can appeal. Democrats contend that Hispanics, particularly new immigrants and members of the working class, are more focused on access to education, health care, and jobs than on social issues. In the coming years, we will see who is right.[13]

CHAPTER SUMMARY

Political parties in Texas are composed of a few full-time professionals, many unpaid volunteers, and the voters who respond to their calls for support on election day. The Democratic and Republican parties are similarly organized. Elected but unpaid party activists serve as precinct, county, state senate district, and state officers. These officers prepare for party conventions and primary and general elections. Political parties develop party platforms, recruit candidates, and contest elections with the goal of winning majority control over government and controlling public policymaking and implementation. Minor-party, independent, and write-in candidates have all they can do just to get their names on the ballot.

The Democratic Party was the majority party of Texas from the initial Anglo settlement of the state through the 1960s and 70s. Democratic dominance was seldom challenged until tensions over FDR's New Deal agenda and civil rights divided the liberal Democrats of Texas from the more conservative Texas Regulars. As Texas Democrats squabbled among themselves, Texas Republicans began a slow, almost imperceptible, rise to majority status.

By 2002, Republicans held every statewide office and majorities in the Texas House and Senate. With the support of powerful Texas Republicans in Washington, Governor Perry, Texas House Speaker Tom Craddick, and Lt. Governor David Dewhurst pushed redistricting through the Texas legislature. In an extremely tumultuous political battle which featured an unusual mid-decade redistricting process and two occasions on which

Democrats fled the state in vain attempts to stop the process, Republicans redrew Texas legislative and U.S. House district lines. Republicans solidified their legislative majorities and gained six congressional seats in 2004.

Nonetheless, social change in Texas renders Republican dominance insecure. The Anglo proportion of the Texas population, which votes mostly Republican, is declining, while the Hispanic proportion of the population, which votes mostly Democrat, is increasing. Democrats won back two U.S. House seats and six Texas House seats in 2006. By 2035, Hispanics will be a majority of Texans, if not of Texas citizens and voters. Despite these great changes, one thing will not change: Democrats and Republicans will continue to struggle for partisan advantage and political dominance.

KEY TERMS

Big tent model	Precinct	Social conservatives
Democrats of Texas	Redistricting	Texas Regulars
Fiscal conservatives	Responsible party model	
Political parties		

SUGGESTED READINGS

Earl Black and Merle Black, *The Rise of Southern Republicanism* (Cambridge, MA: Harvard University Press, 2002).

Norman D. Brown, *Hood, Bonnet, and Little Brown Jug: Texas Politics, 1921–1928* (College Station, TX: Texas A&M University Press, 1984).

Chandler Davidson, *Race and Class in Texas Politics* (Princeton, N.J.: Princeton University Press, 1990).

Ricky F. Dobbs, *Yellow Dogs and Republicans: Allan Shivers and Texas Two-Party Politics* (College Station, TX: Texas A&M University Press, 2005).

John R. Knaggs, *Two-Party Texas: The John Tower Era, 1961–1984* (Austin, TX: Eakin Press, 1986).

WEB RESOURCES

http://www.txdemocrats.org The official website of the Democratic Party of Texas.

http://www.txgreens.org The official website of the Green Party of Texas.

http://www.tx.lp.org The official website of the Libertarian Party of Texas.

http://www.texasgop.org The official website of the Republican Party of Texas.

END NOTES

1. Marjorie R. Hershey, *Party Politics in America,* 13th ed. (New York: Longman, 2008).
2. John F. Bibby and L. Sandy Maisel, *Two Parties—Or More,* 2nd ed. (Boulder, CO: Westview Press, 2003).
3. Gray and Hanson, *Politics in the American States,* p. 84.

4. D. B. Hardeman and Donald C. Bacon, *Rayburn: A Biography* (New York: Madison Books, 1987).

5. Ricky F. Dobbs, *Yellow Dogs and Republicans: Allan Shivers and Texas Two-Party Politics* (College Station, TX: Texas A&M University Press, 2005).

6. John R. Knaggs, *Two-Party Texas: The John Tower Era, 1961–1984* (Austin, TX: Eakin Press, 1986).

7. Carolyn Barta, *Bill Clements: Texian to His Toenails* (Austin, TX: Eakin Press, 1996).

8. Earl Black and Merle Black, *The Rise of Southern Republicanism* (Cambridge, MA: Harvard University Press, 2002), pp. 88–93.

9. Laylan Copelin, "Texas GOP Agrees to Stop Some Campaign Practices," *Austin American Statesman,* November 17, 2005.

10. Chandler Davidson, *Race and Class in Texas Politics* (Princeton, N.J.: Princeton University Press, 1990).

11. Paul Burka, "Almost Blue," *Texas Monthly,* May 2008, pp. 18–22.

12. Michael Ennis, "All Shook Up: The Tectonic Plates of Texas Politics are Once Again in Motion," *Texas Monthly,* October 2006, pp. 80–88.

13. Gromer Jeffers, "Democrat Trust Joins Supporters to Empower Party at Local, State Level," *Dallas Morning News*, October 30, 2007, A1.

CHAPTER 6

The Texas Legislature

Focus Questions

Q1. Who serves in the Texas Legislature?

Q2. How much influence do the leaders of the Texas House and Senate exercise?

Q3. What roles do committees play in the legislative process?

Q4. How does a bill become a law in Texas?

Q5. How does the legislative process differ in the House and Senate?

Democratic theory gives pride of place to the legislative branch of government. Democracy is based on the ideas of **popular sovereignty,** that all legitimate political authority comes from the people, and **legislative supremacy,** that the people's elected representatives should make the laws that bind citizens. But the power to make law might be abused, so bicameralism, separation of powers, and checks and balances are intended to limit and constrain legislative powers.

The authors of the Texas Constitution were intently focused on the potential abuse of government power. They limited all government power, especially executive authority (as we shall see in Chapter 7), but legislative authority was limited as well. In this chapter, we describe the members and leaders of the Texas Legislature. We then ask how the Texas Legislature is organized to do the state's business and how well that business is being done.

Popular sovereignty
The idea that all legitimate governmental authority comes from the people.

Legislative supremacy
The idea that the law making power in government is superior to the executive and judicial powers.

SERVICE IN THE TEXAS LEGISLATURE

Article III of the Texas Constitution mandates a bicameral legislature. The Texas Senate has 31 members, each elected to a four-year term, while the Texas House of Representatives has 150 members, each elected to a two-year term. Each House district contains about 150,000 residents and each Senate district contains about 750,000. In November of even-numbered years, all 150 House seats and half of the Senate seats are up for election.

Rep. Tommy Merritt, R-Longview, celebrates the passing of a bill to allow the Texas Education Agency to limit sexually suggestive cheerleading. Rep. Dan Branch (left), R-Dallas, enjoys the routine. *ERICH SCHLEGEL/Staff Photographer/*Dallas Morning News

Formal Qualifications

Q1. Who serves in the Texas Legislature?

Article III of the Texas Constitution also lays out the qualifications for service in the legislature. To sit in the Texas House, one must be at least 21, a U.S. citizen, a registered voter, and a resident of Texas for two years and of the legislative district for one year. To sit in the Texas Senate, one must be at least 26, a U.S. citizen, a registered voter, and a resident of Texas for five years and of the district for one. These qualifications are very general and exclude few Texans from potential service. Nonetheless, some Texans have a much better chance to serve in the Texas Legislature than do others.

Member Characteristics

Fifty years ago, the Texas Legislature was the preserve of white, middle-aged businessmen, lawyers, and ranchers. Since then, the legislature has become more diverse, but the growth of that diversity has slowed in recent decades. Anglos still hold just over 70 percent of the legislative seats, though they make up only about 48 percent of the adult population.

Hispanics make up about 36 percent of the adult population, but because citizenship rates and voter turnout among Hispanics trail whites and blacks, they hold just over 20 percent of the seats in the Texas Legislature. Blacks, who have made up a steady 12 percent of the Texas population for decades, hold 8.8 percent of the seats. Asians make up just over 3 percent of the Texas population and hold 1 percent of the seats. Women have made gains in the Texas Legislature, but they still hold just over 20 percent of the seats.[1]

TABLE 6.1
Ethnicity and Gender in the Texas Legislature, 1987–2007

Year	%Anglo	%Hispanic	%Black	%Asian-Amer	%Women
1987	78.5	13.3	8.3	0	9.9
1989	77.9	14.4	7.7	0	10.5
1991	78.5	13.3	8.3	0	13.3
1993	73.5	17.7	8.8	0	17.1
1995	72.4	18.8	8.8	0	19.3
1997	73.0	18.5	8.4	0	18.2
1999	71.8	19.3	8.8	0	18.2
2001	71.8	19.3	8.8	0	18.8
2003	69.6	21.0	8.8	.6	19.9
2005	70.2	20.4	8.8	1.1	19.9
2007	70.2	20.4	8.8	.6	19.9
2009	69.0	21.0	8.8	1.1	20.4

Source: Texas Legislature webpage. www.capitol.state.tx.us

Sessions, Salaries, and Support

Texas icon Molly Ivins used to love to quip that the approach of the Texas legislative session meant that "every village is about to lose its idiot."[2] The Texas Legislature meets in **biennial session** for 140 days, beginning on the second Tuesday in January of odd-numbered years. The **regular session** of the Texas Legislature comes to a hectic climax around the end of May. Texas is one of only six states, and the only one of the ten most populous states, to retain biennial sessions.

If the legislature does not complete its work during the regular session, the governor may call one or more 30-day special sessions. After a spate of ten special sessions called by Governors Bill Clements and Ann Richards between 1989 and 1992, there were no special sessions for more than a decade. Then Governor Rick Perry called seven special sessions between 2003 and 2006 to deal with legislative redistricting and school finance.

Texas state legislators receive just $600 a month, or $7,200 a year, for their service. They also receive a *per diem* (daily expenses) of $139 a day during regular and special sessions and for interim service, such as committee work, up to twelve days each month. The Texas Ethics Commission may change the *per diem* rate as it sees fit, but the salary of Texas legislators is set in the constitution. Legislators can, however, increase their retirement benefits, which they did in the 79th (2005) regular session.[3]

Legislators are allocated support for secretarial, administrative, and research assistance both during and between sessions. Each member receives a staff and office allowance. In recent years, Senators have received $37,500 a month for staff and office expenses, while House members have received $12,250. Members must decide how to allocate these funds across an Austin office and one or more district offices. Members also receive some support from staff assigned to committees on which they serve.

Biennial session The Texas legislature meets in regular session every other year, that is biennially, rather than annually.

Regular session The regularly scheduled biennial session of the legislature.

TABLE 6.2

Let's Compare: Legislative Compensation in the Ten Largest States

Texas legislative salaries are very low compared to similar states, though its *per diem* rate is more generous, and its legislative retirement system is very generous. Legislator's retirement benefits are pegged to the retirement salaries of Texas district judges (whose salaries are about fifteen times higher than the legislator's salaries). Legislators who choose to participate in the retirement program, and virtually all do, must pay $48 per month into the system. Legislators at age 60 with eight years of service, or 50 years of age with twelve years service, are eligible for retirement benefits, ranging from $4,800 to $5,700 a month. Not bad on a base salary of $7,200 annually.

States	Salary*	Per Diem**	Retirement***
California	$116,208	$170 per day	None
Texas	**$7,200**	**$151 per day**	**High**
New York	$79,500	$139 per day	Medium
Florida	$31,932	$126 per day	Medium
Pennsylvania	$76,163	$133 per day	Medium
Illinois	$65,363	$129 per day	High
Ohio	$60,484	None	Medium
Michigan	$79,650	$12,000 annually	Medium
North Carolina	$13,951	$104 per day	Low
Georgia	$17,342	$173 per day	Low

*Annual salary

**Daily *per diem* when the legislature is in session or for intersession workdays.

*** Retirement systems are complex. Here we divide them into None, Low, Medium, and High (most generous).

Source: Council of State Governments, *The Book of the States, 2008* (Lexington, KY: 2008), Table 3.9, pp. 97–99; Table 3.13, pp. 112–117. See also National Conference of State Legislatures, *http://www.ncsl.org/programs/legismgt/about/07-legislatorcomp.htm*

Turnover and Experience

Nationally, state legislatures experience an average turnover of 20 to 25 percent in each electoral cycle, though redistricting and the occasional voter revolt can increase turnover. The Texas House had 38 new members (25 percent) in 2003, 24 (16 percent) in 2007, but only 19 (13 percent) in 2005 and 2009. The Senate, usually more stable than the House, had four new members (13 percent) in 2007 but just two new members (6 percent) in 2003, 2005, and 2009.[4]

The average length of service for members of the Texas House in 2007 was 10 years and 12 years for the Senate. Some members serve much longer. Tom Craddick (R-Midland) has served continuously in the House since 1969 and John Whitmire (D-Houston) has served continuously in the Texas House and Senate since 1973. New legislators often take a session or two to learn the ropes. Experienced legislators exercise the most influence because they know how the system works.

Scholars and students of state legislatures often distinguish among professional legislatures, amateur legislatures, and hybrids. **Professional legislatures** look a lot like the U.S. Congress, and their members are full-time

Professional Legislatures State legislatures which pay and support their members well and, in turn, demand nearly fulltime service from them.

Amateur legislatures State legislatures which provide low pay and support to their members. Sessions are generally short and members have other jobs.

politicians. Professional legislatures, like those in California, Michigan, and New York, meet nearly year round and are supported by large and well-trained staffs. **Amateur legislatures,** often called citizen legislatures, are not well-paid or supported, meet less frequently, and their members generally have other jobs and professions. Small or lightly populated states, like Nevada, Wyoming, and the Dakotas, tend to employ amateur or citizen legislatures.

Texas is usually described as having a hybrid legislature. **Hybrid legislatures** have elements common to both professional and amateur legislatures. In Texas's case, a large and well-trained staff is suggestive of professional standards while the biennial session and low pay are characteristic of amateur legislatures. According to the National Council of State Legislatures, Texas is by far the largest state to employ a hybrid legislature.[5]

Hybrid legislatures
State legislatures, including the Texas legislature, that share some of the characteristics of professional legislatures, such as long sessions and good staff support, and some of the characteristics of amateur legislatures, such as low pay and biennial sessions.

PARTIES AND LEADERS IN THE TEXAS LEGISLATURE

In both the U.S. Congress and the Texas Legislature, the majority party controls the legislature and the majority party is controlled by its elected leaders. Republicans have enjoyed a majority in the Texas Senate since 1997 and in the Texas House since 2003. In the 81st (2009) legislative session, the Senate is composed of 19 Republicans and 12 Democrats, while the House is composed of 76 Republicans and 74 Democrats.

Q2. How much influence do the leaders of the Texas House and Senate exercise?

Legislative leaders always exercise more influence and control than regular members, but in some legislatures, such as the U.S. Congress, there are many leaders serving to limit, check, and balance each other. Not so in the Texas Legislature. In the Texas Legislature, the speaker of the House and the lieutenant governor (who serves as the presiding officer in the Senate) have had no peers and few challengers for authority over their respective bodies. The 2007 and 2009 sessions were highly unusual in that there were concerted attempts to depose Speaker Tom Craddick.

The Speaker of the House

The Speaker of the Texas House is elected by House members as the first order of business in each regular session. The Secretary of State presides over the balloting, but the outcome of the election is usually known well in advance. Since 1973, candidates for speaker have been required to keep detailed records of loans, contributions, and expenditures relating to the election. As with most Texas campaign contribution restrictions, these limits are ineffectual. State law also made it illegal for others to spend money trying to influence the speaker's election. However, in August 2008, a federal judge, citing the importance of free speech, struck down the law barring third parties from trying to influence the speaker race.

Speaker of the House Tom Craddick (left) and Lt. Gov. David Dewhurst confer over teacher raises and school funding. *ERICH SCHLEGEL/Staff Photographer/*The Dallas Morning News

Through the 1940s, speakers served a single two-year term and then retired or sought higher office. From 1951 to 1975, most speakers served one or two terms, but no more than two. Since 1975, speakers have served multiple terms. Billy Clayton served four terms, between 1975 and 1983, followed by five terms each for Gib Lewis (1983–1993) and Pete Laney (1993–2003). Laney sought a sixth term, despite the Republican takeover of the House in 2003, but he was pushed aside by Tom Craddick.

The powers of the speaker are grounded in the Texas Constitution and laws, as well as in the rules and traditions of the House. The speaker: (1) defines the jurisdiction of the standing committees; (2) appoints all committee chairs and vice chairs; (3) appoints most committee members; (4) refers all bills and resolutions to the appropriate committee; (5) serves as presiding officer over all House sessions; and (6) appoints all conference committee members, as well as members of special and interim committees.

Speaker Craddick has been a lightning rod. He worked hard in 2002, coordinating Republican-leaning interest groups and channeling campaign contributions to needy members in order to produce the first Republican House majority since the 1870s. He campaigned energetically for speaker and then used his position to assist then-U.S. House Majority Leader Tom DeLay in pushing a partisan redistricting plan through the 2003 Texas Legislature. The new Republican majority was extremely grateful to Craddick for his role in bringing them to power. Craddick ruled the House with an iron hand in 2003 and 2005, but by 2007 the Republican majority effectively exploded.

The 2007 regular session opened on January 9. By late-December 2006, Brian McCall (R-Plano) and Jim Pitts (R-Waxahachie), chair of the powerful Appropriations Committee in the previous session, had declared that they would stand against Craddick for the speakership. McCall withdrew in favor of Pitts and Pitts promised House members to eschew "arm twisting and intimidation" in favor of a new "spirit of cooperation and bipartisanship."[6] The insurgents wanted a secret ballot while Craddick, with his well-deserved reputation for playing hardball, wanted an open vote. On January 9, when the Pitts forces fell five votes short on a key procedural motion, Pitts withdrew and Craddick was elected to a third term as speaker.

Craddick told his colleagues that he had heard their criticisms and concerns and would make changes. But Craddick used his power to appoint members to committees and name the committee chairs to reward his supporters and punish his opponents.[7] Pitts not only lost the chairmanship of Appropriations but was bounced completely off the committee. Tensions built throughout the session as Craddick sought to give members somewhat more autonomy and they increasingly gained a taste for it. In early May the

House overruled one of Craddick's decisions from the chair, the first such instance since 1973. On May 21, Byron Cook (R-Corcicana) called in a floor speech for Craddick to step down, the first such challenge to a sitting speaker since 1959, and Jim Pitts and Jim Keffer (R-Eastland), chair of the tax writing Ways and Means Committee, filed to challenge Craddick for the speakership in any special session or in 2009.

With just three days left in the session, the House descended into chaos. When members sought to offer a motion "to vacate the chair," Craddick recessed the House for more than two hours. When he returned, he declared that there was no such motion in the rules. The House parliamentarian and her assistant disagreed and resigned. Craddick appointed allies to the now vacant parliamentarian positions and proceeded to overrule all attempts to challenge him. Craddick's opponents yelled "dictator" and supporters shouted "anarchists" back at them. Craddick survived, barely, to the end of the session, but a bare knuckled speaker race was guaranteed for 2009.[8]

Further Republican losses in the 2008 Texas House elections fed opposition to Speaker Craddick as the 2009 regular session approached. Though Republicans held a narrow majority on election night, 76 to 74, Irving Republican Linda Harper-Brown clung to a 29 vote lead over challenger Bob Romano. A successful Romano challenge would leave the House divided 75 to 75. Knowing how close this race was likely to be, Craddick had channeled $10,000 into Harper-Brown's campaign in the final week to buttress both her position and his own. Nonetheless, both Republicans and Democrats lined up to challenge him for the speakership. In addition to Craddick, Republicans Tommy Merritt of Longview and Jim Keffer of Eastland, Democrats Pete Gallego of Alpine and Senfronia Thompson of Houston declared while others continued to assess their chances. Keep your seatbelts fastened throughout the flight.

The Lieutenant Governor

The lieutenant governor is a statewide elected official who presides in the Texas Senate by constitutional mandate. Unlike the U.S. vice president, who is constitutionally empowered to preside in the U.S. Senate, the lieutenant governor of Texas is an independent political figure. The vice president is selected by the president and remains subservient to him while in office. The lieutenant governor of Texas is the dominant figure in the Texas Senate. The lieutenant governor: (1) appoints the chairs, vice chairs, and members of all Senate committees, including standing committees, conference committees, and interim committees; (2) assigns all bills and resolutions to the appropriate committee; and (3) presides over the Senate and interprets the rules. He votes only in the case of a tie.

During the past several decades, two lieutenant governors have become legendary figures, on a par with any governor of the period. Bill Hobby, son of a former governor, served as lieutenant governor for 18 years, between 1972 and 1990. Hobby was a quiet, scholarly man, well-liked by his colleagues in the Senate and very effective. Bob Bullock, as bullying and boisterous as Hobby was quiet and retiring, served as lieutenant governor for eight years, between 1990 and 1998. Bullock knew Texas state government

*WILLIAM "BUBBA" FLINT/Special Contributor/*The Dallas Morning News

inside out and was credited with helping a newly elected governor—George W. Bush—learn the ropes. The Bob Bullock State History Museum opened in Austin in April 2001 and is well worth a visit.

Rick Perry, longtime Texas Agriculture Commissioner, moved up to lieutenant governor in 1998 as George W. Bush was winning a second term as governor. When Governor Bush won the presidency in 2000, Rick Perry became governor and the members of the Texas Senate elected one of their own, Senator Bill Ratliff (R-Mount Pleasant), to preside in the Senate. Ratliff declined to run for lieutenant governor in 2002 and the position was won by one-term land commissioner and wealthy businessman, David Dewhurst.

Dewhurst, a novice when he approached the 78th (2003) regular session, won high marks for hard work and a willingness to listen and search for common ground. In the 79th (2005) legislative session, Craddick's unwillingness to compromise on the major issue of the session, school finance, made Dewhurst's search for compromise seem ineffectual, perhaps weak, and left both men seeking to blame the other.[9] Cartoons such as this one were all over the Texas press. Craddick and Dewhurst both benefited when the 2006 special session finally succeeded in passing a school finance bill. Dewhurst is widely expected to run for governor in 2010.

"The team" The Speaker's closest associates, through whom he attempts to control and direct the House. A similar pattern operates in the Senate.

The Team

Supporters and close associates of the presiding officers are commonly referred to as "**the team.**" While the idea of the team applies to both the House and the Senate, it is most clear in the House. Legislators that support the successful candidate for speaker, particularly if they signed on early and worked to build support, are usually rewarded with important committee assignments. If they are senior members of the House, they are likely to be named committee chairs or vice chairs.

Historically, "the team" has not been a strictly partisan group. While the presiding officer usually draws most heavily on the members of his own party, leaders have always tried to include members of the opposition on the team. Drawing support from both sides of the aisle enhances prospects of consistently controlling the body and gives the leader's team an air of bipartisanship. In truth, the willingness of most members of the minority party to join the speaker's "team" is less a matter of bipartisanship than it is a desire to be close to power and share in some of its benefits.

Legislative Institutions and Leadership Power

The lieutenant governor and speaker share control over the legislature's research, budgetary, audit, and oversight staff. The lieutenant governor serves as Chair of the Legislative Council and the speaker serves as vice chair. The 17-member Council is filled out with ten House members appointed by the speaker and five senators appointed by the lieutenant governor. The Legislative Council has a staff director and a professional staff that assists the leaders, committee chairs, and members with interim research as well as bill-drafting services before and during the session. Between sessions, the Legislative Council conducts studies, inquiries, and investigations as directed by the leaders.

The lieutenant governor and speaker also jointly control the powerful Legislative Budget Board (LBB), the Legislative Audit Committee (LAC), and the Sunset Advisory Committee (SAC). The LBB oversees the drafting and monitoring of the state budget and the LAC oversees post-spending audits and investigations. The SAC conducts a review of every state agency, on a twelve-year cycle, to determine whether the agency is still needed. Control of these boards and committees is central to the power of the presiding officers of the Texas Legislature.[10]

Limits on Legislative Leadership

The speaker and the lieutenant governor wield tremendous power, but their power is not unchecked. Obviously, each is in the position to check the other. Moreover, leaders sometimes make demands with which their followers are unwilling to comply. In these contests of will, leaders win some and they lose some.

First, the leaders are well aware that they cannot simply dominate their fellow legislators. Many members have a decade or more of service in the legislature, are skilled legislative tacticians, and have broad contacts in the lobby and the executive branch. The presiding officers tend to communicate closely and continually with senior members of the team to make sure that they are all on the same page.

Second, the leaders know that it is futile to pass something in one house of the legislature, or even in both houses, without insuring that the rest of state government is receptive. Leaders stay in close touch with the governor's office and the elected and appointed officials that run the bureaucracy to be sure that they support and approve legislative actions. Leaders also pay continuous attention to the lobby to get their input and gauge their likely reaction to whatever the legislature might do.

Finally, leaders know that members are more afraid of the voters than they are of them. Members are likely to defect if leaders ask that they take positions or cast votes that might get them defeated in the next election. On the other hand, members that regularly stray from the course set by the leaders often find themselves marooned on a marginal committee and sometimes find themselves opposed for re-election.

THE COMMITTEE SYSTEM

Q3. What roles do committees play in the legislative process?

The committee system is a set of working groups into which the members are divided to more efficiently process the business of the legislature. Committees are frequently called "little legislatures" because each one takes responsibility for a particular aspect of the legislature's work. The Texas Legislature employs several kinds of committees, including standing committees, conference committees, and special and interim committees.

Standing Committees

Standing committees
Continuing committees of the legislature appointed at the start of each legislative session unless specific action is taken to revise or discontinue them.

Standing committees are the most important legislative committees. Each standing committee has a designated area of responsibility, and all bills must be considered by the appropriate standing committee before proceeding to the floor for final action. However, standing committees in the Texas Legislature are less powerful and independent than are standing committees in the U.S. Congress, or even in many other state legislatures. The speaker and lieutenant governor fairly regularly change the number, jurisdiction, leadership, and membership of standing committees.

Standing committees come in two varieties, policy committees and power committees. Policy committees, such as the House committees on Agriculture and Livestock, Border and International Affairs, Criminal Jurisprudence, and Natural Resources, have jurisdiction over particular policy areas. Power committees, such as the House committees on Appropriations, Calendars, and Ways and Means, control how bills come to the floor and how much money is to be raised and spent.

In the 80th (2007) legislative session, the Senate had 15 standing committees and the House had 40. Lieutenant Governor Dewhurst named ten Republicans and six Democrats to chair the Senate's standing committees. In general, the most important committees, including Finance, Education, State Affairs, and Business and Commerce, were not only chaired by Republicans, but given a two-to-one Republican majority. This being

TABLE 6.3
Committees of the 80th Texas Legislature

Senate Committees	
Administration, R, 4R-3D	Intergovernmental Relations, D, 3R-2D
Business and Commerce, R, 6R-3D	International Relations & Trade, D, 4R-3D
Criminal Justice, D, 4R-3D	Jurisprudence, R, 4R-3D
Education, R, 6R-3D	Natural Resources, R, 9R-2D
Finance, R, 10R-5D	Nominations, R, 5R-2D
Government Organization, D, 4R-3D	State Affairs, R, 6R-3D
Health & Human Services, R, 5R-4D	Vet. Affairs & Mil. Installations, D, 3R-2D
Trans. & Homeland Security, R, 6R-3D	

House Committees	
Agriculture & Livestock, R, 4R-3D	Human Services, D, 5R-4D
Appropriations, R, 17R-12D	Insurance, R, 5R-4D
Border & International Affairs, D, 2R-5D	Judiciary, R, 4R-5D
Business & Industry, D, 5R-4D	Juvenile Justice & Family Issues, D, 10R-9D
Calendars, R, 7R-4D	Land & Resource Management, R, 4R-4D
Civil Practices, R, 6R-3D	Law Enforcement, R, 3R-4D
Corrections, R, 3R-4D	Licensing & Admin. Procedure, D, 5R-4D
County Affairs, R, 3R-6D	Local & Consent Calendars, R, 8R-3D
Criminal Jurisprudence, D, 2R-7D	Local Gov. Ways & Means, R, 4R-3D
Culture, Rec. & Tourism, R, 4R-3D	Natural Resources, D, 6R-3D
Defense Affairs & St.-Fed. Rel., R, 2R-7D	Pensions & Investments, R, 2R-4D
Economic Development, D, 3R-4D	Public Education, R, 6R-3D
Elections, R, 3R-4D	Public Health, R, 4R-5D
Energy Resources, R, 5R-2D	Redistricting, R, 10R-5D
Environmental Regulation, R, 5R-2D	Regulated Industries, R, 7R-2D
Financial Institutions, R, 5R-2D	Rules & Resolutions, D, 5R-6D
General Investigating &Ethics, D, 3R-2D	State Affairs, R, 7R-2D
Government Reform, R, 4R-3D	Transportation, R, 8R-1D
Higher Education, R, 5R-4D	Urban Affairs, D, 2R-2D
House Administration, R, 7R-4D	Ways & Means, R, 5R-4D

Source: Texas House and Senate websites. *http://www.house.state.tx.us/committees/welcome.htm*
http://www.senate.tx.us/75r/Senate/Commit.htm

Texas, the Natural Resources Committee was given a nine to two Republican majority. The committees chaired by Democrats were generally of lesser importance and had Republican majorities to boot.

Speaker Craddick appointed 30 Republicans and 10 Democrats to chair standing committees. As in the Senate, the most important committees were reserved for Republican chairs and Republican majorities. The Democrats tapped to lead committees were either charter members of "the team" or were given marginal committees with light policy agendas.

Special or Temporary Committees

The Texas Legislature also employs various special or temporary committees. Conference committees, which are the most common and important of

Interim committees
Legislative committees that work in the interim between regular legislative sessions to study issues, prepare reports, and draft legislation.

the special committees, will be discussed in detail later in the chapter. **Interim committees** are appointed to work during the interim between regular sessions or in preparation for a special session. They may be composed of the members of a standing committee or freshly formed to deal with a particular issue.

HOW A BILL BECOMES A LAW

> **Q4.** How does a bill become a law in Texas?

The journey from bill introduction to final passage is long and arduous. In the 80th (2007) regular session, 6,190 bills (bills are proposed laws) were introduced into one or both chambers, and 1,481 passed. This approval rate of about 25 percent is consistent with the approval rate in past legislative sessions.[11]

The Texas Constitution requires that a bill be read three times, on three separate days, before it is passed. This three-readings requirement is a centuries-old procedure designed to slow the legislative process and assure time for thoughtful consideration.[12] The Texas Legislature's heavy workload, short 140-day regular session, and the general tumult of the legislative process go a long way toward defeating the goals of slow and thoughtful decision-making.

Introduction and Referral

Though the idea behind a bill can come from anyone, only an elected member can introduce a bill into the Texas Legislature. A bill may be introduced into both houses simultaneously, or into either initially, though revenue bills must be introduced into the House first. The legislator that files the bill is called its sponsor and other legislators that sign on to support the bill are called co-sponsors. Texas allows pre-filing, meaning that a bill can be filed during the interim before a regular session, or during the first 60 days of the 140-day regular session. After the 60th day, only local bills effecting one city or county, emergency appropriations, or matters that the governor declares to be emergencies may be filed.

Once a bill is filed, it is assigned a reference or tracking number, such as "H.B.1," or "S.B.1," for House Bill 1 or Senate Bill 1, respectively. Bills are assigned a number in the order in which they are filed, though it has become common for leaders to set aside the first few numbers for the most important bills of the session. After the bill has been filed and a number assigned, the clerk reads the bill (really just author, bill title, and number) for the first time and announces the committee to which the presiding officer has referred the bill.

The presiding officers have great discretion in selecting the committee to which a given bill will be referred. If the presiding officer approves of the bill, he may refer it to a friendly committee, chaired by a member of "the team," and instruct that it be treated positively. If he disapproves of the bill, he may refer it to a committee he knows will "pigeonhole" it. Two-thirds of bills introduced into the Texas Legislature die in committee.

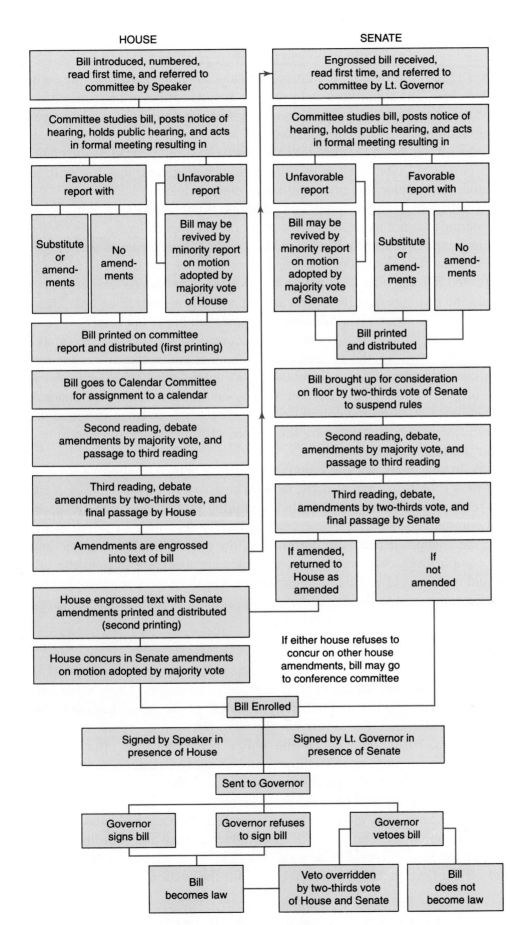

CHART 6.1
The Legislative Process in Texas

This diagram displays the sequential flow of a bill from the time it is introduced in the House of Representatives to final passage and transmittal to the governor. A bill introduced in the Senate would follow the same procedure in reverse. Students who have difficulty understanding this fairly complicated chart should pay close attention to the accompanying text. *Source: Texas Legislature Online.* *www.capitol.state.tx.us*

HOUSE

Bill introduced, numbered, read first time, and referred to committee by Speaker

Committee studies bill, posts notice of hearing, holds public hearing, and acts in formal meeting resulting in

Favorable report with

Unfavorable report

Substitute or amendments

No amendments

Bill may be revived by minority report on motion adopted by majority vote of House

Bill printed on committee report and distributed (first printing)

Bill goes to Calendar Committee for assignment to a calendar

Second reading, debate amendments by majority vote, and passage to third reading

Third reading, debate amendments by two-thirds vote, and final passage by House

Amendments are engrossed into text of bill

House engrossed text with Senate amendments printed and distributed (second printing)

House concurs in Senate amendments on motion adopted by majority vote

SENATE

Engrossed bill received, read first time, and referred to committee by Lt. Governor

Committee studies bill, posts notice of hearing, holds public hearing, and acts in formal meeting resulting in

Unfavorable report

Favorable report with

Bill may be revived by minority report on motion adopted by majority vote of Senate

Substitute or amendments

No amendments

Bill printed and distributed

Bill brought up for consideration on floor by two-thirds vote of Senate to suspend rules

Second reading, debate, amendments by majority vote, and passage to third reading

Third reading, debate, amendments by two-thirds vote, and final passage by Senate

If amended, returned to House as amended

If not amended

If either house refuses to concur on other house amendments, bill may go to conference committee

Bill Enrolled

Signed by Speaker in presence of House

Signed by Lt. Governor in presence of Senate

Sent to Governor

Governor signs bill

Governor refuses to sign bill

Governor vetoes bill

Bill becomes law

Veto overridden by two-thirds vote of House and Senate

Bill does not become law

Committee Action

When a bill is referred to committee, it comes under the control of the committee chair. The committee chair sets the agenda for his or her committee, allocates the committee's staff resources, and determines to which issues the committee will dedicate its time and attention. If the committee chair buries a bill far down the committee's agenda, that bill is dead. If the chairman puts a bill near the top of the committee's agenda, that bill will go through three major stages of committee consideration.

The first stage of committee consideration is public hearings. While public hearings are not mandatory, they are common, especially for major bills. Public hearings acknowledge the public's right to participate in the legislative process. The Texas Open Meetings Law requires that notice of hearings be posted five calendar days before the meeting. Any citizen who wishes to attend the hearings may do so and any citizen who wishes to be heard may fill out a brief witness identification card and wait his or her turn.

The second major stage of committee consideration is committee mark-up. During mark-up, the chairman leads the committee through a line-by-line consideration of the bill, revising and amending it where necessary. The original bill may have been drafted by an interest group, a bureaucrat, a paid lobbyist, or by the committee staff. The mark-up stage is where the committee members, guided by the wishes of the speaker and committee chair, make the bill their own.

Following mark-up, the committee votes whether to approve the bill and pass it on to its parent body, or to disapprove it, thereby killing it for the remainder of the session. If the committee vote is favorable, the chair and committee staff draft a report which briefly describes the intent of the bill, the changes it makes in current law, the cost of implementation, and the comptroller's certification that revenues are available to fund the bill should it become law. Bills that clear committee must then be scheduled for consideration on the floor.

Calendar Assignment

Q5. How does the legislative process differ in the House and Senate?

Legislative calendars Lists of bills passed by committees but awaiting final action on the floor.

Both the House and Senate employ legislative calendars. **Legislative calendars** determine when and under what "rules" of debate bills come to the floor for final action. The House has the more formal and orderly calendaring process. Bills approved by the policy committees go either to the Calendars Committee or to the Local and Consent Calendars Committee. The Calendars Committee places the major bills of the session on the Emergency, Major State, and General State calendars. The Local and Consent Calendars Committee manages three calendars for local bills and various types of resolutions. The Calendar Committees control and coordinate traffic onto the House floor. The general goal is to move minor legislation onto and off the floor quickly to preserve time for the session's major bills.

The Senate employs a single calendar and a process that is quite different than the one used in the House. Formal Senate rules for bringing a bill to the floor, called "the regular order," are similar to the House rules. But for more than half a century, the Senate has ignored the regular order to follow informal rules that promote collegiality and consensus. At the beginning of each legislative session, the lieutenant governor instructs the Secretary of the Senate to place a minor bill with no meaningful support at the top of the calendar. With this "blocker bill" permanently in place, every subsequent bill must come to the Senate floor under suspension of the rules, which requires a two-thirds vote. A senator wishing to bring a bill to the floor must consult with the lieutenant governor, secure the support of two-thirds of his or her colleagues, and file a "notice of intent" with the Secretary of the Senate.[13]

As the legislature moves toward adjournment and time remaining in the session grows short, the management of the calendars by the presiding officers becomes increasingly important. The key bills, especially the state budget, have to be brought to the floor with enough time remaining to complete action. Bills not brought to the floor at least 48 hours prior to final adjournment are doomed.

Floor Action

When a bill reaches the floor of the House, it receives its second reading, and debate begins. The bill's sponsor or floor manager, oftentimes with other senior supporters, stands in the well of the house (down front) to describe the bill, urge support, and answer questions. The bill's manager gets twenty minutes at the beginning and at the close of debate. Other members are restricted to one ten-minute statement in favor of or opposition to the bill. Any member can offer an amendment to a bill, but a majority of members present and voting must approve for the amendment to be adopted.

When the debate concludes, the Speaker calls the vote. Proponents walk the aisles holding up one finger, urging a yes vote, while opponents walk the aisles holding up two fingers, urging a no vote. Members unfamiliar with the issue look to see whether their friends, partisans, or highly respected members are urging a yes or a no vote and follow their lead. If the vote is positive, the bill will be laid over to the next day, given a third reading (debate is uncommon on third reading because amendments require a two-thirds vote), and passed for a final time. To an outsider, the House floor often looks chaotic.

For a bill to reach the Senate floor, it must have the support of the lieutenant governor and two-thirds of the senators. During floor debate, senators speak standing at their desks, as frequently and as long as they like, before voting from their desks. Senate floor action has little of the tumult that characterizes floor action in the House.

Rep. Wayne Smith, R-Baytown signaled his "aye" vote on a transportation bill that he sponsored in the 2007 session.
*Harry Cabluck/*The Associated Press

Conference Committee

Even when bills are introduced simultaneously into both the House and the Senate, they seldom survive committee deliberation and floor action in identical form. In most cases, when differences between the House and Senate versions of the same bill are minor, one house concurs in or accepts the version passed by the other. Where differences are too important to ignore, they must be resolved. The **conference committee** is the device that legislatures use to resolve differences between House and Senate bills. All differences must be resolved and accepted by both houses before the bill can be sent to the governor for his or her signature.

In the Texas Legislature, the speaker and lieutenant governor each name five legislators to form a conference committee. These members usually are the bill's sponsors, the chairs of the committees that produced the bill, and other senior members with knowledge of the subject. Once the conference committee has completed its work, a committee report is drafted comparing the original House and Senate language on each point in disagreement to the new language proposed by the committee. At least three of the five conferees from each house must approve the report before it can be returned to the full House and Senate for their consideration.

Conference committees
Committees composed of members of the House and Senate charged to resolve differences between the House and Senate versions of a bill.

Conference committees frequently do their work late in the session, as adjournment looms, and under great pressure. When conference committees do reach agreement, those agreements are almost always ratified by both bodies. The 80th legislature sent 167 bills to conference committee and 139 of them were reported out and approved by the House and Senate. Though fewer than ten percent of the bills passed in the 80th regular session (139 of 1,481 bills went through the conference committee process), they were many of the most important bills of the session.

The Governor

The governor is involved in the legislative process throughout, though mostly as an adviser, coach, and cheerleader. Legislators know that the governor has a veto and that while he or she normally vetoes only about one percent of bills passed, they take his or her views into account to insure that their bill is not among the unfortunate few vetoed at the close of the term. The powers of the Texas governor will be treated at length in the next chapter.

REFORMING THE TEXAS LEGISLATURE

The Texas Constitution of 1876 was designed to limit and diffuse power. It did so by limiting the legislative session and setting legislative pay low enough to make the office unattractive to those not yet wealthy. In the more than 130 years since the Constitution was approved, much has changed. Modern Texas is a large, populous, and complicated state facing myriad opportunities and challenges. To face them effectively, Texas needs a modern legislature. Several reforms seem obvious.

First, Texas is the only one of the ten largest states in the U.S. to still employ a biennial legislature. Oftentimes, the Texas legislature is so hard pressed in the closing days and hours of the session that critical business is left undone. The Texas Constitution should be amended to require annual, meaning yearly, rather than biennial sessions. Unlike California and New York, the Texas Legislature might not need to meet year around, but it should meet annually and it should be able to stay in session until its most critical business has been completed.

Second, and this comes hard, Texas legislators should be paid more. Historically, southern states paid legislators little so that only "the better sort" could afford to serve. But Texas, at $7,200 a year plus per diem, is among the lowest in the nation. Low pay means legislators must be wealthy, must have jobs that take them away from the public's business, or they must allow themselves to be kept by the lobby. Texas legislators should be paid in the range of $50,000 to $75,000, still well below California's $113,000, but enough to allow full attention to their cities. This too would require a constitutional amendment.

And finally, the powers of the Speaker and the Lieutenant governor, the presiding officers of the Texas House and Senate, should be checked and the individual legislators should be empowered. This could be done simply by changing the House and Senate rules that are adopted at the beginning of each regular legislative session. The key change would be to limit the presiding officers ability to define the number and jurisdiction of committees and name members to them each session. Rather, as in the U.S. Congress, members should have seniority in their committees. This would allow members to remain on committees from session to session once named to the committee and to grow in expertise and rise in influence. Somewhat weaker leaders and somewhat more secure members would, one hopes, restore a lost civility and balance to the Texas Legislature.

CHAPTER SUMMARY

The Texas Legislature was once the preserve of white, male professionals. Most were lawyers, businessmen, and ranchers, so they tended to take a fairly conservative view of politics, government, and public policy. Though there are more women and minorities in the legislature than there once were, the low pay, uncertain schedule, and hectic pace keep expertise low and turnover high. Texas is the only one of the ten largest states whose legislature still meets biennially.

The presiding officers of the Texas Legislature wield extraordinary power. The Speaker of the House and lieutenant governor in the Senate set the number of standing committees and their jurisdiction, appoint all of the committee chairs and most of the committee members, interpret and apply the rules, and preside over the conduct of business on the floor. Members seek to be on "the team," meaning to be among the presiding officer's recognized loyalists in order to receive favorable committee assignments and some modicum of influence.

The presiding officer's chief supporters chair the most important standing committees (especially those that handle the major bills), set the schedule for floor debate, and control the appropriations process. The speaker and the lieutenant governor, working with and through their respective committee chairs and "teams," can usually manage the legislative process to produce the results they desire, or at least those that they find acceptable. Sometimes, however, the presiding officers cannot agree, will not compromise, and have to settle for the lesser satisfactions of blocking each other.

KEY TERMS

Amateur legislatures	Interim committees	Professional legislatures
Biennial session	Legislative calendars	Regular session
Conference committees	Legislative supremacy	Standing committees
Hybrid legislatures	Popular sovereignty	"The team"

SUGGESTED READINGS

Jimmy Banks, *Gavels, Grit & Glory: The Billy Clayton Story* (Burnet, TX: Eakin Press, 1982).

Nancy Baker Jones and Ruthe Winegarten, *Capitol Women: Texas Female Legislators, 1923–1999* (Austin, TX: University of Texas Press, 2000).

Karen Olsson, *Waterloo: A Novel* (New York: Farrar, Strauss, and Giroux, 2005).

Alan Rosenthal, *Heavy Lifting: The Job of the American Legislature* (Washington, D.C.: CQ Press, 2004).

Thomas M. Spencer, *The Legislative Process, Texas Style* (Pasadena, TX: San Jacinto College Press, 1981).

WEB RESOURCES

http://www.ncsl.org National Conference of State Legislatures.

http://www.capitol.state.tx.us Texas Legislature's website.

http://www.house.state.tx.us Texas House of Representatives' website.

http://www.senate.state.tx.us Texas Senate's website.

http://www.lrl.state.tx.us Texas Legislature's Reference Library.

http://www.capitol.tx.us/capitol/legproc/summary.htm Summary of Texas Legislative precedents.

END NOTES

1. Dennis L. Dresang and James L. Gosling, *Politics and Policy in American States and Communities,* 6th ed., New York: Pearson Longman, 2008, pp. 287–288.
2. Katherine Q. Seelye, "Obituaries: Molly Ivins is Dead at 62; Writer Skewered Politicians," *New York Times,* February 1, 2007, A20.
3. Associated Press, "Perry OKs Judge's Pay, Lawmakers' Pension Boost," September 8, 2005.
4. For the national numbers, see Virginia Gray and Russell L. Hanson, eds., *Politics in the American States: A Comparative Analysis,* 9th ed. (Washington, D.C.: CQ Press, 2008), p. 170.
5. See http://www.ncsl.org/programs/press/2004/backgrounder_fullandpart.htm. Updated January 2008.
6. Christie Hoppe, "Another Joins Fray for House Speaker," *Dallas Morning News,* December 29, 2006, p. A1.
7. Laylan Copelin, "Craddick Rewards Loyalists," *Austin American-Statesman,* January 27, 2007, A1.
8. Paul Burka, "Speaker for Life," *Texas Monthly,* September 2007, pp. 14–18.
9. American Statesman Staff, "In the End, Key Goals Unreached," *Austin American-Statesman,* May 31, 2005.
10. Karl T. Kurtz, "Strong Staff, Strong Institution: Custodians of American Democracy," *State Legislatures,* July/August, 2006, pp. 28–32.
11. Texas Reference Library, at http://www.lrl.state.tx.us/legis/profile80.html.
12. Calvin Jillson and Rick K. Wilson, *Congressional Dynamics: Structure, Coordination, and Choice in the First American Congress, 1774–1789* (Stanford, CA: Stanford University Press, 1994), p. 23.
13. Paul Burka, "First, Dew No Harm," *Texas Monthly,* February 2006, pp. 16, 18.

CHAPTER 7

The Governor and the Executive Branch

Focus Questions

Q1. What is the governor's role in Texas politics?

Q2. What are the governor's formal and informal powers?

Q3. What other statewide elected officials share power with the governor?

Q4. What roles do elected and appointed boards and commissions play in Texas?

Q5. What reforms do analysts propose for the executive branch?

Most Texans assume, reasonably enough, that the governor is the chief executive and natural leader of Texas state government. In a sense, he is, but he is not the undisputed leader because the tools he has to make his leadership felt are modest. The Texas Constitution and state statutes create a plural executive with power and responsibility spread diffusely through the system. If the governor of Texas is to lead, it must be by political skill and force of personality.

For much, perhaps even most, of Texas history there was at least as much force of personality as political skill on display in the governor's office. Texas governors James Stephen Hogg (1891–1895), James Ferguson (1915–1917), and W. Lee O'Daniel (1939–41) come easily to mind. Hogg is credited both with political skill and a larger than life personality, but Ferguson and O'Daniel rose and fell, won and lost, on the force of their personalities.

Governor Jim Hogg earned a permanent place in Texas political lore by naming his daughter "Ima" and claiming that he did not see the inevitable result—Ima Hogg—until it was too late. Despite Governor Hogg's unfortunate sense of humor, he was a skilled politician. He created the Texas Railroad Commission, which we will learn more about below, and otherwise sought to limit the free rein previously enjoyed by the railroads and other corporate interests.

Governor James Ferguson, a small town banker, campaigned as "Farmer Jim" to strengthen his connection to rural voters. Jim Ferguson did try to benefit the common people by providing financial relief to tenant farmers, improving farm-to-market roads, and providing free textbooks to the public schools, but he did not forget to benefit himself along the way. Early in his second term, "Farmer Jim" was accused of embezzling state funds, impeached, convicted, and removed from office. Impeachment made him ineligible to hold state office in the future. Undeterred, Jim convinced his wife, Miriam "Ma" Ferguson, to run for governor on the slogan "two governors for the price of one." With "Pa" at her side, "Ma" Ferguson served two terms, 1925–27 and 1933–35, as governor of Texas. "Ma" and "Pa" Ferguson kept Texas politics in an entertaining turmoil for two decades, but their political accomplishments were relatively few.

W. Lee "Pappy" O'Daniel had no discernible political agenda and left public life after a decade as governor and U.S. senator with no major and few minor political accomplishments. "Pappy" was a flour salesman, a radio personality, and leader of the "Hillbilly Boys"—his radio and campaign band. "Pappy" campaigned on "the ten commandments and the golden rule." Texans expect little from state government and "Pappy" gave them just what they expected—along with some country wisdom and a song.

In the past half century, the politics of personality have faded while the politics of partisanship and ideology have become dominant, but Texas governors have become no more effective. They still labor in a political system in which power is diffuse, resources are few, and expectations for the good that government might do are low.

The Texas Constitution of 1876 created a plural executive of five statewide elected officials: the governor, lieutenant governor, attorney general (AG), comptroller of public accounts, and land commissioner. Each statewide elected official has independent constitutional powers and responsibilities. Constitutional amendments and statutes also mandate that the agriculture commissioner and the members of the Railroad Commission be elected statewide. Members of the State Board of Education (SBE) are elected in districts across the state. The governor must work with these elected officials, but he does not control them.[1]

THE GOVERNOR

Q1. What is the governor's role in Texas politics?

Now we explore the structure of the Office of Governor, the qualifications required to hold the office, and the formal and informal powers of the office. Despite a paucity of formal powers, the governor is the focal point of public and media attention. He cannot always determine outcomes, but he has formal and informal powers that allow him to set the public agenda of the state, lead the public and political discussion, and nudge the process toward desired outcomes. Finally, we ask what reforms might strengthen and improve the performance of the executive branch of Texas state government.

Though being governor of Texas may be frustrating at times, it is not a bad job. It pays $150,000 a year and the perks include a mansion in Austin

TABLE 7.1
The Texas Governor and His Peers

Name	State	Salary	Staff	Term	Consecutive Terms Allowed	Campaign Cost (millions)
Arnold Schwarzenegger	California	$212,179	185	4 yrs	2	$129
Rick Perry	**Texas**	**$150,000**	**266**	**4 yrs**	**–**	**$34**
David Paterson	New York	$179,000	180	4 yrs	2	$46
Charlie Crist	Florida	$132,932	293	4 yrs	2	$42
Edward Rendell	Pennsylvania	$170,150	68	4 yrs	2	$41
Rod Blagojevich	Illinois	$158,000	130	4 yrs	–	$48
Ted Strickland	Ohio	$144,830	60	4 yrs	–	$29
Jennifer Granholm	Michigan	$177,000	78	4 yrs	2	$53
Mike Easley	North Carolina	$135,854	74	4 yrs	–	$19
Sonny Perdue	Georgia	$135,281	42	4 yrs	2	$29

Source: The Book of the States, 2008, vol. 40 (Lexington, KY: Council of State Governments, 2008), pp. 170, 180–181, 183.

(badly damaged by fire in June 2008), a fleet of cars and planes (drivers and pilots included), and reimbursement for official travel, business, and entertainment expenses. A staff of 266 serves the governor's personal and political needs.

Despite the nice salary and perks, until recently, job security has been uncertain.[2] During the first century of Texas statehood, no governor was elected to more than two two-year terms. In the 1950s and 60s, governors were commonly elected to three two-year terms. But after the term was lengthened to four years in 1974, governors had difficulty being reelected. George W. Bush was the first Texas governor to be elected to consecutive four-year terms, though he resigned in the middle of his second term to become president.

Lieutenant Governor Rick Perry succeeded Bush as governor on December 21, 2000. Governor Perry was elected to a full four-term of his own in 2002 and reelected in 2006. Midway through his current term, he became the longest serving governor in Texas history. Rick Perry has led a charmed political life. He switched from Democrat to Republican in 1989, just as the Republicans were coming to majority status. After eight years as Agriculture Commissioner, Rick Perry defeated the well-respected Democrat Comptroller John Sharp in 1998 to become lieutenant governor under George W. Bush. Perry became governor when George W. Bush went to Washington and has held the office through two reelection campaigns. Twenty-seven states impose term limits on their governors, but Texas does not.[3] Perry has declared his intention to run for a third full term, though some doubt that he will.

Formal Qualifications

Article IV of the Texas Constitution stipulates that the governor "be at least thirty years of age, a citizen of the United States, and shall have resided in

*John Branch/*San Antonio Express-News

this State at least five years immediately preceding his election." These, obviously, are minimum qualifications. Voters have more than these minimum qualifications in mind when they think about who truly is qualified to be governor of Texas.

Informal Qualifications

All but a very few Texas governors have been wealthy, middle-aged, white, protestant, professional men. Most have been wealthy ranchers, businessmen, or lawyers. Texas has had two female governors, Miriam (Ma) Ferguson (1925–27 and 1933–35) and Ann Richards (1990–94), but no minority governors. Though some Texas governors have seemed loosely constrained by their protestant roots, all have been protestant.

Formal Powers

Q2. What are the governor's formal and informal powers?

Unlike most other governors, the governor of Texas does not prepare the state budget for submission to the legislature, nor does he appoint most of the other top administrators. On the other hand, the Texas Constitution and statutes do award the governor some important executive, budgetary, legislative, judicial, and military powers.

Executive Powers. The Texas Constitution describes the governor as the state's "Chief Executive Officer." The governor does have some of the powers of a chief executive. The governor's **appointment power** extends

TABLE 7.2
Recent Governors of Texas

Name	Party/Home	Term	Occupation	Previous Office
Allan Shivers	D-Port Arthur	1949–1957	Law	Texas Senate Lt. Governor
Price Daniel	D-Liberty	1957–1963	Law/Ranching	Texas House Attorney General U.S. Senate
John Connally	D-Floresville	1963–1969	Law/Business	Secretary of the Navy Secretary of the Treasury
Preston Smith	D-Lubbock	1969–1973	Business	Texas House Texas Senate Lt. Gov.
Dolph Briscoe	D-Uvalde	1973–1979	Rancher	Texas House
Bill Clements	R-Dallas	1979–1983	Business	Deputy Sec. of Defense
Mark White	D-Houston	1983–1987	Law	Secretary of State Attorney General
Bill Clements	R-Dallas	1987–1991	Business	See above
Ann Richards	D-Austin	1991–1995	Teacher/Politician	Travis County Commissioners Court State Treasurer
George W. Bush	R-Midland	1995–2000	Business	None
Rick Perry	R-Austin	2000–present	Farmer/Politician	Texas House Agriculture Commissioner Lt. Governor

Source: Legislative Reference Library of Texas. See *http://www.lrl.state.tx.us/legis/leaders/govbio.html*

to a number of senior officials, including the secretary of state; the adjutant general; the commissioners of education, insurance, health and human services; and the executive director of the department of commerce. Texas governors also make nearly 2,500 appointments during each four-year term to fill and keep filled about 1,900 seats on 275 independent agencies, boards, and commissions.[4] Most such appointments are to staggered six-year terms. Most gubernatorial appoints require approval by a two-thirds vote of the Senate.

Once appointed, however, members of agencies, boards, and commissions are highly independent because they are very difficult to remove. Governors can dismiss members of their personal staff at will, but they can remove persons that they appoint to agencies, boards, and commissions only with the approval of two-thirds of the Senate, and they cannot remove the appointees of previous governors at all. This limited removal power makes it hard for Texas governors to control bureaucrats and guide policymaking and program implementation.

Governors work hard to expand their authority, but others work just as hard to limit and check it. In 2007, Governor Perry argued that the Texas Constitution's declaration that the Governor is the "Chief Executive Officer of the State" allowed him to direct state agencies by "executive order."

Appointment power
The Texas Constitution and statutes empower the governor, often with the approval of two-thirds of the Senate, to appoint many senior government officials.

TABLE 7.3
Let's Compare: Governor's Institutional Powers

For many years, Thad Beyle of the University of North Carolina, Chapel Hill, has been the nation's leading expert on governors. He and Margaret Ferguson compared the institutional powers of the fifty state governors on several dimensions of autonomy, independence, and authority. Beyle ranked them on a five-point scale; Massachusetts, for example, at 4.3 was among the strongest, while Vermont at 2.5 was among the weakest. The Governor of Texas has fewer constitutional and legal powers than most of his or her peers and ranked 3.2.

Massachusetts 4.3	Tennessee 3.8	Florida 3.6	Arizona 3.4	South Dakota 3.0
New York 4.1	Nebraska 3.8	Missouri 3.6	Idaho 3.3	South Carolina 3.0
Alaska 4.1	Pennsylvania 3.8	Washington 3.6	Kansas 3.3	Nevada 3.0
West Virginia 4.1	Iowa 3.8	Arkansas 3.6	Kentucky 3.3	Mississippi 2.9
New Jersey 4.1	New Mexico 3.7	Montana 3.5	California 3.2	Indiana 2.9
Maryland 4.1	Minnesota 3.6	Wisconsin 3.5	New Hampshire 3.2	North Carolina 2.9
Utah 4.0	Ohio 3.6	Delaware 3.5	Virginia 3.2	Oklahoma 2.8
North Dakota 3.9	Connecticut 3.6	Oregon 3.5	Georgia 3.2	Alabama 2.8
Colorado 3.9	Maine 3.6	Hawaii 3.4	Texas 3.2	Rhode Island 2.6
Illinois 3.8	Michigan 3.6	Louisiana 3.4	Wyoming 3.1	Vermont 2.5

Source: Virginia Gray and Russell L. Hanson, *Politics in the American States: A Comparative Analysis*, 9th ed. (Washington, D.C.: CQ Press, 2008, pp. 212–213.)

Perry's spokesman, Robert Black, said "it's the governor's job to provide leadership and direction to the executive branch of government. . . . The governor's ability to lead this branch is inherent in the office." Governor Perry issued executive orders requiring that public schools spend at least 65 percent of state funds in the classroom, speeding up administrative review of coal plant permits, and requiring that sixth-grade girls be vaccinated against the human papillomavirus (HPV).

Others read the Texas Constitution differently. Steve Bickerstaff, former director of constitutional research for the Texas Legislative Council, said "an executive order is a statement by the Governor of Texas about what he thinks is in the best interest of the state. But he can't issue an order and tell that agency or hearing examiner that, 'you have to do this.' "[5] Interest groups, the courts, and the legislature all took the same view, arguing that the Constitution denied the governor such sweeping unilateral powers. This is classic American political theory—separation of powers and checks and balances—it is just that the Governor of Texas is easier to check than most other federal and state executives.

Budgetary Powers. In forty-six states, the governor has a major role in drafting the state's budget.[6] Not so in Texas. Article 4, section 9, of the Texas Constitution requires the governor to submit a **budget message** and an estimate of revenue needs to the legislature at the commencement of its regular session. Traditionally, governors followed their estimate of revenue needs with a detailed spending plan. In recent years, governors "have tended to submit either general outlines or no separate budget at all."[7]

While the governor has little power on the front end of the budgetary process, he has some on the back end. Like most U.S. governors, the Governor of Texas has a **line-item veto.** This means that once the budget is adopted by the legislature and submitted for approval, the governor can

Budget message   The governor is required by law to address the legislature on budget matters in the first thirty days of each regular session.

Line-item veto   The power to strike out or veto individual items in the state budget without striking down the whole budget.

TABLE 7.4
Bills Vetoed and Special Sessions Called by Recent Texas Governors

Governor	Term	Bills Vetoed	# of Special Sessions
Allan Shivers (D)	1949–1957	89	2
Price Daniel (D)	1957–1963	42	8
John Connally (D)	1963–1969	104	2
Preston Smith (D)	1969–1973	93	6
Dolph Briscoe (D)	1973–1979	71	3
Bill Clements (R)	1979–1983	78	3
Mark White (D)	1983–1987	95	5
Bill Clements (R)	1987–1991	113	8
Ann Richards (D)	1991–1995	62	4
George W. Bush (R)	1995–2000	97	0
Rick Perry (R)	2000–2008	208	7

Source: Legislative Reference Library of Texas, *Texas Legislative Sessions and Years.* See *http://www.lrl.state.tx.us/legis/sessionYears.html.* Bills Vetoed 1860–2007. See *http://www.lrl.state.tx.us/legis/vetoes/*

veto individual items in the budget without vetoing the whole budget. Moreover, legislators know that the governor has a line-item veto at the end of the process, so they listen to him throughout the process.

Legislative Powers. The Governor of Texas enjoys three main legislative powers. These are the message power, session power, and veto power. First, the Texas Constitution requires the governor to deliver a **State of the State message** at the beginning of each regular legislative session. This message gives the governor an opportunity to lay out an agenda for the session and to focus the attention of the public and the legislators on that agenda.[8]

Second, once the biennial regular session is over, the governor can call the legislators back to Austin for a **special session.** The governor controls the timing and the agenda for special sessions. Issues not included in the governor's "call" for the special session cannot be taken up. Hence, the governor usually issues a narrow call, requiring the legislators to deal with his key issues first, before broadening the call to allow other issues to be considered. Special sessions of the legislature can last no more than 30 days, but the governor can call two or three special sessions in a row if need be.

Finally, the governor wields both a regular and a line-item veto, either of which can be threatened or actually employed. During a regular or special session, the governor can try to shape the development of a bill by threatening a **veto.** Once the legislature passes a bill, the constitution gives the governor ten days to decide whether to sign or veto the bill. He gets an additional twenty days if the legislature adjourns during the initial ten days. Moreover, as we saw above, the governor has a line-item veto that allows him to strike out particular budgetary items without striking down the whole budget. The governor's regular and line-item veto powers are his greatest sources of influence over the legislature.

Formally, a governor's veto can be overridden by a two-thirds vote of both houses of the Texas legislature. But this rarely happens because most major bills are passed so late in the session that the legislature is adjourned

State of the State message   At the beginning of each regular legislative session, the governor lays out his agenda for the session in a speech to a joint session of the legislature.

Special session   If the legislature does not complete its business in the regular session, the governor can call one or more 30-day special sessions.

Veto   The governor is empowered to veto or strike down acts of the legislature. A veto can be overridden by a two-thirds vote of both houses of the legislature, but it rarely happens.

Gov. Rick Perry delivered his "State of the State" message to the 80ᵗʰ regular session of the Texas Legislature on February 6, 2007. *Erich Schlegel/Staff Photographer,* Dallas Morning News, *Feb. 7, 2007, A1.*

and the legislators are gone before the governor announces his vetoes. Of the nearly 1,857 vetoes cast by Texas governors since 1876, only 26 have been overridden by the legislature, none since 1979.

Judicial Powers. Though the Texas Constitution requires that judges be elected, the governor is empowered to fill judicial vacancies above the level of district judge by appointment. Like other gubernatorial appointments, interim judicial appointments require the concurrence of two-thirds of the Texas Senate. Half of Texas judges first reach the bench by appointment. Once the term of their appointment ends, they must stand for election to a new term, but they have the advantage of running as incumbents.

Beyond the initial selection of many of the state's judges, the governor has few judicial powers. Though many state governors have an independent **clemency** power, the Governor of Texas does not. In Texas, the governor acts in response to recommendations from the seven-member Texas Board of Pardons and Paroles. Once the board acts, the governor has the power to approve or reject their recommendations on pardons, paroles, and sentence reductions. The governor can grant one 30-day reprieve in death penalty cases.

Military Powers. The Governor of Texas has modest military powers. In the normal course of events, the governor appoints the Adjutant General to command the Texas Army and Air National Guard and the Texas State Guard. If the Texas Army and Air National Guard is called up for national service, as some units were in the Afghan and Iraq wars, command passes from the governor to the president. In the event of a statewide or local emergency, the governor has the power to declare martial law and to assume command of the National (if not in national service) and State Guard.

In 2009, the Texas Army and Air National Guard were composed of a headquarters compliment of 628 and 21,900 guardsmen. Nearly 1,600 Texas guardsmen served in Iraq, Afghanistan, and Kosovo during 2007. The 1,400-member Texas State Guard supports the Army and Air National Guard in the event of local emergencies and natural disasters, and fills in for them when they are called to national service.[9]

Clemency Some governors have the power to forgive or lessen the punishment for criminal infractions by granting pardons, paroles, or commutations.

Informal Powers

The formal powers of the Texas governor are fewer than those of most other governors, but one must be careful not to dwell exclusively on these limits. Even if the governor has limited powers, so does everyone else in Texas politics and no one has *more* power than the governor. It is common to suggest that the lieutenant governor may be the most powerful figure in Texas politics. But politics is about winning and using power. So ask yourself this: has any governor ever capped off his or her political career by running for lieutenant governor? (Hint: the answer is no.)

Most Texas governors establish themselves as the leading figure in the state's politics. There are several important reasons for this. First, the governor is the face of his party; he is expected to develop an agenda for the legislature and to speak to major public issues. Second, the governor is the only figure who has a finger in every pie. While his powers do not allow him to control most events, he is in a position to influence them. Third, when the legislature is not in session, which is most of the time, the governor dominates the stage in Austin. Finally, most Texans are only vaguely aware of the real limitations on the power of the governor. They assume that, as governor, he is the leader of Texas state government. Governors use this visibility, centrality, and presumption of authority to direct events more authoritatively than their formal powers alone might allow.

THE BUREAUCRACY

To exercise the influence and leadership that most citizens and voters expect, the governor must distinguish himself on a crowded stage. The lieutenant governor, AG, comptroller of public accounts, commissioner of public lands, and agriculture commissioner are also elected statewide, and with the exception of the lieutenant governor, who is principally a legislative official, they are executive department heads. Hence, Texas is often said to have a **plural executive.** The lieutenant governor is paid a legislative salary of $7,200 a year, plus *per diem,* while the others draw a salary between $137,500 and $150,000.[10]

Plural executive
An executive branch featuring several officials with independent constitutional and legal authority.

The executive branch of Texas state government is made up of about 275 separate departments, agencies, boards, and commissions. Each executive branch office is headed in one of four ways: by elected or appointed single administrators, or by elected or appointed multimember boards or commissions. These executives direct the work of about 340,000 state employees. 750,000 Texans work in county and municipal governments.

Single-Elected Administrators

Like the governor, the lieutenant governor, AG, comptroller of public accounts, agriculture commissioner, and land commissioner are elected to renewable four-year terms.

Q3. What other statewide elected officials share power with the governor?

Lieutenant Governor. While the lieutenant governor is one of the top officials in Texas government, the office is almost exclusively legislative rather than executive. The lieutenant governor's legislative responsibilities were described in Chapter 6, so here we simply note that the lieutenant governor serves as acting governor when the governor is out of state or incapacitated. If the governor should resign or die, the lieutenant governor ascends to the governorship for the remainder of the open term. If the lieutenant governor becomes governor, and then dies, or is forced to resign, the Senate selects one of its own to serve as lieutenant governor until the next general election.

Lieutenant Governor David Dewhurst, formerly a U.S. Air Force officer, C.I.A. and State Department official, and Houston businessman and rancher, first won statewide office as Texas Land Commissioner in 1998. In 2002, Dewhurst was elected lieutenant governor by defeating former Democratic Comptroller John Sharp, 52 percent to 46 percent. Dewhurst was easily re-elected in 2006 and is widely expected to be a candidate for governor in 2010.

Attorney General. The Office of Attorney General (OAG) is mandated by the Texas Constitution. The AG is one of the state's most visible public officials. Texas Supreme Court Justice Greg Abbott was elected AG in 2002 and easily reelected in 2006. The OAG has 4,100 employees, more than 400 of them lawyers, in 70 offices located throughout the state. Most of the department's responsibilities involve legal representation of state agencies and civil administration.

The AG is the principal legal advisor and advocate for Texas state government. The AG represents the officers and agencies of Texas state government in court when they are party to a suit. Moreover, the AG's Opinion Committee issues opinions to the legislature and other state agencies concerning whether existing or proposed laws and regulations comply with the requirements of the U.S. and Texas Constitutions. While these opinions are not legally binding, they are seldom challenged or disobeyed.

Greg Abbott, Attorney General of Texas. *Photo courtesy of Office of the Attorney General of Texas.*

Most of the 38 divisions in the OAG engage in civil administration; they punish delinquency and enforce compliance with Texas laws and regulations. The OAG investigates and punishes violations of family and tax law, consumer and environmental law, antitrust legislation, and worker's compensation and Medicare fraud. Key divisions of the OAG include the Child Support Enforcement Division, the (Tax) Collections Division, the Consumer Protection Division, and the Cyber Crimes Unit.

Comptroller of Public Accounts. The Texas Constitution mandates a Comptroller of Public Accounts. Only a dozen other states have an elected comptroller; the rest have appointed comptrollers or state treasurers. The comptroller is the state's chief accountant, auditor, tax collector, and investment officer. Many credit the legendary Bob Bullock, Texas comptroller from 1975 to 1990 and lieutenant governor from 1990 to 1998, with modernizing the comptroller's office and making it one of the most powerful offices in Texas politics.[11] Carole Strayhorn was elected comptroller in 1998 and 2002. She ran unsuccessfully for governor in

2006. Susan Combs, Texas Agriculture Commissioner since 1998, was elected comptroller in 2006.

The key to the comptroller's political influence lies in her constitutional responsibility to produce a **revenue estimate** at the beginning of each legislative session. The revenue estimate may be updated during the session, but the legislature cannot pass and the governor cannot sign a budget that expends more money than the comptroller predicts will be available. Tensions can build between the governor, legislative leaders, and the comptroller because the comptroller tends to make conservative revenue estimates that other leaders feel make budgetary discussions more difficult than they need to be. In the 2003 and 2005 legislative sessions, these tensions led to open conflict between the governor, legislative leaders, and the comptroller. Tensions have eased since Susan Combs became comptroller.

Land Commissioner. Texas has had an elected land commissioner since independence. The land commissioner oversees the General Land Office. David Dewhurst was land commissioner before he was elected lieutenant governor in 2002. Jerry Patterson, a former state legislator, was elected land commissioner in 2002 and reelected in 2006.[12] He oversees 20.3 million acres of land and 2.2 million acres of Texas submerged lands (often called tidelands) extending three leagues (10.3 miles) into the Gulf. The land commissioner is responsible for leasing state land for oil and gas exploration, mining, and grazing. The commissioner is also responsible for maintaining the environmental quality of Texas lands, waters, wetlands, and coastal areas. Finally, the land commissioner administers the Veteran's Land Board, which provides veterans with loans and other assistance to purchase Texas public lands.

Agriculture Commissioner. The office of agriculture commissioner was established by statute in 1907. Governor Rick Perry first won statewide election as agriculture commissioner in 1990. Susan Combs, the first female agriculture commissioner, succeeded Rick Perry in 1998 and was easily reelected in 2002. Republican Todd Staples, a former member of the Texas House (1995–2001) and Senate (2001–2006), was elected agriculture commissioner in 2006 when Combs moved up to comptroller.

The agriculture commissioner oversees the Texas Department of Agriculture (TDA). The TDA has the dual responsibility of regulating and promoting Texas agricultural interests and products. As a regulator, the TDA enforces laws and regulations regarding land use, pesticide use, product certification, and inspection. The TDA also inspects and certifies measuring devices like gas pumps, electronic scanners, and scales. Finally, the TDA promotes Texas agricultural products through research and public education.

Revenue estimate The Texas Comptroller is empowered to make revenue estimates that the Texas state budget must stay within.

Single-Appointed Administrators

The governor, with the approval of two-thirds of the Texas Senate, is empowered to appoint several key officials of the executive branch to renewable two-year terms of office. While these are not officials of the first rank, they do oversee and administer important elements of Texas state government.

Secretary of State. The Secretary of State (SOS) is the chief election officer for Texas. The SOS interprets the election code, enforces election laws throughout the state, and maintains the voter rolls. Prior to election day, the SOS trains election officials and distributes election supplies. On election day, the SOS receives, reviews, and officially reports election results. Between elections, the SOS receives reports of campaign contributions and maintains a list of lobbyists registered with the state. Finally, the SOS issues corporate charters and licenses notary publics.

The incumbent Secretary of State, Esperanza "Hope" Andrade, was appointed by Governor Perry in 2008. In addition to the traditional responsibilities of the office, Secretary Andrade will serve as the governor's liaison on border and Mexican affairs.

Commissioner of Insurance. The Commissioner of Insurance (COI) monitors and regulates the insurance industry in Texas. Governor Perry named Mike Geeslin to be insurance commissioner in 2005. The commissioner's office educates the public on insurance matters, licenses agents and investigates complaints against them and their companies, and monitors the financial health of insurance companies operating in the state. In recent years, the COI has attempted to roll-back home and auto insurance rates.[13]

Commissioner of Health and Human Services. Governor Perry named Albert Hawkins to be Executive Commissioner of Health and Human Services (HHSC) in 2003. The executive commissioner has oversight and coordination and review responsibility over five health and welfare agencies, running 200 programs from 1,300 locations around the state. HHSC employs 48,000 workers. Each agency is administered by its own appointed board or commission. The commissioner's responsibility is to review their activities, identify overlaps and redundancies, and recommend efficiencies.[14]

Adjutant General. The Adjutant General, the top military official in Texas state government, is appointed by and reports to the governor. He oversees and manages the Army and Air National Guard and the Texas State Guard.

Elected Boards and Commissions

Q4. What roles do elected and appointed boards and commissions play in Texas?

Much of Texas state government is administered by multimember boards and commissions. The members of most boards and commissions are appointed by the governor with the consent of the Senate, but a few of the most important win their seats in partisan elections.

The most important elected board is the Texas Railroad Commission (TRC). The TRC was founded in 1891 to regulate the railroads. Over the course of the 20th century, the TRC's regulatory mandate was extended to cover the oil and natural gas industries. The modern TRC's principal responsibilities involve regulating oil and natural gas exploration, drilling, recovery, storage, and transportation while protecting the state's environment. Critics always contend that the commission leans toward exploiting natural resources rather than environmental protection.

The three members of the TRC are elected statewide to staggered six-year terms. One member is up for election every two years and the member next up for election serves as the commission chair. Elizabeth Jones, first appointed by Governor Perry in 2005, was elected to a full term in 2006. Michael Williams was appointed to the TRC by Governor George W. Bush in 1998. He won a full term in 2002 and another in 2008. Victor Carrillo, appointed by Governor Perry in 2003, won a full term in 2004.

The State Board of Education (SBE) is composed of fifteen persons, elected to four-year terms from single-member districts. The governor appoints a member of the SBE, currently Dr. Don McLeroy of Bryan, to serve a two-year term as chair. The SBE nominates three persons to be Commissioner of Education, from whom the governor, with the consent of the Senate, picks one to serve a four-year term. Governor Perry appointed Robert Scott in 2007 to be Texas Commissioner of Education.

The Commissioner of Education is the chief executive officer of the SBE and head of the 1,200 employee Texas Education Agency (TEA). The Commissioner, SBE, and TEA set and administer policies and standards for the state's 1,227 school districts and 7,900 individual campuses. Texas public schools employ 590,000 teachers and staff to teach more than 4.5 million students.[15]

Don McLeroy is chairman of the State Board of Education. The Associated Press.

Appointed Boards and Commissions

With the consent of two-thirds of the Senate, the governor appoints members to more than 275 agencies, boards, and commissions. Most gubernatorial appointees serve for a six-year renewable term without pay. The boards and commissions of Texas state government set general policy for their agencies, approve agency budget requests and major personnel decisions, hire the agency's executive director, and oversee agency implementation of state and federal law.

Governors try to appoint people who are accomplished and knowledgeable and who share their partisan and ideological commitments and principles. Surprisingly (or not), governors often find their appointees among their political contributors. One-third of Governor Perry's appointees between December 5, 2002 and February 22, 2006 were contributors. They contributed an average of $3,769 to his campaigns. The more important the board, the more likely the appointee was a contributor, and the more likely that the contribution was large. Appointees to the higher education governing boards gave an average of $10,616 to Governor Perry's campaigns.[16]

To serve on some boards and commissions, generous contributors will also need to have appropriate professional credentials. For example, there are 38 examining boards that license individuals to practice particular professions, from dentistry to home building. Service on these boards allows members of these professions to ensure that state law aids the profession and does it no harm. Finally, all gubernatorial appointments are scrutinized for appropriate regional, racial, ethnic, and gender balance.

TABLE 7.5
Gubernatorial Appointments: Gender, Race, and Ethnicity

	Texas Population	Ann Richards Administration	George Bush Administration	Rick Perry Administration
Male	50%	54%	69%	68%
Female	50%	46%	31%	32%
Anglo	49%	63%	80%	74%
Black	12%	15%	7%	9%
Hispanic	36%	20%	11%	15%

Source: Dallas Morning News, August 7, 2006, A2.

Table 7.5 shows that while white men still fill most seats on state boards and commissions, qualified female and minority candidates are present. Governor Ann Richards, a female Democrat, directed 46 percent of her appointments to women, 15 percent to blacks, and 20 percent to Hispanics. Governors Bush and Perry, both male Republicans, gave two-thirds of their appointments to men. Perry did somewhat better than Bush in regard to black and Hispanic appointments, giving 9 percent of appointments to blacks and 15 percent to Hispanics.

EXECUTIVE BRANCH REFORM

> **Q5.** What reforms do analysts propose for the executive branch?

Texas's plural executive and extensive use of independent boards and commissions has created a weak and diffuse executive branch. Historically, Texans have been wary of executive power. But today's Texas is the second most populous state in the Union, with three of the nation's ten largest cities. Some Texans wonder whether the powers of the governor and the structure of the executive branch are adequate. The most frequently mentioned reforms involve making the executive branch in Texas work more like the executive branch at the national level. The goal of these reforms would be to make Texas state government stronger and more hierarchical.

Advocates of reform contend that the governor's ability to energize and direct the executive branch would be dramatically enhanced by the adoption of several key reforms. First, candidates for governor, like candidates for the presidency, should pick their running mates. A lieutenant governor, selected by and working with the governor, would pull together the executive branch. The Senate would likely reduce the power of the lieutenant governor as a presiding officer, making him more of an executive than a legislative figure, but that would allow him or her to take on major tasks assigned by the governor.

Cabinet government
An executive branch in which the governor has broad appointment and budgetary powers.

Second, reformers argue that the governor, like the president, should have the power to appoint and remove executive branch department heads. These department heads would then form the governor's cabinet. **Cabinet government** would empower the governor to initiate, coordinate, and implement executive policy. Advocates of reform also propose that many of the state's boards and commissions be rolled into the major departments of the state government.

Finally, reformers argue that the governor, again like the president, should have the power to initiate and submit an executive budget. Today, the governor just goes through the motions of drafting a budget proposal because the legislature favors the budget drafted by the Legislative Budget Board. Reformers suggest that the Texas legislature must be able to consider and revise the governor's budget proposal, but that proposal should be the basis for the legislature's budget considerations.

CHAPTER SUMMARY

The Texas Constitution of 1876 established a plural executive and a diffuse executive branch. The governor of Texas shares leadership of the executive branch with five other statewide elected officials. Each is elected to a four-year term of office, each has his or her own constitutional or legislative authority, and each operates with a great deal of independence.

In addition to the major departments of Texas state government, there are approximately 275 agencies, boards, and commissions that administer important aspects of state government. While the governor appoints the members of these agencies, boards, and commissions, with the consent of two-thirds of the Senate, they are difficult to remove and are essentially independent once appointed. These bodies set policy within the area of their responsibility, select the executive directors of their agencies, and monitor the agencies' performance.

Critics of Texas state government call for reforms that would strengthen the governor's hand and streamline the executive branch. The strengthened governor and streamlined executive branch is often called cabinet government and employs the presidency as the model for the modern governorship.

KEY TERMS

Appointment power

Budget message

Cabinet government

Clemency

Line-item veto

Plural executive

Revenue estimate

Special session

State of the State message

Veto

SUGGESTED READINGS

Jimmy Banks, *Money, Marbles, and Chalk: The Wondrous World of Texas Politics* (Austin, TX: Texas Publishing Company, 1971).

Carolyn Barta, *Bill Clements: Texian to his Toenails* (Austin, TX: Eakin Press, 1996).

William R. Childs, *The Texas Railroad Commission: Understanding Regulation in America in the Mid-Twentieth Century* (College Station, TX: Texas A&M University Press, 2005).

Jean Houston Daniel, Price Daniel, and Dorothy Blodgett, *The Texas Governor's Mansion: A History of the House and Its Occupants* (Austin, TX: Texas State Library and Archives Commission, 1984).

Margaret R. Ferguson, *The Executive Branch of State Government: People, Process, and Politics* (Santa Barbara, Calif.: ABC CL10, 2006).

Kenneth E. Hendrickson, *The Chief Executives of Texas: From Stephen F. Austin to John B. Connally, Jr.* (College Station, TX: Texas A&M University, 1995).

Dave McNeely and Jim Henderson, *Bob Bullock: God Bless Texas* (Austin, TX: University of Texas Press, 2008).

WEB RESOURCES

http://www.nga.org Website of the National Governor's Association

http://www.governor.state/tx/us Website of the Governor of Texas

http://www.senate.state.tx.us Website of the Lieutenant Governor of Texas

http://www.oag.state.tx.us Website of the Attorney General of Texas

http://www.tsl.state.tx.us/trail/agencies.html List of all Texas stage agency websites

END NOTES

1. For a full list of Texas governors, lieutenant governors, statewide elected officials, and a description of key agencies, see the *Texas Almanac, 2008–2009*, pp. 466–471, 481–495.
2. Elizabeth C. Alvarez, *Texas Almanac: 2008–2009* (Dallas, TX: *Dallas Morning News*, 2008), pp. 466–467.
3. John J. Harrigan and David C. Nice, *Politics and Policy in States and Communities*, 9th ed. (New York: Pearson Longman, 2006), p. 222.
4. The governor's office provides a list of all the agencies, boards, and commissions to which the governor makes appointments and the number of appointments made to each. See http://www.governor.state.tx.us/divisions/appointments/positions.
5. Christy Hoppe, "Does Perry Really Have the Power?," *Dallas Morning News*, February 23, 2007, A1, A6. See also Corrie MacLaggan, "Abbott: Perry's HPV Mandate Does Not Carry the Weight of Law," *Austin American-Statesman*, March 13, 2007, A1.
6. Dennis L. Dresang and James L. Gosling, *Politics and Policy in American States and Communities*, 6th ed. (New York: Pearson Longman, 2008), p. 257.
7. House Research Organization, "Writing the State Budget," 80th Legislature, State Finance Report, no. 80-1, p. 8.
8. Kelley Shannon, AP, "Governor Wins Some, Loses Some in Past State of the State Proposals," *Austin American-Statesman*, February 5, 2007, A1.
9. Legislative Budget Board, *Fiscal Size-up, 2008–09 Biennium*, "Adjutant General's Department," pp. 287–288.
10. Robert T. Garrett, "Officials Beg Off Big Raises," *Dallas Morning News*, June 7, 2007, A1, A12.
11. Dave McNeely and Jim Henderson, "The Devil and Bob Bullock," *Texas Monthly*, January 2008, pp. 132–137, 190–198.
12. S.C. Gwynne, "This Land Is His Land," *Texas Monthly*, pp. 146–151, 254–259.
13. W. Gardner Selby, "Four Years After Emergency: Texas Still #1 in Homeowner Insurance," *Austin-American Statesman*, April 23, 2007, A1.
14. Carrie MacLaggan, "State Has Little to Show for Social Service Innovation Plan," *Austin-American Statesman*, April 25, 2007, A1.
15. http://www.tea.state.tx.us/sboe_history_duties.html
16. Jane Elliott, "1 in 3 Perry Donors Get Post," (This story title was later corrected to say one-third of appointees were donors, not one-third of donors got posts) *Houston Chronicle*, April 11, 2006, B2; see also Christy Hoppe, "In Perry Appointees: Dallas Lagging Across the Board," *Dallas Morning News*, August 7, 2006, A1, A2.

CHAPTER 8

The Judicial System in Texas

Focus Questions

Q1. How do we define law?

Q2. What is the difference between trial courts and appellate courts?

Q3. How are judges selected in Texas?

Q4. What role does money play in judicial selection?

Q5. Why are the incarceration and execution rates so high in Texas?

Though Article VI of the U.S. Constitution declares that the federal constitution, laws, and treaties are "the supreme law of the land," most legal activity occurs in state courts. The federal courts have a comparatively narrow jurisdiction, while state courts are responsible for resolving many of the disputes of daily life. The state courts are organized and empowered to resolve disputes that range from disagreements between homeowners and traffic violations to burglary and murder. The Texas courts alone process five times as many cases each year as do the federal courts.

Article III, section 2, of the U.S. Constitution provides that the judicial power of the federal courts "shall extend to all Cases . . . arising under this Constitution, the Laws of the United States, and Treaties made . . . under their Authority." Most cases that arise in the federal courts fall into three categories: "First are the criminal and civil cases that arise under the federal laws, including the Constitution." These include such crimes as bank robbery, counterfeiting, mail fraud, and violations of federal civil rights laws. "Second are cases in which the U.S. government is a party . . . Third are civil cases involving citizens of different states, if the amount in question is more than $75,000."[1] The federal court system, composed of the U.S. Supreme Court, the 13 federal courts of appeals, and the 94 federal district courts, employs about 1,000 judges to apply the U.S. Constitution and federal laws. In 2007, they handled about 1.3 million cases, over 800,000 of which were bankruptcy cases.

The Texas judicial system, composed of several types of municipal and county courts, as well as three levels of state courts, employs more than 3,268 judges.[2] In 2007, the Texas courts processed 10 million cases. More than 7.8 million cases moved through the municipal courts and nearly 85 percent of those were traffic cases. County and state courts dealt with most of the serious cases, in which significant fines and even jail time were possible. State courts touch the lives of more citizens than any other level or branch of government. Many of those lives are permanently changed.

In this chapter, we begin by defining law and discussing several key principles and concepts that underlie American legal thought. Second, we look at the organization and structure of the judicial system in Texas. Third, we ask why Texas incarcerates and executes more people than any other state in the union. Finally, we ask what concerns people have about law, the courts, and justice in Texas and whether reforms might be appropriate.

TEXAS LAW AND JUSTICE

Courts are dispute-resolution mechanisms. Some disputes are minor, squabbles between neighbors or between a home owner and a contractor, while others involve serious wrongdoing and violence. Courts resolve conflicts by publicly proving criminal and civil wrongdoing and applying relevant law. Judges are expected to be impartial, evenhanded, and fair. In fact, courts are carefully designed to reinforce the idea that justice is being done—think of the black robes, the formalities ("All rise, this honorable court is now in session."), and the liberal use of Latin (*writ of mandamus*—say what?).

Law Defined

Q1. How do we define law?

Courts apply the law. So before we study courts, we must define **law.** Political scientist Herbert Jacob has offered the best simple definition, saying that laws are "authoritative rules made by government."[3] A slightly more elaborate definition is offered by Henry Abraham, highlighting not just authoritative rulemaking, but enforcement. Abraham defines law as "rules of conduct . . . backed by the organized force of the community."[4]

Those civilized definitions even apply in Texas today, though it was not always so. One of the iconic figures of late 19th century Texas was Judge Roy Bean. Judge Bean described himself, accurately for a time, as the only "law west of the Pecos." Today, of course, legislatures make laws and executives enforce them. But when the normal course is breached, when society's authoritative rules of conduct are broken, or when disputes arise between citizens about what the law requires in a particular instance, the courts are charged to restore order and define justice. It is a critical social role and a very tall order.

Judge Roy Bean was the "Law West of the Pecos" from about 1882 to 1902.

Civil and Criminal Law

The broadest distinction within both U.S. and Texas law is between civil law and criminal law. They differ in the nature of the disputes that come before them, the parties involved, and the evidence required for decision. **Civil law** generally covers disputes between individuals, as in tort law (damage claims), family law (divorce and child custody), and contracts. The individual who brings the case is the **plaintiff** (sometimes called the complainant, because this is the person complaining) and the person defending against the plaintiff is the **defendant.** The goal of civil law is to protect individual and property rights and to hold persons to their obligations and responsibilities. Judges and juries resolve civil cases based on "a preponderance of the evidence" and then order the parties to fulfill their obligations, stop engaging in illegal activities, and/or pay a fine. Jail time is unusual in civil cases unless one party resists an initial court order.

Criminal law covers the "Law and Order," "CSI," "Without a Trace," stuff—murder, rape, assault, theft, and fraud. Under **criminal law** the complaining party is "the state" or "the people." The person charged is still referred to as the defendant. In criminal cases, especially those involving the most heinous crimes, punishments range beyond judgments and fines to long prison terms and even death. Hence, the standard of proof required for conviction is not just a "preponderance of the evidence," but guilt "beyond a reasonable doubt."

Surely the most famous example of the difference between criminal law and civil law and the penalties related to each involves the prosecutions of O.J. Simpson for the deaths of Nicole Brown Simpson and Ronald Goldman. In the criminal trial the charge was murder, and the penalties ranged up to imprisonment for life (Simpson was lucky he was tried in California and not in Texas). He was acquitted. He was later convicted on the charge of wrongful death in the civil trial, where that standard of evidence is not as great, and the jury awarded the Brown and Goldman families large monetary awards for damages. These outcomes, acquittal in the criminal case and conviction in the civil case, reflect the differences in standards of proof and punishment between criminal and civil law.

Courts and Jurisdiction

The structure of the Texas judicial system and the broad jurisdiction of the courts are set in the Texas Constitution. The broadest structural distinction among Texas courts is between trial courts and appellate courts. As we shall see more fully below, **trial courts** take evidence, hear testimony, determine guilt or innocence, and apply relevant law. **Appellate courts** do not take testimony or scrutinize facts; rather, they hear appeals from the losing party at the lower-court level claiming that procedures were unfair or the law wrongly interpreted and applied.

Civil law   Deals primarily with relations between individuals and organizations, as in marriage and family law, contracts, and property.

Plaintiff   The individual who brings a case before a court is called the plaintiff or complainant.

Defendant   The person defending against a charge in court.

Criminal law   Criminal law prohibits certain actions and prescribes penalties for those who engage in the prohibited conduct.

Q2. What is the difference between trial courts and appellate courts?

Trial court   Trial courts take evidence, hear testimony, determine guilt or evidence, and apply relevant law.

*ALEX GREGORY/*The New
Yorker

*"So he got a trophy for good sportsmanship—that
doesn't mean he won't go to law school."*

Appellate courts
Appellate courts review
trial court records to
insure that the trial was
fair and the law correctly
applied.

Jurisdiction   The
constitutional or legal
right of a court to hear
certain types of cases.

The Texas Constitution left it to the state legislature to determine how many courts there would be, how many judges would be assigned to each court, and precisely what kinds of cases the various courts would hear. A court's **jurisdiction** is its constitutional or legal mandate to hear certain kinds of cases. Some courts hear civil cases, some hear criminal cases, and some hear both. Other courts specialize in juvenile, drug, or probate cases and may hear either civil or criminal cases or both.

The Texas Bar

Texas judges and lawyers are required to be members of the Texas bar and to pay annual dues. The Texas bar is an agency of state government, a professional organization that looks out for the interests of the legal community, and a powerful interest group. Both judges and the lawyers that practice before them tend to be white men from comfortable, and often privileged, families. Of the 79,409 members of the Texas bar, about 85 percent are white and 69 percent are male. Still, the Texas bar is more diverse than it once was; today, about 31 percent are female, 7 percent are Hispanic, 4 percent are African American, 2 percent are Asian, and 0.3 percent are Native American.[5]

Texas judges are a good reflection of the broader bar. Texas judges are 69 percent male and 31 percent female. They are 80 percent Anglo, 15 percent Hispanic, 3.7 percent black, with both Asians and American-Indians registering under 1 percent.[6]

THE STRUCTURE OF TEXAS COURTS

Each of the 50 states, including Texas, uses municipal and county courts to handle minor civil and criminal matters. Above the local level, most states use a three-tier system of state courts, much like that of the federal

FIGURE 8.1   The Texas Courts

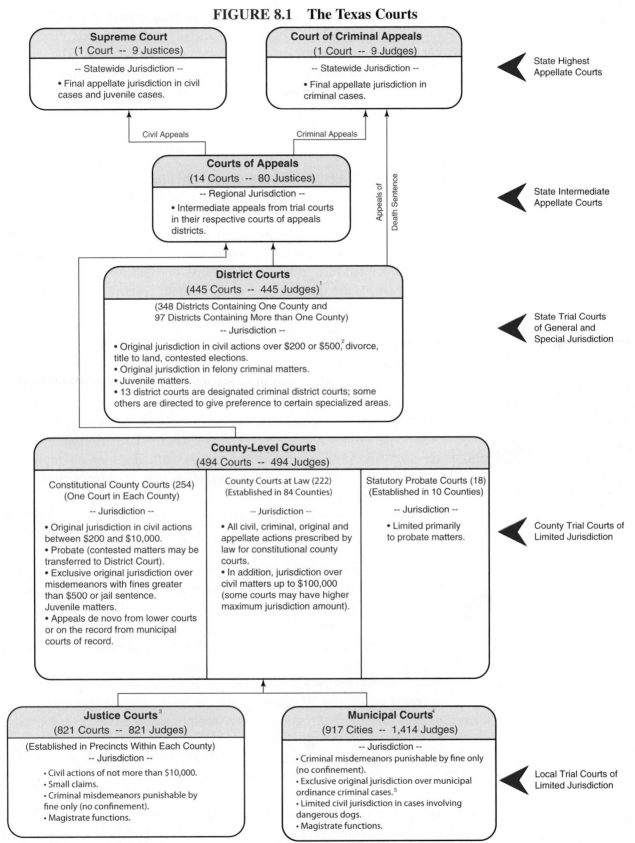

Source: Office of Court Administration, P.O. Box 12066, Austin, TX, 78711.

government, with a lower level of district or trial courts, a middle tier of appellate courts, and a high court that is usually called the Supreme Court. Texas and Oklahoma are the only states with dual high courts. The chart on page 131 shows that the top court for civil cases is the Texas Supreme Court, while the top court for criminal cases is the Texas Court of Criminal Appeals.

Trial Courts

Trial courts are the courts of original jurisdiction that actually try cases: they hear witnesses, accept evidence, assess guilt, and declare appropriate remedies and punishments. Texas has a number of trial courts, each with a geographic and a substantive jurisdiction. Local government courts are commonly called municipal courts or justice of the peace courts. County courts are either constitutional county courts or statutory county courts at law. District courts are the trial courts of the state system. Finally, there are a number of special courts, dealing with controversies relating to juveniles, domestic relations, and probate. The Texas penal code, summarized on page 133, describes the types of crimes recognized in Texas law.

Municipal Courts. Municipal courts deal with minor criminal matters. They are authorized to deal with all Class C misdemeanor traffic violations that occur within the city. Class C misdemeanors carry fines of no more than $500. These cases constitute approximately 85 percent of their case load. Municipal courts also try minor violations of state criminal law, such as petty theft and public intoxication, again with fines of no more than $500. Municipal courts have exclusive jurisdiction over enforcement of city ordinances, such as zoning and code enforcement, with fines up to $2,000. Finally, municipal courts have magistrate functions, including issuing arrest and search warrants and holding preliminary hearings in cases involving serious crimes.

There are about 917 municipal courts in Texas. In 2007, they disposed of just over 7.8 million cases. Most municipal court judges are appointed by city officials to two-year renewable terms. Compensation varies by size of city and court workload. These often are courts of non-record, meaning that no formal transcript is kept and if either party chooses to appeal the result, the case begins anew in the district courts.

Justice of the Peace Courts. Justice of the peace courts (also called justice courts or simply JP courts) have exclusive jurisdiction over minor civil matters and share jurisdiction over minor criminal matters, or Class C misdemeanors, with the municipal courts. Texas has 821 JP courts hearing about 3.1 million criminal cases and 400,000 civil cases each year. Justices of the peace are elected to four-year terms.

Traffic cases account for 70 percent of the criminal caseload of the justice courts. Justice courts also serve as small claims courts in Texas with exclusive jurisdiction over cases in which $200 or less is at issue and concurrent jurisdiction with county and district courts in cases involving up to $5,000. Like municipal courts, justice courts also issue arrest and search warrants and handle preliminary hearings. Finally, JPs can act as coroners.

Texas Penal Code: Crimes and Punishments

Offenses are designated as misdemeanor or felonies.

Classification	Example	Jail or Prison Term	Maximum Fine
Misdemeanors (classified into three categories, from less to more serious)			
Class C Misdemeanor	Theft under $50 Most traffic violations Public intoxication Simple assault	None	$500
Class B Misdemeanor	Theft over $50 Prostitution 1st offense DOI	180 days	$2,000 or both
Class A Misdemeanor	Theft over $500 Assault with injury Resisting arrest	1 year	4,000 or both
Felonies (classified into five categories from less to more serious)			
State Jail Felony	Theft over $1,500 Auto theft Forgery	180 days to 2 years	$10,000 or both
Third Degree Felony	Involuntary Manslaughter Kidnapping Escape	2–10 years	$10,000 or both
Second Degree Felony	Theft over $100,00 Burglary of a home Sexual assault	2–20 years	$10,000 or both
First Degree Felony	Theft over $200,000 Murder Aggravated Sexual assault	5–99 years	$10,000 or both
Capital Felony	Murder of a police officer Murder of a child Serial murder	Life without parole or death	

Source: Texas Penal Code, Title 3, Chapter 12, "Punishments."
http://tlo2.tlc.state.tx.us/statutes/statutes.htm

County Courts. Texas has two types of county courts: constitutional county courts, about which we will hear more in Chapter 9, and statutory county courts at law. The Texas Constitution mandates a county court that is presided over by a county judge in each of the state's 254 counties. In the state's rural counties, these constitutional county courts have administrative responsibilities as well as judicial responsibilities for criminal and civil matters. In criminal matters, county courts have original jurisdiction over Class A and B misdemeanors punishable by more than a $500 fine and/or imprisonment. They also have appellate jurisdiction over cases initially tried in the municipal and JP courts. Their civil jurisdiction extends to cases involving up to $5,000 and probate (verifying wills).

In 30 of the state's most populous counties, where the county courts perform almost exclusively administrative responsibilities, the state legislature has created 222 statutory county courts at law. The jurisdiction of county courts at law varies depending upon the initiating stature. Some have broad criminal and civil jurisdiction, while others specialize in civil, criminal, probate, or juvenile matters. Judges of the constitutional county courts need only be well-informed in the law, while judges of the statutory county courts at law must be lawyers. Both are elected to four-year terms by the voters of the county. County courts and county courts at law handle nearly one million cases each year; 70 percent of their cases are criminal, 20 percent are civil, while the remaining 10 percent are juvenile, probate, and mental health cases.

District Courts. District courts are the top trial courts in Texas. They have both civil and criminal jurisdiction, though their case loads are two-thirds civil and one-third criminal. Their civil case load leans heavily to family law, especially divorce and child custody, as well as state tax matters, land disputes, workers' compensation claims, and personal injury suits. Criminal cases include all felonies for which jail time might be assessed.

The state legislature creates new district courts as the judicial workload requires. Today there are 445 district courts in Texas. Some populous counties have several dozen district courts while several lightly populated counties often share one district court. District court judges run in partisan elections for four-year terms. Vacancies that occur between elections are filled by gubernatorial appointment. Salaries of district court judges now stand at $132,500. Texas district courts handle more than 900,000 cases each year.

TABLE 8.1

Let's Compare: What the Ten Most Populous States Pay Their Judges

With their 2005 raises, Texas state judges went from being among the least well-paid judges in the country to being better paid than the national average, though still not as well-paid as most judges in comparably large and complex states. Of the ten largest states, only Ohio and North Carolina consistently pay their judges less than Texas. Clearly, California and Illinois are the pace-setters on judicial compensation, paying their judges an average of 15 percent more than Texas.

	Highest Court	**Appellate Court**	**District Court**
California	$210,000	$196,000	$172,000
Texas	**$150,000**	**$145,000**	**$140,000**
New York	$151,200	$144,000	$136,700
Florida	$161,000	$153,000	$145,000
Pennsylvania	$175,000	$165,000	$152,000
Illinois	$189,000	$178,000	$163,000
Ohio	$138,000	$128,000	$118,000
Michigan	$164,610	$151,441	$139,919
North Carolina	$134,000	$128,000	$121,000
Georgia	$162,000	$161,000	$117,000
50 State Average	**$143,669**	**$139,694**	**$128,953**

Source: National Center for State Courts, *"Survey of Judicial Salaries,"* vol. 32, no. 2, as of July 1, 2007, p. 11.

Appellate Courts

Appellate courts review the work of trial courts to insure that legal rules were followed and the law correctly applied. Appellate courts do not hear witnesses or review evidence; they review the written record of lower-court deliberations and decisions and the written briefs and recorded oral arguments of lawyers challenging and defending the decisions of the lower court. The Texas appellate courts hear all civil and criminal cases, except those criminal cases in which the death penalty has been levied, which go directly to the Court of Criminal Appeals.

Texas has 14 appellate court districts served by 80 judges. Each court has from three to 13 judges, elected to staggered six-year terms, in partisan elections. Court of Appeals judges are paid $137,500 annually. The judges in each court hear cases in three-judge panels or en banc (all together). Appellate court decisions are made by a simple majority of the judges hearing the case. Texas' appellate courts hear about 11,300 cases each year; evenly divided between criminal and civil cases.

Dual High Courts

The Federal Government and 48 of the 50 states cap their judicial systems with a single high court, usually called the Supreme Court. Texas and Oklahoma employ dual high courts. In Texas, the Supreme Court (created in 1845) is the highest appellate court for civil matters, while the Court of Criminal Appeals (created in 1891) is the top court for criminal matters. The Supreme Court is composed of a chief justice and eight associate justices, while the Court of Criminal Appeals is composed of a presiding judge and eight serving judges. All are elected statewide in partisan elections to six-year staggered terms. Vacancies are filled by gubernatorial appointment. Most cases are heard by all nine justices or judges, though some cases are heard by three-judge panels. High court judges are paid $150,000 annually.

Texas Supreme Court. The Texas Supreme Court hears only civil cases and issues formal opinions in about 150 cases each year. While these formal opinions receive most of the attention, the Supreme Court is also empowered to issue writs of mandamus or orders to corporations, persons, and public officials (except the governor) to take certain actions. The court takes formal action on 800 to 1,000 matters each year. In 2007 the Supreme Court began offering live video webcasts of oral arguments on its website.[7]

The Supreme Court also has important administrative responsibilities. It sets judicial rules and policies for all Texas courts, including the criminal courts, and it has the exclusive right to approve new law schools in the state. It appoints the Board of Legal Examiners whose responsibility it is to develop, administer, and score the bar examination by which aspiring lawyers earn the right to practice law in Texas. The Texas Supreme Court issues law licenses and oversees the Texas bar.

Texas Court of Criminal Appeals. The court of criminal appeals hears only criminal cases. These cases, except death penalty cases that come directly from the district courts, come on appeal from the 14 appellate courts. Convictions in death penalty cases must be reviewed by the court of criminal appeals. Lawyers for convicted defendants argue that the trial and appeals court judges erred in the way the cases were handled or in the application of Texas law. The court of criminal appeals decides about 250 to 300 cases each year and writes about 500 to 600 majority, minority, concurring, and dissenting opinions.

SELECTION OF TEXAS JUDGES AND JURIES

> **Q3.** How are judges selected in Texas?

How are judges and juries selected to play their critical roles in the judicial system? Federal judges are nominated by the president, with the advice and consent of the Senate, for lifetime appointments. Lifetime appointments are thought to allow federal judges to ignore partisanship and to apply their unbiased judgment. Texas judges are viewed somewhat differently; they are expected to be competent legal practitioners, independent and fair-minded, but also responsive to political and social expectations.

Different states seek to balance judicial competence, independence, and responsiveness in different ways. Some states use gubernatorial appointment of state judges, like presidential appointment of federal judges, to assure judicial competence. Others seek to balance competence and independence with responsiveness through nonpartisan elections. Others, including Texas, focus on responsiveness by subjecting most judges to partisan elections and all of the public speaking, campaigning, and fund raising that go along with it. Still others seek to balance competence, independence, and responsiveness through a system of initial appointment of judges followed by retention elections.[8]

Texas Judges

Texas has 3,268 judges, more than any other state. Though municipal judges are usually appointed by city officials, every other Texas judge is elected. Texas is one of only twelve states to elect most of its judges in partisan elections. Over the past decade, Texas legislators have introduced several bills calling for nonpartisan election of trial court judges and merit selection of appellate court judges. All of these bills have failed, but the debate is sure to continue.

Partisan Elections. Partisan election of judges puts a heavy burden on Texas voters. Voters have a difficult time assessing the credentials, relevant experience, and personal qualities of judicial candidates. It is quite common for voters to confront a ballot that asks them to decide more judicial races than executive or legislative races. Voters frequently respond either by declining to vote for the lesser judicial offices or by voting a straight partisan ticket. Advocates of partisan election of judges contend that even when voters do not know much about the particular candidates, they usually know whether they prefer Democrat or Republican judges. Opponents argue that it would be far better to have a well-informed panel screen potential judges and make recommendations to the governor or some other responsible appointing authority.

The Missouri Plan. The **Missouri plan** or merit system for selecting judges tries to balance judicial qualifications with judicial independence and accountability. Fifteen states use the Missouri plan for selecting trial judges and twenty-one use it for selecting appellate judges. The Missouri plan begins with a panel of eminent legislators, judges, law professors, and citizens reviewing judicial candidates and nominating the best among them to the governor. The governor makes an initial appointment, usually for four years, after which the judge must stand in a retention election. If retained by majority vote, the judge serves a six- or seven-year term. Under the Missouri plan, qualifications determine the initial appointment of judges, but voters are allowed to remove judges of whom they disapprove.

Missouri plan To balance competence and accountability, governor's appoint judges who later stand in retention elections.

Texas's Mixed Appointive/Elective System. The Texas Constitution and laws call for election of most judges, but, in fact, nearly 50 percent of judges first come to the bench by appointment. Judges often resign before the end of their terms, others become ill, and some die. County commissioner's courts are allowed to fill vacancies in J.P. and county courts while the governor is allowed to fill vacancies in the district, appellate, and high courts. These appointed judges serve to the end of the term they are appointed to and then they must stand for election if they wish to continue in office. A sitting judge is rarely defeated for re-election; in fact, about 80 percent of Texas judges are unopposed for re-election.

Texas Juries

Judges are half of the judicial system, juries are the other half (assuming you do not count the lawyers and the crooks). The place of juries in the American judicial system is highlighted by the phrase "a jury of your peers." The idea is that a citizen's liberty is more secure if it rests in the hands of other citizens than if it rests in the hands of government officials. Citizens participate in two kinds of juries: grand juries and petit (or trial) juries.

Grand Juries. Grand juries are charged with deciding whether enough evidence exists against a person to charge him with a serious crime and to proceed to trial. In Texas, grand juries are selected by district judges to serve three- to six-month terms. Most district judges use a three- to five-person panel of jury commissioners to nominate a pool of potential grand jurors from which the district judge picks twelve. The **grand jury** hears the evidence relating to a particular crime presented by the district attorney and then votes on whether it is sufficient to proceed to trial. If at least nine grand jurors vote yes, an indictment (criminal charge) is issued and a trial is scheduled.

Grand jury A grand jury assesses a prosecutor's evidence against a potential defendant to be sure it is sufficient to proceed to trial.

Jury trial   A trial conducted before a jury of citizens who hear testimony, weigh evidence, and assess guilt.

Trial Juries. Texans have the right to a **jury trial** in all felony cases and in most major civil cases. As a practical matter, most legal disputes are resolved through mediation or plea bargaining, and those that do go to trial are usually, by agreement of the parties, conducted before a judge without a jury. At both the county-court and the district-court levels, less than one percent of trials are conducted before a jury. When juries are present, they are responsible for weighing evidence and determining guilt. Texas jurors are selected from driver's license and voter registration rolls; they must be at least 18, a U.S. citizen, and not an indicted or convicted felon.

Texas instituted reforms intended to improve jury participation and jury selection. First, juror pay was increased in 2006, the first increase in 52 years, from $6 a day to $40 a day. Juror participation had fallen below 20 percent in both Dallas and Houston. The hope was that the improved pay would encourage more people to show up for jury duty when they are called.[9] It has not worked. Three-quarters of people continue to ignore jury summons. Second, the U.S. Supreme Court ruled in 2005 that Texas prosecutors had illegally excused black jurors in the 1986 murder trial of Thomas Miller-El. The Texas Supreme Court is considering changes to jury selection procedures to insure that juries are unbiased.[10]

ARE THE TEXAS COURTS JUST?

Most Texans believe that judges should be competent, independent, and accountable. Yet many close observers of the Texas judiciary believe that judges are too accountable, especially to those who fund their campaigns, to be truly independent. Texas lawyers and judges laugh nervously at the jibe that Texas offers "all the justice you can afford."[11]

SARGENT © 2005 Austin American-Statesman. *Reprinted with permission of UNIVERSAL PRESS SYNDICATE. All rights reserved.*

Money in Judicial Elections

Citizens and voters know that governors and legislators are partisan politicians. They represent political parties and organized interests and they raise money from those interests to conduct their campaigns. Politicians, once elected, are expected, within limits, to serve the partisan and special interests that helped them win office. Texas judges are expected to stand for election in partisan contests, to raise campaign cash from friendly interests, and to treat everyone who comes before them in court fairly and equally. While there are always concerns about the undue influence of money in politics, those concerns are simply much greater in regard to judges.[12]

> Q4. What role does money play in judicial selection?

Voters, lawyers, and judges all believe that money affects the openness and fairness of the courts. A ten-year legal battle between Bob Perry Homes, owned by Bob Perry, the top Republican contributor in Texas (in fact, in the nation in 2006), and a Mansfield, Texas, couple named Bob and Jane Cull highlight the issues. The Culls, believing that their Perry-built home was defective, initially thought to sue Perry, but changed their mind and sought arbitration. The arbitrator awarded the Culls $800,000, which was upheld in district and appellate courts. Perry appealed to the Texas Supreme Court. Perry had made $260,000 in political contributions to the nine Republican judges of the Supreme Court. (Question to students—if you were the Culls, how would you like your chances?)

Andrew Wheat of Texans for Public Justice said: "What is shocking is that the judges that took all this money have agreed to hear Perry's appeal of a lemon-home case—one that he already lost in front of an arbitrator and two Texas courts. It's three strikes and you're out in the Texas justice system—unless you own the league."[13] In May 2008, the Texas Supreme Court ruled in favor of Mr. Perry, overturning the Culls' $800,000 award.

The Texas legislature attempted, ineffectually, to address the role of money in judicial elections in the 1995 Judicial Campaign Fairness Act (JCFA). The JCFA limits the amount that individuals, law firms, and PACs can contribute to judicial candidates and forbids corporate contributions entirely. Individuals are allowed to give up to $5,000 to statewide judicial candidates, and law firms are allowed to give up to $30,000. Candidates are restricted to accepting no more than $300,000 from PACs. Candidates who accept the JCFA guidelines also accept spending limits tied to the population of the district in which they are running. The spending limits range from $100,000 for trial courts in districts of less than 250,000 people; to $500,000 for court of appeals candidates in districts of more than a million; to $2 million for candidates in statewide races for seats on the Texas Supreme Court and Court of Criminal Appeals. The JCFA guidelines are voluntary and a candidate can opt out by a simple public declaration (if you are not laughing, you do not yet understand Texas politics). One recent study by the public interest group, Texans for Public Justice, entitled "Lowering the Bar: Lawyers Keep Texas Appeals Judges on Retainer," reported that 72 percent of the campaign contributions to the judges of the 14 appeals courts came from lawyers and law firms with interests before the courts.[14]

The death chamber in Huntsville, Texas is the most active in the nation. *Pat Sullivan/*The Associated Press

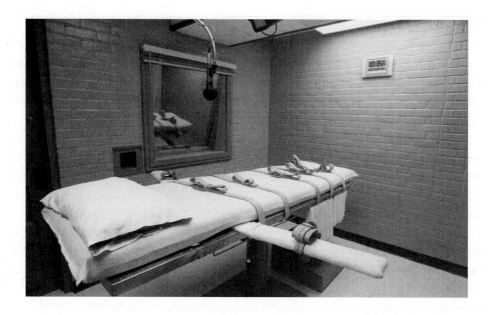

Incarceration and Execution in Texas

Q5. Why are the incarceration and execution rates so high in Texas?

We do not have the time or the space to explore Texas incarceration and execution rates in detail, but we can demonstrate that both are higher, a lot higher, than any other state in the nation. Table 8.2 compares the total population, prison population, and the number of inmates per 100,000 people in the nation's ten most populous states. The national average is 533 prisoners per 100,000. Incarceration rates vary a great deal by state, but Texas is far higher than any other state.

Though California has 36 million citizens to 23 million for Texas, Texas has more people in prison than does California. The Texas incarceration rate is 734 persons per 100,000 of population; the California rate is 482 per 100,000. Even more strikingly, New York, the third most populous state, with 19.3 million people to 23 million for Texas, has a prison population only about 45 percent the size of Texas' prison population. Several of the nation's largest states, including Pennsylvania (366), New York (324), and Illinois (355) incarcerate people at less than half the Texas (734) rate.

What explains these high incarceration rates? Does it make sense to believe that Texans are much more disorderly and violent than say the good people of California, New York, and Pennsylvania? OK, maybe so, but twice as disorderly and violent! A better explanation is that Texas legislators have made more things illegal and attached more jail time to more of them than have legislators in other states. This not only involves more Texans in the criminal justice system, but it is extremely expensive. The average cost of holding a prisoner for one year in a Texas prison about $20,000, though some point out that the cost of having them on the street might be higher.[15]

Texas does not just put people in prison; it uses capital punishment more frequently than any other state in the nation. In the early 1970s, the U.S. Supreme Court suspended capital punishment and required the states to clarify the procedures and circumstances for its use. Since the death penalty was reinstated in 1976 and executions resumed in 1982, 1,117 people have been executed in the U.S. Well over one-third of those executions—411—have occurred in Texas. No other state employs the death penalty with anything like the frequency that Texas does: Virginia is second (102), followed by Oklahoma (87), Missouri (66), and Florida (65).

Twelve states do not employ the death penalty, 38 do. Ten states declared a moratoria on the death penalty in 2006, most of the rest declared a moratoria in 2007 as the Supreme Court reviewed whether lethal injections constituted cruel and unusual punishment. Texas did not pause. In 2006, Texas executed 24 persons, fully 45 percent of the 53 persons executed in the U.S. that year. In 2007, Texas executed 26 of 42, fully 60 percent of those executed in the U.S.

What explains the high incarceration and execution rates in Texas? First, while Texas stands apart, it does not stand alone. High incarceration rates, and even more distinctively, high execution rates, are a southern phenomenon. Of the 1,117 executions carried out in the U.S. since 1976, 919 have been carried out in the South, compared to 127 in the Midwest, 67 in the West, and just 4 in the Northeast. Second, southern judiciaries reflect the traditionalistic political culture of the region, with its focus on elite control, law and order, and security for persons and property.

TABLE 8.2
The Ten States with the Largest Prison Populations

State	State Population	Prison Population	Inmates/100,000
California	36,458,000	176,059	482
Texas	**23,508,000**	**172,626**	**734**
New York	19,306,000	63,536	324
Florida	18,090,000	95,078	526
Illinois	12,832,000	45,565	355
Pennsylvania	12,441,000	45,563	366
Ohio	11,478,000	50,418	439
Michigan	10,096,000	50,648	502
Georgia	9,364,000	53,226	568
North Carolina	8,857,000	38,179	431
National	**299,398,000**	**1,595,034**	**533**

Sources: U.S. Census Bureau, *Statistical Abstract of the United States: 2008*, Table No. 12, "Resident Population—States, 2006," p. 20. Bureau of Justice Statistics, "Prison Inmates at Midyear 2007," Table 2, p. 3.

TABLE 8.3
The States That Use the Death Penalty Most Frequently 1976 to Present

State	Executions	State	Executions
Texas	**411**	North Carolina	43
Virginia	102	Georgia	42
Oklahoma	87	South Carolina	39
Missouri	66	Alabama	38
Florida	65	Louisiana	27

Source: Death Penalty Information Center, *"Number of Executions by State and Region Since 1976,"* last updated August 6, 2008. *http://www.deathpenaltyinfo.org/*

JUDICIAL REFORM IN TEXAS

Three aspects of the judicial culture in Texas seem to cry out for reconsideration and reform. The first two, judicial selection and money, are closely related and potential reform should take both into account. The third, capital punishment, sees Texas strikingly, even radically, outside the national mainstream.

Most states elect at least some of their judges. Texas elects all of its judges, above the level of municipal judge, and fundraising rules are essentially discretionary. Hence, Texas judicial races are funded, not by regular citizens generally, but by interested parties—mostly lawyers and PACs. Moderate reform might entail movement in the direction of the Missouri system for judicial selection and real limits to campaign contributions in judicial races. Perhaps the governor might make initial judicial appointments based on an expert panel's professional assessment of credentials. Sitting judges might then stand in retention elections. Removing judges from the partisan electoral process would also allow strict limits on campaigning and advertising since they would be running in retention elections rather than against other candidates.

Texas must also take a serious look at its use of capital punishment. Texas has executed one-third of all persons executed in the U.S. since 1976. More sobering still, when many states instituted death penalty moratoria in 2006 and 2007 as the Supreme Court considered whether the three drug cocktail used in executions was unconstitutionally cruel, Texas first declined to institute a moratorium and did so only grudgingly as the Supreme Court began staying executions. In 2006, Texas conducted 45 percent (24 of 53) of all executions in the U.S., and in 2007, fully 60 percent (26 of 42) of all executions. Any state, even Texas, so far out of step with its sister states must ask itself why.

CHAPTER SUMMARY

The U.S. Constitution declares federal law to be "supreme" over state law, but, as a practical matter, most legal activity takes place in state courts and under state law. Federal courts deal with violations of the U.S. Constitution, federal laws and treaties, and disputes between citizens of different states. State courts deal with violations of their constitutions and laws. These cover most of the legal requirements and controversies of daily life, including tort law, family law, contracts, zoning, and traffic.

Texas has organized its judicial system in seven types of local, county, and state courts. Local government courts are municipal courts and JP courts. County courts are constitutional county courts and legislative county courts at law. The state trial courts are called district courts. Above the district courts are 14 courts of appeals and two high courts. The Texas Supreme Court hears civil matters and the Texas Court of Criminal Appeals hears criminal matters.

Three questions are frequently raised about Texas courts, judges, and justice. One is whether partisan elections are the best way to select judges. Another is whether the amount of money circulating in Texas judicial elections biases the judicial system in favor of contributors. And the third is whether Texas incarcerates and executes more people than is either advisable or just. All of these questions remain open and will be disputed for years to come.

KEY TERMS

Appellate courts	Grand jury	Missouri plan
Civil law	Jurisdiction	Plaintiff
Criminal law	Jury trial	Trial courts
Defendant	Law	

SUGGESTED READINGS

Kyle Cheek and Anthony Champagne, *Judicial Politics in Texas: Politics, Money, and Partisanship in State Courts* (New York: Peter Lang, 2005).

John Hubner, *Last Chance in Texas: The Redemption of Criminal Youth* (New York: Random House, 2005).

Jack K. Selden, *Texas Justice: The Life and Times of the Third District Court of Texas* (Palestine, TX: Clacton Press, 1997).

Robert M. Utley, *Lone Star Justice: The First Century of the Texas Rangers* (New York: Oxford University Press, 2002).

Robert Walker, *Penology for Profit: A History of the Texas Prison System* (College Station, TX: Texas A&M University Press, 1988).

WEB RESOURCES

http://www.courts.state.tx.us Organization of the Texas judiciary

http://www.texlaw.com Information on recent Texas court cases

http://www.Texasbar.com Texas Bar Association

http://www.deathpenaltyinfo.org Death Penalty Information Center

http://www.cjpc.state.tx.us Texas Criminal Justice Policy Center

END NOTES

1. Lawrence Baum, *The Supreme Court,* 9th ed. (Washington, D.C.: Congressional Quarterly Press, 2007), pp. 5–6.
2. Annual Statistical Report for the Texas Judiciary, Fiscal Year 2007, Office of Court Administration, December 2007, pp. 31–55. See http://www.courts.state.tx.us/pubs/AR2007/published-annual-report-2007.pdf
3. Herbert Jacob, *Law and Politics in the United States* (Boston: Little, Brown, 1986), 6–7.
4. Henry J. Abraham, *The Judicial Process,* 7th ed. (New York: Oxford University Press, 1998), 147.

5. State Bar of Texas, Department of Research and Analysis, Annual Report on the Status of Women and Racial/Ethnic Minorities in the State Bar of Texas (2006–2007), May 1, 2007, p. 2.

6. Annual Statistical Report of the Texas Judiciary, p. 13.

7. Mark Trachtenberg, "Webcasts Open a Window to the Texas Supreme Court," *Houston Chronicle,* March 30, 2007, B11. See http://www.supreme.courts.state.tx.us/.

8. Former Supreme Court Justice Sandra Day O'Connor, "How to Save Our Courts." *Parade,* February 24, 2008, pp. 4–5.

9. Michael Grabell, "Majority Called for Jury Duty Aren't Showing Up," *Dallas Morning News,* December 27, 2006, 9B.

10. Warren Richey, "Court Hits Jury Race Bias," *Christian Science Monitor,* January 14, 2005.

11. Ralph Blumenthal, "DeLay Case Turns Spotlight on Texas Judicial System," *New York Times,* November 8, 2005, A19.

12. Former Supreme Court Justice Sandra Day O'Connor," Justice for Sale: How Special Interest Money Threatens the Integrity of Our Courts," WSJ.com Opinion Journal, *Wall Street Journal,* November 15, 2007.

13. Wayne Slater, "Couple's Dream Home a 10-Year Legal Nightmare," *Dallas Morning News,* January 21, 2007, A1, A24.

14. See Texans for Public Justice website at http://www.tjp.org/press_releases/.

15. Gray and Hanson, *Politics in the American States,* p. 273.

CHAPTER 9

Local Government in Texas

Focus Questions

Q1. What is the legal relationship between state and local governments?

Q2. How important are counties in contemporary Texas government?

Q3. What are the key differences between general-law and home-rule cities?

Q4. Why do most Texas cities conduct elections within single-member districts?

Q5. Why are there so many special district governments in Texas?

Only recently have social scientists, urban planners, and the best public officials begun to think more clearly and systematically about the importance of local communities and their governments. Each of us lives in the United States and in the state of Texas. We all live under the national security umbrella of the U.S. and within the open entrepreneurial culture of Texas. Still, there are vast differences between and among Texas communities. Some Texans live in the impoverished *colonias* of the lower Rio Grande Valley while others live in the beauty and security of gated communities. Locality, place, and community provide the contexts for our lives.

Think for a moment about the myriad ways in which the most attractive community you know differs from an average community, let alone the least attractive community you've seen. The most attractive communities are not just clean and safe, they are interesting and vibrant, offering good schools, good jobs, and all the amenities that add up to a good quality of life. They are places you want to be.[1]

Local officials and the governments in which they serve are responsible for the streets that you drive on every day, the schools that most of you went to as children, and the parks where you walk your dog. And if you want to shake your fist at government, you can easily do so—at the local school board meeting, at the planning commission, or at city hall. Local

> **Q1.** What is the legal relationship between state and local governments?

Claudia Fowler, a former school board member, told an April 2005 school board meeting: "I think Wilmer-Hutchins is being picked on." *MEI-CHUN JAU/Staff Photographer/The Dallas Morning News*

governments are open to citizen input and influence in ways that state and national government simply are not and cannot be.

Despite the importance of local governments and all that they do, they have less independence and authority than most people think. Most Americans assume that there are three levels of government in American federalism—national, state, and local—each with its own powers and responsibilities. But this common assumption is simply wrong. State governments define and limit the structure, resources and responsibilities of local governments. Not surprisingly, local governments spend a lot of time and money trying to influence what state government demands, allows, and forbids them to do.

In this chapter we begin by asking how Texas organizes and empowers its county and municipal governments. We will see that while the structure and powers of county governments are explicitly defined in the Texas Constitution, municipalities, depending upon their size, have some flexibility in choosing their form of government. Finally, we will describe the special district governments that operate in Texas and ask what reforms might make Texas local governments more effective and responsive.

TEXAS AS A FEDERAL SYSTEM

Dillon's Rule   A legal concept holding that local governments are the creatures or creations of state governments.

The U.S. and each of the fifty states, including Texas, are sovereign governments. The U.S. and Texas have their own constitutions and their own chief executives, legislatures, and high courts, all making critical decisions. Texas local governments do not have their own constitutions; they have only those powers granted to them by the state's constitution and laws. In fact, according to a long-standing legal principle known as **Dillon's Rule,** local governments are "creatures of state government."

The Texas Constitution gives the state the power to create, revise, and reform its county and municipal governments. In the 19th century, Texas state government authorized the creation of new cities, revised their charters, increased the number of counties, and redrew their boundaries as population growth and economic development required. In the 20th century, as the number of counties stabilized and cities grew in size and complexity, the political relationship between the state and its cities and counties evolved and matured.

While local governments are constitutionally and legally dependent on state government, they enjoy considerable political influence over it. While governors and legislative leaders often take a statewide view, the average state legislator thinks of him or herself much more as a local official than as a state official. In Austin full-time only five months every other year, state legislators tend to work closely with the local officials from their area.

Perhaps the most interesting recent example of local governments and officials working to thwart state action that they believed would be detrimental to them involved property tax appraisal caps. Property tax revenues are critical to local governments, so state attempts to limit these revenues met with broad opposition from local governments. The Texas Constitution limits property tax appraisal increases to no more than 10 percent a year. Since 1997, Governors Bush and Perry, taxcutters both, have urged legislation to limit the maximum annual increase in property tax appraisals to 3 to 5 percent, unless more was approved by a vote of the affected public. The legislature has taken up a series of bills over more than a decade, but all were opposed by the Texas Association of Counties (TAC) and the Texas Municipal League (TML) and none have passed.

In an attempt to break through this impasse, Governor Perry appointed a 15-member Texas Task Force on Appraisal Reform in 2006. The task force was chaired by Tom Pauken, a former chair of the Texas Republican Party and an anti-tax hawk. In charging the task force, Perry argued that "if people are going to pay higher taxes at the local level, it ought to come with a public vote and not by . . . the appraiser's pen."[2] Local government officials argued that lowering the cap would limit their ability to fund construction and services, particularly in fast growing areas.

Knowing the sentiment in the legislature, Perry's task force declined to recommend reducing the cap to 5 percent, but they did advocate limiting local government spending growth and allowing counties a half cent sales tax increase if they used the money to reduce property taxes. Neither idea passed and Pauken knew why. He blamed "the vigorous opposition of the Texas Municipal League and the Texas Association of Counties; . . . and unfortunately they had support from a number of legislators, including some Republicans."[3]

Still, the fight is not over. Perry continues to support appraisal reform and both Speaker Craddick and Lieutenant Governor Dewhurst assigned committees to study the issue in preparation for the 2009 regular session. Who should decide issues of local government taxing and spending? Should it be local officials or state officials? The Texas Constitution and law say state officials, but so far shrewd politics has allowed local governments to fight off tighter caps. Let's see what local governments in Texas actually do.

THE COUNTIES

Texas has more counties—254—than any other state (see Table 9.1, Let's Compare). Texas counties were originally intended to serve an overwhelmingly rural population that needed only occasional access to government services.[4] As the settlement line moved west, county lines were drawn and redrawn to insure that county government was accessible to most citizens. The Texas Constitution mandates the structure and powers of county government, firmly limiting both.

TABLE 9.1
Let's Compare: Local Governments in Texas and Beyond

Texas is the second most populous state, behind only California, and the second largest, behind only Alaska (not shown here). Texas is organized into far more counties (254) than any other state, and more cities than any state but Illinois. Texas also has more school districts than any other state, though that number has been declining slowly as smaller districts combine with larger districts. Texas also makes extensive use of special district. For a small government state, Texas has a lot of governments, though this may also mean that they are closer to the people.

State	Population	Area in Square Miles	Counties	Cities	School Districts	Special Districts	Total Governments
California	36,458,000	163,696	57	475	1,047	2,830	4,409
Texas	**23,508,000**	**268,581**	**254**	**1,196**	**1,089**	**2,245**	**4,784**
New York	19,306,000	54,556	57	616	683	1,135	2,491
Florida	18,090,000	65,755	66	404	95	626	1,191
Illinois	12,832,000	57,914	102	1,291	934	3,145	5,472
Pennsylvania	12,441,000	46,055	66	1,018	516	1,885	3,485
Ohio	11,478,000	44,825	88	942	667	631	2,328
Michigan	10,096,000	96,716	83	533	580	366	1,562
Georgia	9,364,000	59,425	156	531	180	581	1,448
New Jersey	8,725,000	8,721	21	324	549	276	1,170

Source: U.S. Census Bureau, *Statistical Abstract of the United States, 2008* (Washington D.C.: Government Printing Office, 2008), Tables 12 and 415. New York, Illinois, Pennsylvania, Ohio, Michigan, and New Jersey organize very small communities as townships. Townships are not included in the totals above.

Origins and Purposes

Q2. How important are counties in contemporary Texas government?

In early Texas, county governments brought state law and services to a widely scattered rural population. Texans went to the county courthouse to file birth and death certificates; apply for a marriage license; register deeds, contracts, and wills; pay taxes; and register to vote. The county built and repaired roads and provided law enforcement through the county sheriff. As modern Texas emerged over the course of the 20th century, rural counties changed little, but some urban counties added services like libraries, parks, hospitals, and community colleges. Every Texas county, whether its services are few or many, has the same structure and powers mandated by the Texas Constitution of 1876.

Structure of County Government

Each Texas county is governed by a commissioners court made up of a county judge and four county commissioners. These officials are elected to four-year terms on a partisan ballot. The county judge is elected countywide and the commissioners are elected within geographical districts called precincts. In addition to the commissioners court, several key officials, including a county sheriff, county clerk, county or district attorney, county tax assessor/collector, county treasurer, and county surveyor are elected countywide and act as independent administrators.[5]

As we shall see below, the commissioners court has broad management responsibility for county government. But other countywide elected officials, like the county sheriff and county clerk, have a great deal of discretion in running their own departments. They have the authority to set policy, let contracts, and hire and fire within their own departments. Ultimately, each countywide elected official is responsible to the voters and removable only by the voters. County government, like state government, features a plural executive in which no single official is "in charge."

Commissioners Court

Commissioners court, despite the name, is not simply, or sometimes even mainly, a court. In all Texas counties, it is the chief policymaking (legislative) and administrative (executive) institution of county government. In the smaller, rural counties the commissioners court still has some modest judicial duties. While the commissioners court does not have direct authority over most other county officials, it does derive significant influence from its control of the county budget. However, once county officials get their annual appropriation, they generally seek to re-assert their independence.

Commissioners court The chief policymaking and administrative institution of Texas county government.

The commissioners court passes ordinances; sets the property tax rate; adopts the budget; appoints senior administrators; awards contracts for building, road construction, and repair; and generally monitors county government. In most Texas counties the budget for road and bridge construction and repair is divided among the four commissioners and administered independently by each. This encourages overlap, inefficiency, and, at least occasionally, corruption, but it is the basis for commissioners' job and contract patronage.[6] In the rural counties, road building and maintenance is the chief role of county government. In fact, in many rural counties, the county commissioners are simply called "road commissioners." Counties are also responsible for law enforcement outside of cities and towns.

The state's urban counties often do more than offer basic county services. Some administer a county hospital, parks, libraries, airports, and sports authorities, as well as a range of welfare, health, and education programs.

County Judge

The **county judge** is elected on a partisan ballot, to a four-year term, by the eligible voters of the county. Though the office is called county judge, the incumbent does not have to be a lawyer, just "well-informed in the law." Only in the state's rural counties, where the workload is light, do county judges have even minor judicial responsibilities. The county judge is the county's chief legislator and executive.

County judge The county judge is elected countywide and presides over the county Commissioners Court.

The county judge presides over the commissioners court, sets the agenda, and participates in all of the debates. In some counties, the tradition has developed that the county judge votes only in case of ties, but the judge is entitled to vote on all issues that come before the court. As the only

FIGURE 9.1   County Government in Texas

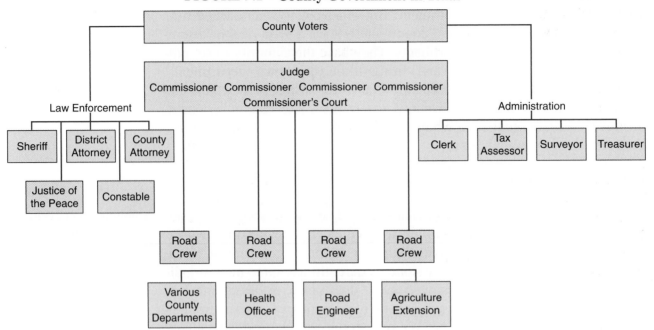

Source: Derived by the author from various sources, including John A. Gilmartin, et. al., *County Government in Texas*, V. G. Young Institute of County Government, Texas A&M University System. See also George D. Braden, "Citizens' Guide to the Texas Constitution," prepared for the Texas Advisory Commission on Intergovernmental Relations by the Institute of Urban Studies, University of Houston, 1972.

member of the court elected countywide, the judge is often in a position to resolve disputes and broker compromises between the four commissioners that represent individual districts.

The county judge's executive and administrative responsibilities also create opportunities for influence. The judge has the power to fill vacancies on the court, to appoint commissioners to important boards and commissions, and to draft the county budget for the consideration and approval of the full commissioners court. The county judge's legislative and executive powers generally allow him or her to emerge as the county's leading public official.

Other County Administrators

The county clerk, county tax assessor/collector, county treasurer, and county surveyor are each elected county wide to a four-year term. These offices vary somewhat in their structure and responsibilities, depending upon the size and complexity of the county.

County Clerk. The county clerk maintains the county's legal files, official records, and vital statistics. Some county clerks oversee the work of a few assistants while others oversee a staff of hundreds. The county clerk's office is responsible for maintaining the records of the commissioners court as well as the justice of the peace and county courts. The county clerk maintains records of births, deaths, marriages, deeds, wills, and contracts. The county clerk also serves on the county elections board and is responsible for conducting elections.

In counties with a population of over 8,000, the workload of the district court justifies the election of a district clerk. The district clerk is elected to maintain the records of the district court. The district clerk manages all court filings, schedules cases, and sends out the feared jury summons for the district court.

County Tax Assessor/Collector. Until 1978, tax assessors actually set the value of property for tax purposes. Since 1978, the state has established 180 tax assessment districts with uniform assessment procedures and criteria to streamline and rationalize the assessment process. Today's tax assessor/collector collects state and county taxes as well as vehicle license and title fees and, in some counties, operates as the registrar of voters. Counties of under 10,000 may leave the office of assessor/collectors unfilled and devolve its duties onto the county sheriff.

County Treasurer/Auditor. County treasurers receive, deposit, and expend county funds. State law requires counties over 35,000 to supplement the treasurer with an appointed auditor. The district judge with jurisdiction in the county appoints an auditor to a two-year term to monitor the financial practices of the county to insure that they comply with state law.

County Surveyor, The office of county surveyor dates back to the Republic of Texas. Throughout the 19th century, county surveyor was an influential and often lucrative position. Surveyors record and verify land boundaries for individuals, developers, and municipalities. Today, most Texas counties no longer elect a surveyor. Survey work is still required, but it is contracted for on a fee-for-service basis.

County Law Enforcement

The county sheriff and the county attorney are elected at-large to four-year terms. They are the principal non-judicial law enforcement officials of Texas county government.

County Sheriff. The county sheriff is a powerful figure in county government, often second only to the county judge. He or she is the county's chief law enforcement officer, responsible for enforcing state laws and county ordinances within the county and for administering the county jail. Oftentimes, the sheriff's office patrols the unincorporated parts of the county, leaving urban law enforcement to city police forces. Constables are law enforcement officers attached to the justice of the peace courts. They perform many of the same duties as deputy sheriffs.

District/County Attorney. Texas counties may have a county attorney, a district attorney, or both. County and district attorneys serve as legal advisers to county government and represent the county in court. Urban counties usually divide the workload between a county attorney and a district attorney. County attorneys usually handle minor criminal matters and juvenile cases in the justice of the peace and county courts. District attorneys handle the major criminal cases in the district courts.

CITIES AND MUNICIPALITIES

Texas cities have more flexibility than counties in selecting the structure and powers of government that will work best for them. In early Texas, cities worked directly with the legislature to craft city charters specially designed to their purposes. As the state grew, legislators sought to simplify and regularize the process of incorporating and organizing municipal governments.

Though the needs of larger cities continued to be addressed by special charters, by 1858 the legislature had devised general-law charters that cities meeting particular criteria could adopt. In 1912, a series of constitutional amendments were adopted that permitted municipalities of more than 5,000 residents to design and adopt "home rule" charters so long as they met certain criteria and did not violate other state laws. A municipal charter, like a constitution, lays out the basic structure and powers of government. Each of Texas's nearly 1,200 municipalities is organized as a general-law or home-rule city.

General-law and Home-rule Cities

Q3. What are the key differences between general-law and home-rule cities?

Article XI of the Texas Constitution declares that all cities and towns of under 5,000 residents must adopt a general-law charter. State law authorizes three general-law charters (the mayor-council, the council-manager, and the commission form) with multiple options for structure and powers within each. About 900 small Texas cities operate under a general-law charter. Most of Texas's 300 larger cities operate under a home-rule charter of their own design.

Each year three or four Texas cities replace general-law charters with home-rule charters. As a city's population grows past 5,000, the issues that confront them seem to demand more time and attention. Home-rule charters allow cities to replace part-time mayors with full-time city administrators, increase their property tax rate from $1.50 per $100 of assessed value to as much as $2.50, and to exercise more control over their growth.

Incorporation and Annexation

Incorporation The legal process by which cities are established.

Annexation A legal and political process by which cities absorb adjacent territory.

Incorporation is the legal process by which cities are born and **annexation** is the process by which they grow. Once an area reaches 200 residents, those residents can petition the county judge to authorize and conduct an incorporation election. The ballot proposes one of the general-law forms of government for adoption. If a majority of voters approve incorporation, the state issues the appropriate municipal charter.

State law recognizes that cities, once founded, need the power and authority to manage their growth. Cities have the right to pass ordinances, deliver services, and levy taxes within their borders. They also have certain rights, called **extraterritorial jurisdiction** (ETJ), outside their immediate borders. A city of under 5,000 has ETJ over zoning and building for half a mile beyond its formal boundaries. Big cities, over 100,000 residents, have ETJ up to five miles beyond their borders.

The growth of cities generally occurs by annexation of adjacent territory. Existing cities can annex land within their ETJ in amounts no greater than 10 percent of their existing territory per year and no more than 30 percent over a three-year period. Home-rule cities can annex territory by a simple majority vote of the city council. They do not require the approval of the residents of the area to be annexed. General-law cities must get majority approval of a referendum among the people living in the area to be annexed. No new cities can be incorporated within an existing city's ETJ without the approval of the existing city.

Extraterritorial jurisdiction (ETJ)
ETJ describes the limited power that cities exercise over territory just beyond their boundaries.

Forms of City Government

The Texas Constitution and laws permit three general forms of municipal government: the mayor-council form of government, which is often discussed in terms of strong mayor and weak mayor forms; the council-manager form; and the commission form. Though the commission form was instrumental in helping Galveston recover from the devastating hurricane and flood of 1901, it is rarely used today and will not be discussed at length below. There are many variations on both the mayor-council and manager-council systems and several of Texas's larger home-rule cities have sought to combine mayoral leadership, council representation of neighborhoods, and professional city management.

Mayor-Council. Most large American cities operate under the mayor-council form of government. In Texas, many small towns employ the mayor-council structure, but among the state's largest cities, only Houston does. The mayor-council form of government reflects, in varying degrees, the classic separation of powers between the executive (mayor) and legislative (council) branches of government. It also reflects the feeling that cities should be led by elected officials rather than appointed managers.

In the mayor-council system, the council ranges from five to fifteen members, elected at-large or in single-member districts. The council makes policy and passes ordinances for the city. It authorizes city programs and services, sets tax rates, and adopts the city budget. Council committees engage in planning, community outreach, investigations, and oversight.

A **strong mayor** is elected citywide and has the classic powers of an American chief executive. Like the president or a strong governor, a strong mayor hires, manages, and, if necessary, fires the principal department heads and prepares the city budget and submits it to the council for adoption. A strong mayor may also preside over council meetings, participate in their debates, and wield a veto over their actions. A strong mayor is the acknowledged representative and leader of his or her city. Houston is the only large Texas city to adopt the strong-mayor form of government.

Strong mayor An elected city executive with strong appointment, budgetary, and council management powers.

FIGURE 9.2   Strong Mayor-City Council Form

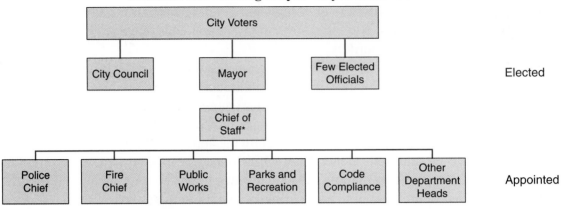

* Chief of Staff is optional, though common in larger cities

Source: Produced by the author.

FIGURE 9.3   Weak Mayor-City Council Form

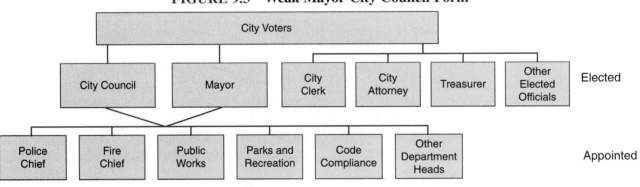

Source: Produced by the author.

From left: Mayors Bill White, Houston; Tom Leppert, Dallas; Phil Hardberger, San Antonio; and Will Wynn, Austin, applaud the 2007 lighting of a granite Texas map. *J. Michael Short/ The Associated Press*

The difference between a strong mayor and a weak mayor is often a matter of degrees. Every power that a strong mayor has can be checked a little or a lot to produce a weaker mayor. Most small Texas towns employ a weak-mayor form of government. A **weak mayor** may require council approval, perhaps by a two-thirds vote, for their hires. A weak mayor may be checked in the budgetary process by an appointed or elected treasurer or comptroller. A weak mayor may not have a veto over council action, or may have a veto that is easily overridden. Politically though, a poor politician can struggle to achieve his or her goals in a strong mayor's office, and a good politician can achieve great things even though the mayoral tools are weak.

FIGURE 9.4   Council-Manager Form

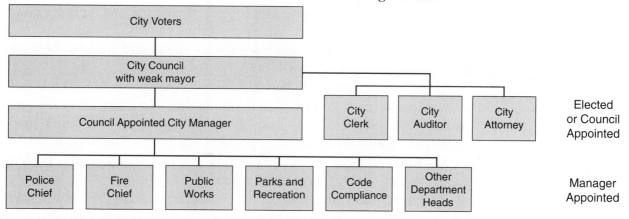

Source: Produced by the author.

Council-Manager. The council-manager form of municipal government is composed of an elected city council of five to fifteen members, of which one will be a weak mayor, and a professional city manager appointed by the council. The council-manager form of government arose early in the 20th century, during the Progressive Era, in an attempt to clean up city government by separating the politics of council policymaking from the non-partisan administration of city services by a professional city manager. The council-manager form of government is popular with medium-sized cities (50,000 to 250,000) throughout the U.S., but in Texas it is preferred even by the state's larger cities. San Antonio, Dallas, and El Paso all use council-manager governments.[7]

In the council-manager system, the **city council** is the policymaking branch of city government. Council members are elected at-large in some small Texas cities and in single-member districts in most large cities. The city council hires the city manager, adopts ordinances, approves the budget, and oversees city government, holding inquiries and hearings as problems and issues arise. A mayor may be appointed by the council or elected citywide, but his or her powers are limited to presiding over council meetings, managing the agenda, and otherwise exercising the powers of a council member.

The **city manager** is responsible for hiring and firing department heads, including the police and fire chiefs; preparing the city budget for council approval; and administering the city on a day-to-day basis. The city manager usually holds a degree in public administration or urban studies and has experience in the law and practice of personnel management, budgeting, and finance.

Municipal Elections

Unlike county and state elections, which are partisan, municipal elections in Texas are nonpartisan. Parties and partisanship are not absent from

Weak mayor   An elected city executive with few meaningful appointment, budgetary, and council management powers.

City council   The policymaking or legislative branch of city government.

City manager   A city manager is an appointed professional executive hired, usually by the city council, to manage or administer city government.

Q4. Why do most Texas cities conduct elections within single-member districts?

municipal elections, but they tend to be a shadowy, behind-the-scenes presence. Candidates do not run as nominees of their party and there are no partisan symbols on the ballot, but voters often know the candidates' background and candidates sometimes wink at voters and suggest their party background if they think it will help.

Most Texas cities hold their elections in the spring of odd-numbered years, separate from county, state, and national elections. They do this to insulate their local elections from the more glamorous and better funded issues and candidates at the state and national levels. The hope is that voters will focus on local issues and candidates if there are no distractions, but usually voters simply ignore local elections.

At-Large Elections. During the first quarter of the 20th century, Progressive Era reformers sought to clean up the partisan corruption that plagued many American cities. Non-partisan elections were thought to be an obvious part of the solution. So were **at-large elections** of city council members. When city council members are elected at-large, meaning citywide, voters cast a ballot for as many candidates as there are open seats, and the top vote-getters win the seats. The benefit of at-large elections was thought to be that persons of citywide reputation and expertise would be elected. The weakness was that the (usually) white majority elected all of the city council seats and minority candidates were closed out.

Place or Ward System. Two variations on at-large elections have been common in Texas. In the place system, city council seats are designated as Place 1, Place 2, Place 3, and so on. Candidates file for a particular place and run only against those who file for that place, but candidates can live anywhere in the city and voters from throughout the city elect all of the places. Under the ward system, the city is divided into geographical wards and candidates are required to live in the ward in which they stand for election, but voters throughout the city still vote for candidates in each of the wards. The ward system tries to balance the sense that all parts of the city should be represented on the city council with the sense that voters should elect persons they believe will serve the broad interests of the city.

Single-Member District Elections. Over the past several decades, most Texas cities over 50,000 adopted **single-member district elections.** The move to single-member districts occurred both because cities were growing larger and more complex and because the courts were demanding that minorities have a better chance to elect their own representatives. To create single-member districts, the city council divides the city into equal population wards or districts. Candidates must live within the district they seek to represent, and voters cast ballots for candidates only in the district in which they live.

The move to single-member districts has changed the balance in local politics. In many cities, neighborhoods are segregated (not legally any more, but practically) by race and people generally tend to vote for a mem-

At-large elections
Elections held throughout a jurisdiction, such as a city or county, rather than in wards or single-members districts within the jurisdiction.

Single-member district elections Elections held within geographical districts, with one candidate elected in each district.

ber of their own race when that option is available to them. Single-member districts, therefore, enhance the prospects that minority districts will send a minority person to the council. On the other hand, some argue that single-member districts encourage council members to focus on their districts to the detriment of the city itself.

Citizen Participation and Voter Turnout

Municipal elections do not generate the interest and excitement of statewide, let alone national, elections. That is not accidental. Holding municipal elections off the cycle of more exciting elections and holding them as non-partisan elections keeps turnout low. In a low turnout election, a few well-organized interests and activists can have a decisive influence on the outcome. Municipal elections are usually controlled by business groups, municipal unions, neighborhood associations, and social group activists.

Occasionally, the presence of a particularly compelling candidate, match-up, or issue will draw voters to the polls in unusual numbers. When Henry Cisneros, an immensely popular Hispanic first ran for mayor of San Antonio in 1981, 43 percent of registered voters turned out. When Bob Lanier challenged Kathy Whitmire, the incumbent mayor of Houston in 1991, 40 percent of voters turned out. But more frequently, with just average candidates and no compelling issues, turnout falls into the teens and below. Mayoral elections in 2003 produced turnout levels of 23 percent in Houston, 15 percent in Austin, 10 percent in Dallas, and just 6 percent in San Antonio. Mayoral elections in 2005 produced similar results, 18 percent in Houston, and 19 percent in San Antonio. Austin's 2006 mayoral race produced a turnout of 11 percent, and Dallas's 2007 mayoral election produced 15 percent.

SPECIAL DISTRICTS

Texas has more than 3,300 special district governments. These are special-purpose local governments set up to deliver a particular service within a defined geographical area. The geographical areas served by special districts range from multi-county regional planning districts to small town water districts. **Special districts** are established by general-purpose governments, usually counties and municipalities, to deliver a service that the general-purpose government cannot or does not wish to deliver. School and water districts are common examples of special district governments.[8]

Special districts are usually administered by an appointed or elected multi-member board. The board hires an executive director or professional manager to run the day-to-day operations of the district. Funding may come as transfers from general-purpose governments, fees charged for services, or taxes that the board is authorized to levy, collect, and spend.

Special districts
Special purpose local governments, established by cities and counties, to deliver a particular service within a limited geographical area.

Types of Special Districts

Q5. Why are there so many special district governments in Texas?

Special districts are employed for dozens of purposes, but several general types predominate. Texas has more than 1,200 independent school districts, 500 economic development and redevelopment districts, and 500 flood control and water sanitation and delivery districts. Fifty Texas counties run community college districts. Metropolitan areas are often served by regional transportation districts, as well as utility, hospital, and airport districts. Rural Texans depend upon fire, soil conservation, and flood control districts.

School Districts

The most common special districts in Texas are the state's independent school districts (ISD). Each ISD is administered by an elected school board. School boards usually have five to nine members, depending on the size and population of the district. Board members are selected, usually for four-year terms, in nonpartisan elections. Rural districts may conduct their elections at-large, but urban districts usually conduct their elections within single-member districts.

School boards are responsible for setting tax rates and budgets, building and maintaining facilities, hiring senior administrators, selecting textbooks and curricula, and setting general policy for the district, all within guidelines set by the Texas Education Agency. Perhaps the most important decision that the board makes is the selection of the district's educational leader, the superintendent of schools. School superintendents, especially in the state's largest urban districts, are visible public figures and often work in an intensely political environment.

Councils of Governments

Councils of governments COGs are voluntary planning districts that provide training, planning, and coordination services to member local governments.

The proliferation of special districts and the increasing complexity of issues facing Texas municipalities have highlighted the need for regional planning and coordination. Texas is divided into 24 regional planning districts, called **councils of governments** (COGs), to facilitate voluntary cooperation between local governments. COGs provide training to local officials; coordinate regional land use, transportation, economic development, and environmental protection programs; and assist in the preparation of grant applications to state and federal governments.[9] Effective COGs can facilitate the spread of best practices, avoid duplication of effort across local governments and special districts, and improve regional planning.

COUNTY AND MUNICIPAL REFORM

As with Texas state government, critics complain that Texas county government is outmoded and in serious need of reform. There are several common criticisms. First, the Texas Constitution requires the same single, rigid structure of government for both Loving county with its several dozen residents and Harris county with its several million residents. More flexibility, perhaps even county home rule, is frequently recommended.

Second, the election of plural executives leaves no one in charge of county government. Empowering the county judge to appoint some of the officials who are now elected would focus authority and promote unity in county government. Third, patronage thrives in county government. Savings and efficiencies that might be achieved are sacrificed to politics and personal agendas, especially in county road building and maintenance. Modernizing county personnel and contracting systems and implementing a unified road maintenance and building budget are pressing needs.

Local governments in Texas have more flexibility in their organizational design and powers. Nonetheless, unlike large cities in most of the country, most large Texas cities still use a council-manager form of government. In most of the country, council-manager governments are employed by medium-sized cities, from 50,000 to 250,000 while large cities use the mayor-council form of government. The mayor-council form of government, especially in its strong mayor variant, is seen as more capable of forcefully leading large and complex cities in dealing with their many problems and opportunities. Houston has a strong mayor, Dallas, San Antonio, and Austin should probably consider it.

CHAPTER SUMMARY

Local government lacks some of the distant majesty of state and national government. Yet, most government, most of the time, for most people, is local. But as we have seen, local government is a "creature" of state government. State constitutions and laws determine what form local governments will take, what powers they will enjoy, and what resources they will have to meet their responsibilities. Texas has more counties, at 254, than any other state (Georgia is second with a measly 156) and more municipalities, at 1,196, than every state but Illinois (1,291).

The Texas Constitution mandates that counties be governed by a five-member commissioners court, composed of a county judge and four county commissioners. Other countywide elected officials include the sheriff, district attorney, clerk, tax assessor/collector, and treasurer/auditor. Urban counties offer more programs and services than rural counties and rural counties are permitted to consolidate some county offices, but the key deficiency of county government is a lack of flexibility.

Texas municipal governments have more flexibility. Towns under 5,000 residents select some variation on the mayor-council, council-manager, or commission forms of government. But larger cities may design their own home-rule charters and most do. Texas also employs more than 3,300 special district governments to deliver particular services. Twenty-four regional planning districts, called COGs, seek to coordinate this welter of local government activity.

KEY TERMS

Annexation

At-large elections

City council

City manager

Commissioners court

Councils of
governments

County judge

Dillon's Rule

Extraterritorial
jurisdiction

Incorporation

Single-member
district elections

Special districts

Strong mayor

Weak mayor

SUGGESTED READINGS

Stephen L. Elkin, *City and Regime in American Politics* (Chicago: University of Chicago Press, 1987).

Richard L. Florida, *The Rise of the Creative Class: And How It's Transforming Work, Leisure, Community, and Everyday Life* (New York: Basic Books, 2002).

Mario T. Garcia, *The Making of a Mexican-American Mayor: Raymond L. Telles of El Paso* (El Paso, TX: Texas Western Press, 1998).

Michael Phillips, *White Metropolis: Race, Ethnicity, and Religion in Dallas, 1841–2001* (Austin, TX: University of Texas Press, 2006).

Linda Scarbrough, "Road, River, and ol' boy Politics: A Texas County's Path from Farm to Supersuburb," Austin: Texas State Historical Association, 2005.

WEB RESOURCES

http://www.nlc.org National League of Cities.

http://www.ci.dallas.tx.us Instead of Dallas, type in any Texas city you want.

http://www.co.harris.tx.us Instead of Harris, type in any Texas county you want.

http://www.tml.org Texas Municipal League.

http://www.tac.org Texas Association of Counties

END NOTES

1. Peter Engardio, "Slicker Cities: The Real Contest Is Among Cities, Not Nations," *BusinessWeek,* August 21–28, 2006, pp. 108–110.

2. Clay Robison, "Panel to Study Law Appraisal Caps," *San Antonio Express News,* August 21, 2006, A1.

3. Will Lutz, "Tom Pauken on Appraisal Reform," Dallasblog.com, September 4, 2007.

4. Ralph Blumenthal, "1 Cafe, 1 Gas Station, 2 Roads: It's America's Emptiest County," *New York Times,* February 25, 2006, A1, A11.

5. John A. Gilmartin, Richard O. Avery, and Eric S. Cartrite, *County Government in Texas: A Summary of Major Offices and Officials,* V.G. Young Institute of County Government, Texas A&M University System, 2000.

6. Molly Bloom, "New Accusations Against Bastrop Commissioner," *Austin American-Statesman,* December 18, 2007.

7. David Crowder, "Mayoral Race Is for a Different City Role," *El Paso Times,* March 7, 2005, A1. See also Paul Burka, "Fed Up," *Texas Monthly,* April 2008, pp. 12–16.

8. Susan Berfield, "There Will Be Water," *BusinessWeek,* June 23, 2008, pp. 40–45.

9. Kevin Krause, "County Roadwork: Responsive Service or Separate Fiefdoms?," *Dallas Morning News,* August 22, 2006, A1, A2.

CHAPTER 10

Financing State Government: Budgets, Revenues, and Expenses

Focus Questions

Q1. What role do budgets play in the political process?

Q2. Who are the leading participants in the budgetary process?

Q3. What key revenue sources support Texas state government?

Q4. What are the principal expenses of Texas state government?

Q5. Where do issues of fairness fit into discussions of taxing and spending?

Much of politics is clashing ideologies, contrasting campaign promises, and conflicting partisan agendas. **Budgets,** on the other hand, force concrete decisions about who pays and who benefits. Officials in Texas state government make critical decisions about how much revenue to raise, through what kinds of taxes and fees, levied against whom. It makes other decisions, just as critical, about how to spend those revenues, on what services, for whose benefit.

Budgets Moral and political documents that seek to balance a community's revenue sources with its spending obligations.

Because budgets declare what government will do, who will pay, and who will benefit, they are often said to be moral documents. They are. But honorable people can differ fundamentally about what morality requires. Moreover, people are motivated not just by what they think is right, but by what they think is best for them. Hence, the budgetary process is both a moral debate about what the political community should do and a political struggle over who benefits and who pays.

Q1. What role do budgets play in the political process?

In states with moralistic political cultures (states like Massachusetts, Minnesota, and Washington) the moral requirements of budgetary decision-making are often thought to demand more—more spending for education, health care, and parks. But in states with traditionalistic political cultures (states like Georgia, Florida, and Texas) the moral injunction to keep government's hands out of people's pockets is thought to be equally compelling. Texas politicians frequently make the case that low taxes expand opportunity and encourage personal responsibility. Texas politicians rarely acknowledge that low taxes severely limit the state's ability to aid its most vulnerable citizens.

In this chapter, we describe how budgets are drafted in Texas, how revenues are raised, and how the money is spent. In general, the legislature dominates the budgetary process, taxes are kept low, and revenues are directed to basic, no frills programs in education, health and human services, and transportation. The 2007 regular session of the Texas legislature approved a 2008–2009 biennial state budget totaling $152.5 billion. Governor Perry trimmed the budget to $151.9 billion before signing it. The technical requirement that monies dedicated to property tax relief be "appropriated" as expenditures raised the final budgetary total to $167.8 billion. The numbers are large and the struggle over them is intense.

THE BUDGETARY PROCESS

The Texas Constitution and laws establish what taxes can be levied, what services can be delivered, and who has the power and responsibility to create the budget.[1] For example, the Texas Constitution and related laws prohibit a state income tax and a statewide property tax, permit a state sales tax and user fees, and require that the state provide basic services, including an "efficient system of public free schools"—all within a balanced budget.

The responsibility for navigating the budgetary process is distributed across the legislative and executive branches of Texas state government. The state legislature has the dominant role, but the governor's line-item veto gives him important leverage late in the process. Occasionally, as with the troublesome school finance issues, the Texas courts become involved as well. There are two broad stages to the budgetary process: preparation and consideration for approval.

Budgetary Preparation

> **Q2.** Who are the leading participants in the budgetary process?

The Texas state legislature meets in regular session for 140 days, from January to May, in odd-numbered years. The most important bill to move through the legislative process in each regular session is the state budget. Budget planning occurs during the even-numbered year prior the legislative session. The actors driving the process are the governor, lieutenant governor, speaker, and comptroller.

The Texas Constitution identifies the governor as the state's chief budget officer, but, in fact, the legislature crafts the budget. Specifically, the ten-member **Legislative Budget Board** (LBB), co-chaired by the lieutenant governor and speaker, prepare a budget for submission to the legislature. The lieutenant governor and speaker each appoint four additional members to complete the LBB, usually including the chairs of the key revenue and spending committees. While the governor also submits a budget, or at least a budget outline, to the legislature, the legislature concentrates on the work of its own leaders and generally ignores the governor's budget.

Legislative Budget Board　The ten-member LBB, co-chaired by the Lieutenant Governor and the Speaker, drafts the state's biennial budget.

The governor and legislative leaders set the strategic planning and budgeting process in motion in the spring of even-numbered years by defining the goals and priorities for the coming biennium (see Figure 10.1). Each agency then embarks on a review of their role in meeting those goals and priorities. Agencies update their strategic plans, request adjustments in their broad budget structures, and develop new budget requests. Agencies are usually instructed to develop alternative budget scenarios. For example, in a normal budget year, they might be required to plan for a three percent increase, no increase, a five percent cut, and a ten percent cut.

Agency budget requests are submitted to the LBB and the Governor's Office of Budget, Planning, and Policy (GOBPP) in July and August of even-numbered years. From August through October, the LBB and GOBPP hold joint hearings in which the agencies are required to explain, justify, and defend their budgetary priorities and funding requests. Agencies respond to the LBB and GOBPP with additional information and often with revised priorities and requests. Between September and December, both the LBB and GOBPP develop budget proposals for submission to the legislature.

Before the legislative session begins in January of each odd-numbered year, the comptroller is constitutionally required to issue a **revenue estimate.** On January 8, 2007, the Comptroller Susan Combs estimated that state revenues for the 2008–2009 biennium would total $156.8 billion. The comptroller usually makes a conservative estimate at the beginning of the session so that legislative leaders wishing to spend more have to include her preferences in their plans. Unless the comptroller raises her initial revenue estimate, the governor and legislature cannot spend more without a 4/5th vote of the House and the Senate.

Revenue estimate
The Texas Comptroller is empowered to make revenue estimates that the Texas state budget must stay within.

Budget Consideration and Approval

The 80th regular session of the Texas legislature opened on January 9, 2007. The LBB is required by law to submit a budget bill during the first week of the session.[2] The LBB's budget bill was submitted to both the Appropriations Committee in the House and the Finance Committee in the Senate on January 15. The chairs of the Appropriations and Finance committees, together with the presiding officers in each chamber, are members of the LBB, so, in a critical sense, they submit the budget to themselves.

The governor is required to deliver a State of the State message and submit his budget proposal to the legislature within the first week of the session as well. The governor's State of the State message, delivered to a joint session of the legislature, is his opportunity to outline goals for the state, set priorities, and argue for his funding preferences. The legislators know and the governor subtly reminds them that, while they control the process during the session, he must ultimately approve the budget they produce.

In the 80th regular session of the Texas legislature, the House Appropriations Committee included 29 members, all appointed by Speaker Craddick. The Speaker named Warren Chisum (R-Pampa) to chair the committee and

FIGURE 10.1   The Budgetary Process in Texas

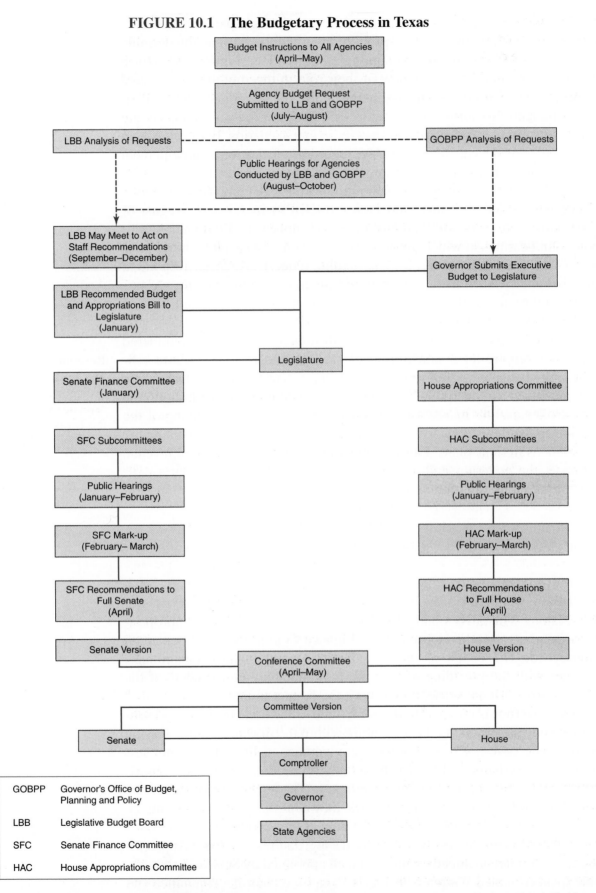

Source: http://www.llb.state.tx.us/The_LBB/Access/Other_Documents.htm On the LBB website, see Budget 101: A Guide to the Budget Process in Texas Courtesy of the Senate Research Center, p. 5.

Ryan Guillen (D-Rio Grande City) to serve as vice chair. Each of the 27 regular members of the Appropriations Committee was liaison to another standing committee of the House where he or she chaired a subcommittee on budget and oversight. Speaker Craddick's goal was to formalize and tighten the relationship between the Appropriations Committee and the substantive committees of the House. Chairman Chisum divided the Appropriations Committee into five subcommittees: education, health and human services, criminal justice, regulation, and general government.

The Senate Finance Committee included 15 members, all appointed by Lieutenant Governor Dewhurst. Steve Ogden (R-Bryan) chaired the committee and Judith Zaffirini (D-Laredo) served as vice chair. Chairman Ogden generally held hearings before the full Finance Committee, though four working groups were named to hear testimony on specific areas of the budget. The legislative phase of the budgetary process involves four stages: committee hearings, mark-up, floor debate, and conference committee deliberations.

Hearings. The House Appropriations and Senate Finance Committees began hearings on the LBB's budget bill in late January, 2007. Some hearings were held before the committees' subcommittees and working groups, some before the full committees. Hearings provide an opportunity for citizens, lobbyists, interest groups, agency representatives, and spokesmen for the governor's office to voice their concerns to the committee before it takes any action.

Mark-up. In many legislatures, mark-up is the stage in the budget writing process where the committees get to place their mark on the document. But in Texas, the budget is drafted by the legislative leaders serving on the LBB. Hence, the presiding officers and committee chairs work hard to defend their handiwork from tampering by committee members. Mark-up in the Texas legislature takes place before the full Appropriations and Finance committees, under the watchful eyes of the presiding officers and committee chairs.

Floor Debate. When the committees finish their work, the House version of the budget goes to the House Calendars Committee and the Senate version is placed on their daily calendar to await floor action. The Calendars Committee writes a special rule scheduling floor action on the budget and limiting amendments to changes that do not affect the "bottom line." Amendments that propose to add money somewhere in the budget must propose cuts somewhere else in the budget. Floor action in the House involves consideration of many amendments, but little real change. Senate rules require approval of the presiding officer and two-thirds of the senators before any bill, including the budget, can come to the floor, so most member concerns are argued out before floor consideration even begins. The Senate usually passes the budget with no amendments from the floor.

Conference Committee Deliberations. Once a budget bill has cleared both the House and the Senate, the differences between the two versions of the bill, and there are always differences, must be resolved. A House-Senate conference committee is the vehicle for resolving the differences

Comptroller Susan Combs told a news conference in Austin the day before the legislature convened that she expected a surplus of $14.2 billion in the coming biennium but that a cooling economy could cut state revenue. *Harry Cabluck*/Associated Press

between the two bills. The lieutenant governor and speaker each appoint five members to the conference committee, usually senior members including the Appropriations and Finance chairs. The conference committee works under great pressure, in the closing days of the session, so the resolutions hammered out in the conference committee are usually approved by the full House and Senate just prior to adjournment.

Even after the legislature has completed its work, two hurdles remain before approval of the budget is final. First, the comptroller must certify, based on the latest information available, that the revenues required to fully fund the budget will be available in the coming biennium. In the closing days of the 2007 regular session, the comptroller declared that anticipated revenue would cover the $152.5 billion for 2008–2009 and leave a significant surplus.

Second, the budget goes to the governor for his consideration. The governor can sign the budget, putting it into immediate effect, which governors sometimes do, or they can veto the whole budget, which they rarely do. Generally, governors exercise their line-item veto by striking out those appropriations that they think ill-advised. It is the line-item veto, and the legislators fear of it, that give Texas governors their influence, modest, but still appreciable, over the state budget. Governor Perry trimmed the 2008–2009 budget by about one-half of one percent (from $152.5 billion to $151.9 billion) before signing it.

REVENUES: WHERE THE MONEY COMES FROM

Q3. What key revenue sources support Texas state government?

Most state constitutions carefully define the general kinds of taxes that may be levied by state and local governments. Broadly, there are four kinds of taxes: taxes on income, sales, property, and special fines and fees. Most states employ them all. Seven states (Alaska, Florida, Nevada, South Dakota, **Texas,** Washington, and Wyoming) do not levy a state income tax and five (Alaska, Delaware, Montana, New Hampshire, and Oregon) do not use a general sales tax. Most local and special district governments depend heavily on property tax revenues.

Texans and their elected representatives have acted to keep taxes low and to restrict their growth. The Texas Constitution prohibits a state income tax and a state property tax. To buttress these constitutional defenses, Texas adopted a constitutional amendment in 1978 limiting general revenue growth to no more than the estimated growth of the Texas economy. Texans are nothing if not wary of taxes.

Tax Revenues

Texas has long derived the bulk of its tax revenues from a general sales tax and several specialized sales taxes. It derived lesser amounts from a corporate franchise fee, oil and gas severance taxes, motor fuels taxes, and taxes on alcohol and tobacco, often called sin taxes. The spring 2006 special session of the Texas legislature, called under court order to

"Bring 'em down," Gov. Rick Perry told John Sharp and the Texas Tax Reform Commission about property taxes in November 2005. *RODOLFO GONZALEZ*/Austin American-Statesman

address school funding issues, replaced the corporate franchise fee with a new general business tax and increased state taxes on cigarettes by $1 a pack. State taxes provide about half the money that flows into Texas

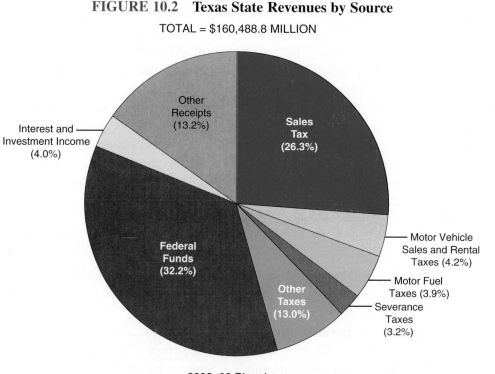

FIGURE 10.2   Texas State Revenues by Source

TOTAL = $160,488.8 MILLION

Other Receipts (13.2%)

Sales Tax (26.3%)

Interest and Investment Income (4.0%)

Federal Funds (32.2%)

Other Taxes (13.0%)

Motor Vehicle Sales and Rental Taxes (4.2%)

Motor Fuel Taxes (3.9%)

Severance Taxes (3.2%)

2008–09 Biennium

Source: Legislative Budget Board, *Fiscal Size-Up, 2008–2009 Biennium,* "Estimated State Revenue Collections," Figure 32, p. 21.

Sales tax　Taxes charged on the sale of designated goods. In Texas the general sales tax is 6.25 percent, with localities permitted to charge up to an additional 2 percent.

coffers. The other half comes from non-tax revenues. These include transfers from the federal government and various license, use, and admission fees. Texas revenues for the 2008–2009 biennium were $160.5 billion.

General Sales Tax. The largest source of tax revenue is the general **sales tax.** During the 2008–2009 biennium, Texas collected $42.2 billion, or 26.3 percent of its total revenues, from the general sales tax. Texas has one of the highest general sales taxes in the U.S., at 6.25 percent. Moreover, local governments are permitted to add up to 2 percent to the state sales tax, which most urban areas do. To ease the burden on the poor, most groceries, prescription drugs, medical services, housing, and utilities are excluded from the sales tax.

Specialized Sales Taxes. Texas also taxes the sale, rental, and operation of motor vehicles. Though Texas records it separately, it levies the same 6.25 percent sales tax on the purchase of motor vehicles as it does on other purchases. It charges a higher tax, 10 percent, on motor vehicle rentals of less than 30 days. Motor vehicle sales and rental taxes brought in $6.8 billion, or 4.2 percent of total revenues, during the 2008–2009 biennium. Motor fuel taxes provided another $6.2 billion, or 3.9 percent. The state receives twenty cents a gallon on gas and diesel purchases (on top of fourteen and a half cents in federal tax) and fifteen cents on liquefied gas.

Corporate franchise fee A business activity tax that in 2005 impacted one in six Texas businesses, mostly corporations and sole proprietorships.

Business Taxes. Through 2006, Texas corporations paid a **corporate franchise fee** of 0.25 percent of taxable capital (value of the corporation) or 4.5 percent of earned income (corporate taxable profits). Limited partnerships and professional associations, including most legal, accounting, and financial management firms, were not subject to the franchise tax. Many businesses that were initially subject to the fee avoided paying by converting to limited partnerships or incorporating out of state. In 2006, only about one in six Texas businesses paid the franchise fee.

The spring 2006 special session of the Texas legislature revised the way business is taxed in the state. It replaced the franchise fee with a broad new business tax. The new tax, commonly called the margins tax, is 1 percent on gross receipts, minus either the cost of employee compensation or the cost of goods sold, whichever is greater. Retailers and wholesalers pay one-half of 1 percent. Sole proprietors, general partnerships, and businesses grossing less than $300,000 annually are exempt and those between $300,000 and $900,000 pay a discounted rate. About 300,000 Texas businesses pay the new margins tax. While the old franchise tax would have brought in $5.8 billion, the new margins tax will bring in $11.9 billion or 7.4 percent of total revenues.

Oil and Gas Severance Taxes. As late as the 1970s, oil and gas severance taxes provided one-quarter of state tax revenue. Texas taxes oil production at 4.6 percent of market value and natural gas at 7.5 percent. Oil and gas production in Texas are both declining slowly. The 2008–2009 biennium saw oil and gas contribute $5.2 billion, or 3.2 percent, to Texas revenues.

Other Tax Revenues. Another 13 percent of revenues come from taxes on several types of economic and business activity. Sales taxes on tobacco and alcohol provided about $4 billion, or 2.5 percent of total revenues, during the 2008–2009 biennium. Business activity taxes on insurance companies, utility companies, and hotel occupancy, accounted for about $4.8 billion, or 3 percent, of revenues.

Non-Tax Revenues

Fully half of the revenues taken in by Texas state government are listed in the state budget as non-tax revenues. The largest streams of non-tax revenues are federal transfer payments. Recall that Texans pay federal income and other taxes, so this is just some of that money coming home. These revenues still come out of the pockets of Texans, just less directly than the sales or business activity taxes. The other sources of non-tax revenues are licenses, fees, fines, profits from the Texas state lottery, interest income, and borrowing.

Federal Transfers. The federal government provides funds to the states to support key state services, including health care, education, and transportation. **Federal transfer payments** provided about 20 percent of state funds during the 1980s and 30 percent during the 1990s. During the 2008–2009 biennium, Texas received $51.6 billion, or 32.2 percent of its total revenues from federal transfer payments.

Federal transfer payments Funds provided by the federal government to state and local governments to support key services such as health care, education, and transportation.

Fines, Fees, Licenses, and Penalties. If you have ever paid a fee to camp in a Texas state park, bought a hunting license, or seen a state trooper's light flashing in your rear view mirror, you have helped fund Texas state government. Assorted fines, fees, licenses, and penalties accounted for $12.6 billion, or 7.9 percent of total revenues, during the 2008–2009 biennium.

Investment and Lottery Income. Interest and investment income on state funds and accounts totaled $3.1 billion, or about 2 percent, of total revenues during the 2008–2009 biennium. The Texas state lottery raised $2 billion, or about 1.2 percent, of total revenues.

Borrowing. State governments, like individuals, sometimes find it convenient to borrow rather than to spend from savings or current income. States borrow by issuing bonds. Texas issues bonds to finance construction, usually of roads, prisons, or university buildings, and to assist veterans to buy land and students to afford college. Not surprisingly though, the Texas Constitution and laws limit state borrowing quite stringently (no more than 5% of state budget). At the close of the 2006 fiscal year, Texas had a per capita indebtedness of just $1,047, compared to the average per capita state indebtedness of $2,902.[3]

EXPENDITURES: WHERE THE MONEY GOES

Like most Americans, Texans demand low taxes and high quality public services. When push comes to shove, as it always does in government finance, Texans demand low taxes more insistently than they demand high quality public services. As a result, Texas spends much less per person

Q4. What are the principal expenses of Texas state government?

FIGURE 10.3   Texas State Expenditures by Purpose

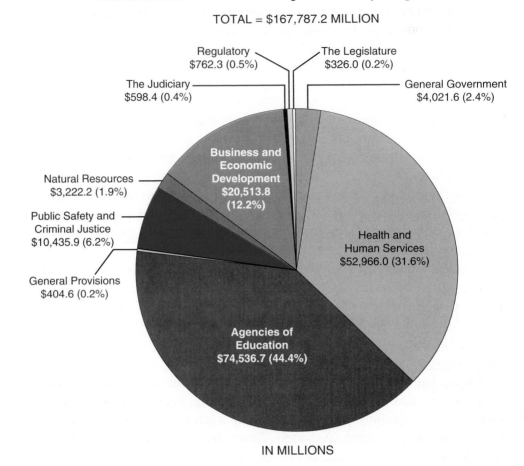

TOTAL = $167,787.2 MILLION

Regulatory $762.3 (0.5%)

The Legislature $326.0 (0.2%)

The Judiciary $598.4 (0.4%)

General Government $4,021.6 (2.4%)

Business and Economic Development $20,513.8 (12.2%)

Natural Resources $3,222.2 (1.9%)

Public Safety and Criminal Justice $10,435.9 (6.2%)

Health and Human Services $52,966.0 (31.6%)

General Provisions $404.6 (0.2%)

Agencies of Education $74,536.7 (44.4%)

IN MILLIONS

Source: Legislative Budget Board, *Fiscal Size-Up, 2008–2009 Biennium,* "All Funds, 2008–2009 Biennium," Figure 2, p. 2.

($3,549) than the average ($4,959) state government.[4] Nearly 85 percent of spending is directed at three broad areas—education, social services, and transportation.

Education

Texas spent almost $75 billion, or 44.4 percent of its total budget of $167.8 billion for 2008–2009, on education. Just over 70 percent of education funding went to elementary and secondary schools ($53.5 billion) and just under 30 percent ($21 billion) went to colleges and universities. The education funding reforms passed in 2006 involved a tax swap of increased state taxes for decreased local property taxes. Little new money was added beyond what was required to accommodate new students and inflation.

As we shall see, these latest reforms raise but do not resolve issues of educational access, quality, and funding that Texas has been wrestling with for more than half a century. Because these issues have been at the top of the political agenda for so long and are so consistently in the news, we will give them special attention here.

Elementary and Secondary Education. The Texas Constitution of 1876 mandated an "efficient system of public free schools" in which whites and blacks would attend separate schools. Hispanic students, not mentioned in the constitution, were treated differently in different districts; sometimes they were allowed to attend the white schools and sometimes not. Many rural counties had no schools at all until the early 20th century. Free school textbooks were made available by the state in 1918. In 1920, Texas made its first concerted attempt to improve public schools. The Better Schools Amendment of 1920 sought to relieve some of the burden on the state by allowing more local funding. Financial disparities between rich and poor districts soon emerged as an issue.

Rural and minority Texans spent the next half century working to insure that their children got the same educational opportunities as more privileged children. In 1930, Jesus Salvatierra, in *Del Rio ISD v. Salvatierra,* claimed that segregation and inadequate school funding denied Mexican-American children an adequate education. Salvatierra lost in the Texas courts. Not until 1948, in the case of *Delgado v. Bastrop ISD,* did the federal courts rule that segregation of Mexican-American students was illegal. Six years later, the landmark case of *Brown v. Board of Education* declared that racial segregation was an unconstitutional violation of the equal protection clause of the 14th Amendment to the U.S. Constitution.

Meanwhile, though many Texas public officials and school districts would continue to resist integration for decades, the state did undertake major educational reforms. The Gilmer-Aikin Laws of 1949, named for Representative Claud Gilmer and Senator A. M. Aikin, reduced the number of independent school districts in Texas from 4,500 to 2,900, equalized school funding, increased teacher pay, reorganized the State Board of Education (SBE), and established the Texas Education Agency (TEA).

The state of Texas, through the SBE and the TEA, sets the standards and expectations for elementary and secondary education in the state. But education is expensive, so battles over funding barely slowed, especially after the U.S. Supreme Court, in the landmark *Pyler v. Doe* (1982) case, declared that school districts must provide the children of illegal immigrants with free public education. As the proportion of school funding provided by the state continued to decline, local school boards were forced to increase property taxes to maintain adequate resources. Wealthy districts managed to cope while poor districts struggled.

In the early 1980s, Texas parents, teachers, school administrators, and public officials brought a new focus to issues of education quality and funding. Dallas billionaire H. Ross Perot was appointed to lead a blue ribbon committee on education reform. In 1984, the legislature passed a number of the Perot reforms, including teacher competency testing, student achievement testing, stricter attendance standards linked to school funding, and "no pass-no play."

Equal funding for rich and poor districts was again raised in 1984. The Mexican-American Legal Defense and Education Fund (MALDEF) filed suit in *Edgewood ISD v. Kirby* claiming discrimination against children in poor school districts. In 1986, the Texas Supreme Court declared that large

*WILLIAM "BUBBA" FLINT/*The Dallas Morning News

differences between rich and poor districts violated the state constitution's mandate of an "efficient" education for all Texas school children. In 1993, Senator Bill Ratliff (R-Mount Pleasant) guided Senate Bill 7 through the legislature. SB 7, known as the "Robin Hood Bill," required wealthy school districts to share some of their money with the poorer districts in the state. Some wealthy districts, such as the Highland Park ISD near Dallas, sent fully 70 percent of their property tax revenues to the state for redistribution to poor districts.

By 2004, two-thirds of the state's school districts were at or near the state-mandated local property tax cap of $1.50 per $100 of assessed property value. Poor districts were at the cap and still unable to raise adequate resources while wealthy districts were at the cap because they had to fund their schools and send Robin Hood contributions to the state. The Texas Supreme Court again intervened, holding that the state had violated the constitution's prohibition on a statewide property tax by forcing most of the state's school districts to the property tax cap. The Court ordered the legislature to reform the school funding system to give local school boards more flexibility.

In the 2005–2006 school year, Texas spent $7,547 per student while the national average was $9,100.[5] The state provided 35 percent of school funding while Texas's 1,026 local school districts provided 55 percent. The federal government provided a little less than 10 percent of school funds. Governor Perry and the Texas legislature responded to the Court's demand for funding reform by lowering local property taxes by one-third, enacting a broad new business tax, increasing the state cigarette tax from $.41 to $1.41 a pack, adjusting a couple of other minor tax streams, and drawing on the state surplus. With the new school funding plans fully in place, the state's

Students marched through the University of Texas campus in December 2007 to demonstrate against tuition hikes. *JAY JANNER/* Austin American-Statesman

share of funding rose to about 50 percent, the localities provide about 40 percent, and federal funds continue at about 10 percent. While these reforms do represent progress, school funding will remain a flashpoint of Texas politics.

The 2006 legislation also allowed local school districts to raise taxes from $1 per $100 of assessed value to $1.04 as needed and to as much as $1.17 with voter approval. About 98 percent of school districts did raise their rate to $1.04 by 2008. About 10 percent of districts asked voters to approve higher rates and most of them asked to go to the max—$1.17. Many more school districts will be emboldened to approach their voters for increases in the next few years. Texas parents, far more than Texas legislators, are focused on their children's need for a high quality education.[6]

Higher Education. About 1.2 million students attend 150 public and private colleges and universities in Texas. Nearly 90 percent of these students attend public colleges and universities and about half of these attend one of the 50 community college districts in the state.[7] Two issues have roiled Texas higher education in recent years. One is how to divide the cost of higher education between the state and the student. Should the state appropriation to colleges be high and tuition charged to students low, or should the appropriation be low and tuition high?

Historically, Texas had among the lowest college tuition and fees in the country. As late as the 1994–95 academic year, average tuition and fees at Texas state universities was only 60 percent of the national average ($1,608 in Texas versus $2,689 nationally). In 2003, the legislature reduced state funding and allowed the colleges and universities to set their own tuition and fees. Texas tuition and fees still compare favorably with many other states, but they have been rising fast, up 52 percent since 2003. Students attending Texas public four-year universities during the 2007–08 academic year paid slightly above the national average ($6,437 versus $6,185 nationally). Under pressure from students, parents, and legislature, the UT system scrapped anticipated tuition increases of 15% over the 2008–2009, and 2009–2010

Hopwood v. Texas
(1992) The U.S. Fifth
Circuit Court of Appeals
agreed with Cheryl
Hopwood and others that
the affirmative action
program run by the
University of Texas gave
race too dominant a role
in the admissions
process.

Grutter v. Bollinger
(2003) Also known as the
Michigan case, the U.S.
Supreme Court upheld
affirmative action
programs taking race into
account as one factor
among many.

school years, and instituted a 5% per year cap. Texas community colleges are still a bargain at $1,695 compared to a national average of $2,361.[8]

A second major issue in higher education, both nationally and in Texas, is affirmative action. Admissions criteria are always sensitive, especially when issues of race, ethnicity, and gender are in play. Beginning in the 1970s, Texas universities managed admissions to assure that the student body reflected the diversity of the state. In 1992, Cheryl Hopwood charged in *Hopwood v. Texas* that the University of Texas Law School discriminated against her by rejecting her and admitting minority students with lower grades and test scores. The U.S. Fifth Circuit Court of Appeals found for Hopwood, saying that race should not be a factor in law school or undergraduate admission.

Fearing too great a drop in minority enrollment in Texas colleges and universities, the legislature adopted a program by which the top 10 percent of each high school graduating class in the state would be eligible for admission to the state's top universities. Because many of the state's high schools have a clear ethnic or racial identity, some overwhelmingly Anglo, others overwhelmingly Hispanic or black, admitting the top 10 percent of each graduating class assured some diversity.

The U.S. Supreme Court's 2003 *Grutter v. Bollinger* decision, better known as the Michigan decision, overturned Hopwood and restored the right of colleges and universities to consider race in admissions decisions, so long as it was just one of a list of factors considered. Public colleges and universities in Texas employ the top 10 percent rule but they also consider race as a criterion in admission. Some contend that Texas universities should simply take the very best students without regard to non-academic criteria like race or ethnicity. Others point out that non-academic criteria are used in admissions all the time—think of that not so bright quarterback with the great arm and that great dancer that does not test so well. Several attempts have been made, including three bills in the 2007 legislative session, to weaken or strike down the top 10 percent rule but all have failed.

Health and Human Services

Health and human services programs include Medicaid, child health care, mental health and retardation programs, welfare, unemployment compensation, and workmen's compensation for those injured on the job. These programs are among the fastest growing elements of the state budget.

About $53 billion, 31.6 percent of the state budget, goes to health and human services. The cost of these programs is usually shared between the federal and state government, with the federal government setting the basic rules and providing base funding and the states adding to the federal funding and administering the program. Federal funds account for almost 60 percent of Texas spending for health and human services. In fact, Texas frequently leaves federal money on the table so that it will not have to raise and allocate additional state revenues.

Nowhere is Texas's reluctance to spend on social welfare programs clearer than in regard to income support for the poor. The Texas Constitution prohibits spending more than one percent of the Texas state budget on welfare.

Business, Transportation, and Economic Development

During the 2008–09 biennium, Texas spent $20.5 billion, about 12.2 percent of its total budget, on business and economic development. This spending category includes the Texas Department of Transportation (TxDOT), the Department of Economic Development, and the Department of Housing and Community Affairs. About 43 percent of the funds spent in this category come to Texas as federal grants.

Eighty-two percent of the money spent in the business and economic development category of the state budget goes to TxDOT. While TxDOT is responsible for planning, maintenance, and development of the state road, rail, and air transportation infrastructure, most of its resources go to maintain and extend the state's nearly 80,000 miles of roads and highways.[9] Texas's $16.8 billion roads budget for 2008–2009 comes principally from federal and state gas taxes.

In 2002, Governor Perry developed a plan for the state's future transportation needs that has generated great controversy. Perry unveiled plans for the Trans-Texas Corridor, a 4,000 mile corridor, a quarter-mile wide including six lanes for cars, four lanes for trucks, as well as railroad tracks, oil and gas pipelines, and utility lines, running from the Mexican border to the Red River and from El Paso to Houston. Construction of the Trans-Texas Corridor is envisioned to begin in 2010, take many years to complete, and cost $184 billion.

As always, Governor Perry sought to deliver this major project without raising taxes. Initial contracts were awarded to a Spanish-led consortium, Cintra-Zachry, which promised to fund the project in exchange for the right to charge tolls later. Critics complain about lost farmland, foreign contractors, and the prospect of paying tolls far into the future. The 2007 legislative session overwhelmingly, 139-1 in the House and 30-1 in the Senate, passed a bill declaring a two-year moratorium on toll roads.

Prisons and Public Safety

Texas spent about $8.7 billion, or 5.4 percent of its 2008–2009 budget, to house nearly 155,000 inmates in the state's 106 prisons and jails. Texas ranks 39 among the states in spending per prisoner. The Department of Criminal Justice is responsible for the prisons while the Department of Public Safety (DPS) provides police services throughout the state. Within the DPS, the Texas Highway Patrol (2,706) and the Texas Rangers (134) field about 2,840 uniformed officers.

Parks and Recreation

Finally, the decade-long struggle to fund Texas's 120 state parks highlights the state's budgetary practices. Texas officials try to limit the pressure on state general funds by identifying dedicated funds for particular programs. In 1993, the legislature dedicated a tax on sporting goods to fund Texas

TABLE 10.1
Let's Compare: State Tax Burden of Ten Largest States

Throughout this book, we have argued that Texas has a traditional political culture that has worked to keep taxes low, regulations light, and elites in social and political control. Not surprisingly, Texas ranks 48 among the states in the proportion of income taken in state taxes. Texans differ as to whether this is a source of pride or shame.

State	State Tax Per Capita	Rank Among 50 States	% of Personal Income	Rank Among 50 States
California	$3,139	11	8.0%	15
New York	$3,273	9	7.4%	22
Michigan	$2,368	29	7.0%	27
Pennsylvania	$2,480	24	6.8%	32
Illinois	$2,297	32	6.0%	43
Ohio	$2,164	38	6.5%	35
North Carolina	$2,496	22	7.9%	18
Florida	$1,958	41	5.4%	46
Georgia	$1,953	43	6.2%	41
Texas	**$1,686**	**48**	**4.9%**	**49**
U.S. Total	**$2,484**		**6.8%**	

Source: See *http://www.taxadmin.org/fta/rate/07taxbur.html*. Data is drawn from the U.S. Bureau of the Census and the Bureau of Economic Analysis.

parks. In 1995, though the tax produces more than $100 million annually, the legislature capped park funding at $32 million and directed the rest into the general fund. As state budgets tightened after 2001, park funding was further reduced to $20.5 million in 2005, before rebounding to $33.9 million in 2007. Park fees bring in an additional $32 million annually, but the parks continue to lay off workers and defer maintenance. Texas ranks 49 among the fifty states in spending on parks.[10]

EXPLORING THE TAX BURDEN IN TEXAS

Q5. Where do issues of fairness fit into discussions of taxing and spending?

Texas ranks among the lowest of the low tax states. Our state takes just 4.9 percent of personal income in state taxes (compared to a national average of 6.8 percent), placing Texas 49 among the 50 states. The per capita tax burden, $1,686 in 2007 (compared to the national average of $2,487) places Texas 48.[11] In a sense, all taxes are paid out of income. But, as discussed earlier in this chapter, Texas does not have a classic income tax whereby employers withhold taxes from paychecks. Rather, Texas state and local governments at least let you get your income home before they charge you sales taxes, property taxes, and other fines and fees.

Clearly, governments need to claim revenue, but how they choose to do so raises issues of fairness. As a result, taxes are often described in terms of who pays them. **Progressive taxes** take a larger percentage share of the income of the wealthy than they do of the poor. Nationally, the most com-

Progressive taxes
Taxes that take a higher proportion of the income of the wealthy than of the poor.

mon progressive tax is the income tax, and Texas does not employ an income tax. **Regressive taxes,** which are common in Texas, draw a higher proportion of the income of the poor than they do of the wealthy. A 2003 study by the Institute on Taxation & Economic Policy found that poor Texans pay 11.4 percent of their income in state and local taxes while the wealthy pay about 5 percent.[12]

The reason that the poor in Texas pay a higher proportion of their income in taxes than the wealthy is that our state depends so heavily on the general and special sales taxes. Poor Texans must spend all of their money on consumption, for food, gasoline, and clothing, and hence pay the sales tax on more of their total income. Wealthy Texans can shield some of their income by saving and investing rather than spending it. Saving and investing are good things to be sure, they drive economic growth, but they do allow the wealthy to shield their income while the poor cannot.

Regressive taxes
Taxes that take a higher proportion of the income of the poor than of the wealthy.

CHAPTER SUMMARY

Some of the most critical decisions made in politics, whether in Washington or Austin, concern taxing and spending. These are decisions about who pays taxes, what kinds of taxes they pay, and how much they pay. Closely related decisions involve what services will be funded and who will benefit from them.

Texas is a low tax state. To keep taxes low, Texans have used the constitution and laws to prohibit a state income tax and a state property tax. Even following the recent increase in business taxes, they remain modest by national standards. On the other hand, Texas has some of the highest sales taxes in the country. Texas deploys its limited resources, supplemented by federal transfers that comprise one-third of the Texas budget, to fund basic programs in education, social services, highways, and prisons.

Texans have long favored small government and low taxes. Most Texans applaud careful spending. But the taxes that Texas does levy, especially the general sales tax and the gas tax, bear hard on those who have little. Tight budgets leave many Texans with less education, health care, and job training than a healthy and productive life requires.

KEY TERMS

Budgets

Corporate franchise
   fee

Federal transfer
   payments

Grutter v. Bollinger

Hopwood v. Texas

Legislative Budget
   Board

Progressive taxes

Regressive taxes

Revenue estimate

Sales tax

SUGGESTED READINGS

Council of State Governments, *Book of the States, 2007 Edition,* vol. 39, Lexington, KY, 2007.

House Research Organization, Texas House of Representatives, *Writing the State Budget,* State Finance Report, No. 80-1, February 14, 2007. See the LBB website.

Legislative Budget Board, 80th Texas Legislature, *Fiscal Size-Up, 2008–2009 Biennium.* See the LBB website.

WEB RESOURCES

http://www.window.state.tx.us/revenue.html Historical view of state revenue by source

http://www.window.state.tx.us/expend.html Historical view of state expenditures by category

http://www.lbb.state.tx.us LBB website

http://www.cbpp.org Center on Budget and Policy Priorities. Comparing state budgets

http://www.taxadmin.org and http://www.taxfoundation.org More good comparative data

END NOTES

1. House Research Organization, Texas House of Representatives, *Writing the State Budget,* State Finance Report, No. 80-1, February 14, 2007. See the LBB website.
2. See LBB website at: http://www.lbb.state.tx.us/ Under Publications, Reports, and Links, see Appropriations Bills, 2008–2009.
3. Legislative Budget Board, *Fiscal Size-Up, 2008–2009 Biennium,* "State Indebtedness," p. 15. See LBB website as noted above.
4. *Fiscal Size-Up, 2008–2009,* "Per Capita State Government Expenditures," Figure 61, p. 50.
5. *Fiscal Size-Up, 2008–2009,* Figure 178, p. 200.
6. Paul Burka, "No Nino Left Behind," *Texas Monthly,* December 2007, pp. 20–26. See also the National Center for Education Statistics, Digest of Education Statistics Tables and Figures, 2006, Table 159.
7. *Fiscal Size-Up, 2008–2009,* "Higher Education Enrollment," Table 193, p. 217.
8. Special Update, University of Texas System, June 17, 2008.
9. *Fiscal Size-Up, 2008–2009,* "State Highway Fund # 006," Figure 306, p. 384.
10. R. A. Dyer, "Texas Parks in a State of Neglect," *Fort Worth Star-Telegram,* July 2, 2006.
11. See http://www.taxadmin.org/fta/rate/07taxbur. See also, *Fiscal Size-Up, 2008–2009,* Figure 55, p. 45.
12. See the Institute on Taxation & Economic Policy website at http://www.itepnet.org/whopays.htm

Glossary

Amateur legislatures   State legislatures which provide low pay and support to their members. Sessions are generally short and members have other jobs.

Anglo   A Spanish term referring to non-Hispanic whites.

Annexation   A legal and political process by which cities absorb adjacent territory.

Appellate courts   Appellate courts review trial court records to insure that the trial was fair and the law correctly applied.

Appointment power   The Texas Constitution and statutes empower the governor, often with the approval of two-thirds of the Senate, to appoint many senior government officials.

At-large elections   Elections held throughout a jurisdiction, such as a city or county, rather than in wards or single-members districts within the jurisdiction.

Balcones Escarpment   A geological fault line that separates the lowlands of East Texas from the prairies and plains of West Texas.

Biennial session   The Texas legislature meets in regular session every other year, that is biennially, rather than annually.

Big tent model   Sees political parties as organizations that appeal to the broadest range of potential voters rather than seeking to implement a coherent ideological program.

Budget message   The governor is required by law to address the legislature on budget matters in the first thirty days of each regular session.

Budgets   Moral and political documents that seek to balance a community's revenue sources with its spending obligations.

Cabinet government   An executive branch in which the governor has broad appointment and budgetary powers.

City council   The policymaking or legislative branch of city government.

City manager   A city manager is an appointed professional executive hired, usually by the city council, to manage or administer city government.

Civil law   Deals primarily with relations between individuals and organizations, as in marriage and family law, contracts, and property.

Civil War   The U.S. Civil War, pitting the northern states against the southern states, occurred between 1861 and 1865.

Clemency   Some governors have the power to forgive or lessen the punishment for criminal infractions by granting pardons, paroles, or commutations.

Commissioners court   The chief policymaking and administrative institution of Texas county government.

Conference committees   Committees composed of members of the House and Senate charged to resolve differences between the House and Senate versions of a bill.

Constitution   Basic or fundamental law that lays out the structure of government, the powers of each office, the process by which officials are elected or appointed, and the rights and liberties of citizens.

Corporate franchise fee   A business activity tax that in 2005 impacted one in six Texas businesses, mostly corporations and sole proprietorships.

Councils of governments   COGs are voluntary planning districts that provide training, planning, and coordination services to member local governments.

County judge   The county judge is elected countywide and presides over the county Commissioners Court.

Criminal law   Criminal law prohibits certain actions and prescribes penalties for those who engage in the prohibited conduct.

Defendant   The person defending against a charge in court.

Democrats of Texas   Liberal faction of the mid-20th century Democratic party, led by elected officials like Lyndon Johnson and Ralph Yarborough.

Devolution   The return of political authority from the national government to the states.

Dillon's Rule   A legal concept holding that local governments are the creatures or creations of state governments.

Elitism   The belief that the interest group system is skewed toward the interests of the wealthy.

Enumerated powers   The specifically listed, or enumerated, powers of the Congress and president found in Article I, section 8, and Article II, section 2, of the U.S. Constitution.

Extraterritorial jurisdiction (ETJ)   ETJ describes the limited power that cities exercise over territory just beyond their boundaries.

Federal transfer payments   Funds provided by the federal government to state and local governments to support key services such as health care, education, and transportation.

Federalism   A form of government in which some powers are assigned to the national government, some to the states, and some, such as the power to tax, are shared.

Fiscal conservatives Conservative faction that focused on fiscal and economic issues such as taxation, spending, and business regulation.

General elections A final or definitive election in which candidates representing their respective parties contend for election to office.

Grand jury A grand jury assesses a prosecutor's evidence against a potential defendant to be sure it is sufficient to proceed to trial.

Grovey v. Townsend (1935) U.S. Supreme Court found that the Democratic Party in Texas was a private organization and could exclude blacks from its primary elections.

Grutter v. Bollinger (2003) Also known as the Michigan case, the U.S. Supreme Court upheld affirmative action programs taking race into account as one factor among many.

Hopwood v. Texas (1992) The U.S. Fifth Circuit Court of Appeals agreed with Cheryl Hopwood and others that the affirmative action program run by the University of Texas gave race too dominant a role in the admissions process.

Hybrid legislatures State legislatures, including the Texas legislature, that share some of the characteristics of professional legislatures, such as long sessions and good staff support, and some of the characteristics of amateur legislatures, such as low pay and biennial sessions.

Incorporation The legal process by which cities are established.

Interest groups Organizations that attempt to influence society and government to act in ways consonant with their interests.

Interim committees Legislative committees that work in the interim between regular legislative sessions to study issues, prepare reports, and draft legislation.

Jurisdiction The constitutional or legal right of a court to hear certain types of cases.

Jury trial A trial conducted before a jury of citizens who hear testimony, weigh evidence, and assess guilt.

King Ranch Founded in 1853 by Captain Richard King, the 825,000 acre King Ranch south of Corpus Christi epitomizes the huge dry land cattle ranches of Texas.

Law Authoritative rules made by government and backed by the organized force of the community.

Legislative Budget Board The ten-member LBB, co-chaired by the Lieutenant Governor and the Speaker, drafts the state's biennial budget.

Legislative calendars Lists of bills passed by committees but awaiting final action on the floor.

Legislative supremacy The idea that the law making power in government is superior to the executive and judicial powers.

Line-item veto   The power to strike out or veto individual items in the state budget without striking down the whole budget.

Lobby Registration Act   A 1973 Texas law requiring groups and individuals attempting to influence state government to register and report on certain of their activities.

Lobbyists   Hired agents who seek to influence government decision making in ways that benefit or limit harm to their clients.

Missouri plan   To balance competence and accountability, governors appoint judges who later stand in retention elections.

Motor Voter   A 1995 law, also known as the National Voter Registration Act, that permits persons to register to vote at motor vehicle and other state government offices.

Necessary and proper clause   The last paragraph of Article I, section 8, of the U.S. Constitution, states that Congress may make all laws deemed necessary and proper for carrying into execution the powers specifically enumerated in Article I, section 8.

Nixon v. Herndon   (1924) U.S. Supreme Court held that Texas could not exclude blacks from voting in state sanctioned primary elections.

Peak associations   Peak associations, like the U.S. Chamber of Commerce, represent the general interests of business.

Permian Basin   A geological formation in West Texas, around Midland, where oil discoveries were made in the 1920s that remain productive today.

Plaintiff   The individual who brings a case before a court is called the plaintiff or complainant.

Plural executive   An executive branch featuring several officials with independent constitutional and legal authority.

Pluralism   The belief that the interest group system produces a reasonable policy balance.

Political action committee   Legal entity, often associated with interest groups, through which campaign contributions and other forms of support can be given to parties and candidates.

Political culture   Widely held ideas concerning the relationship of citizens to their government and to each other in matters effecting politics and public affairs.

Political participation   All of those activities, from attending campaign events, to voting, and even running for office, by which individuals and groups undertake to affect politics.

Political parties   Organizations designed to elect government officeholders under a given label.

Poll tax   In 1902 Texas adopted a poll tax of $1.50 to discourage the poor and minorities from voting.

Popular sovereignty   The idea that all legitimate governmental authority comes from the people.

Precinct   Geographical area within which voters go to a polling place to cast their ballots on election day.

Preclearance   The Voting Rights Act requires states and communities with a history of racial discrimination in voting to seek prior approval from the Justice Department for changes to their election codes to insure against dilution of minority electoral impact.

Primary elections   A preliminary election in which voters select candidates to stand under their party label in a later general election.

Professional associations   Organizations formed to represent the interests of professionals in occupations like medicine, law, accounting, and cosmetology.

Professional Legislatures   State legislatures which pay and support their members well and, in turn, demand nearly fulltime service from them.

Progressive taxes   Taxes that take a higher proportion of the income of the wealthy than of the poor.

Reconstruction   The period of post Civil War (1867 to 1872) military occupation of the South during which the North attempted to reconstruct southern social, political, and economic life.

Redistricting   The political process by which electoral district boundaries are redrawn to reflect changes in population and party power.

Regressive taxes   Taxes that take a higher proportion of the income of the poor than of the wealthy.

Regular session   The regularly scheduled biennial session of the legislature.

Republic of Texas   Texas was an independent nation from 1836 until it became a U.S. state on December 29, 1845.

Reserved powers   The 10th amendment to the U.S. Constitution declares that powers not granted to the national government by the Constitution are reserved to the states or their citizens.

Responsible party model   Sees political parties as organizations that campaign on coherent ideological platforms and then seek to implement their policies if elected.

Revenue estimate   The Texas Comptroller is empowered to make revenue estimates that the Texas state budget must stay within.

Right-to-work   Legal principle prohibiting mandatory union membership.

Rio Grande   Spanish for Grand River, the Rio Grande forms Texas's southern border with Mexico from El Paso to Brownsville.

Rio Grande Valley   Texas's four southernmost counties, often referred to simply as "the valley," are heavily Hispanic. The phrase is sometimes used more expansively to refer to all of South Texas.

Sales Tax   Taxes charged on the sale of designated goods. In Texas the general sales tax is 6.25 percent, with localities permitted to charge up to an additional 2 percent.

Sharpstown scandal   1972 scandal in which Houston financier Frank Sharp and a number of prominent Texas politicians were accused of trading political for financial favors.

Single-member district elections   Elections held within geographical districts, with one candidate elected in each district.

Smith v. Allwright   (1944) U.S. Supreme Court overturned *Grovey*, declaring that political parties are 'agencies of the state' and must abide by the 15th amendment's prohibition on racial discrimination in voting.

Social conservatives   Conservative faction that focuses on social issues such as abortion, school prayer, and gay marriage.

Sovereign immunity   The 11th amendment to the U.S. Constitution declares that states cannot be sued in their own courts except as federal or state law explicitly allows.

Special districts   Special purpose local governments, established by cities and counties, to deliver a particular service within a limited geographical area.

Special election   Special elections are held to decide constitutional amendments, local bond proposals, and other nonrecurring issues.

Special session   If the legislature does not complete its business in the regular session, the governor can call one or more 30-day special sessions.

Spindletop   A.F. Lucas's spindletop well near Beaumont came in on January 10, 1901, kicking off the 20th century Texas oil boom.

Standing committees   Continuing committees of the legislature appointed at the start of each legislative session unless specific action is taken to revise or discontinue them.

State of the State message   At the beginning of each regular legislative session, the governor lays out his agenda for the session in a speech to a joint session of the legislature.

Strong mayor   An elected city executive with strong appointment, budgetary, and council management powers.

Suffrage   Another term for the legal right to vote.

Supremacy clause   Article VI of the U.S. Constitution declares the U.S. Constitution, federal laws, and treaties to be the supreme law of the land.

"The team"   The Speaker's closest associates, through whom he attempts to control and direct the House. A similar pattern operates in the Senate.

Texas Ethics Commission   Created in 1991, the TEC administers the state's ethics, campaign finance, and lobbying laws.

Texas regulars   Conservative faction of the mid-20th century Democratic party, led by elected officials like Coke Stevenson and Allan Shivers.

Trade associations   Associations formed by businesses and related interests involved in the same commercial, trade, or industrial sector.

Trial court   Trial courts take evidence, hear testimony, determine guilt or evidence, and apply relevant law.

Unfunded mandates   States frequently complain that the federal government mandates actions, like improving education, without providing sufficient funds to fulfill the mandate.

U.S. v. Texas   (1966) U.S. Supreme Court struck down the poll tax in state elections.

Veto   The governor is empowered to veto or strike down acts of the legislature. A veto can be overridden by a two-thirds vote of both houses of the legislature, but it rarely happens.

Voter turnout   That portion of the eligible electorate that actually turns up to cast a vote on election day.

Weak mayor   An elected city executive with few meaningful appointment, budgetary, and council management powers.

White primary   In 1906 Texas Democrats adopted a white primary, meaning that only whites were permitted to vote in the Democratic primary.

Index